The Theatre of
Peter Barnes

The Theatre of
Peter Barnes

by

Bernard F. Dukore

Heinemann : London and Exeter, N.H.

Heinemann Educational Books Ltd
22 Bedford Square, London WC1B 3HH

Heinemann Educational Books Inc
4 Front Street, Exeter, NH 03833, USA

LONDON   EDINBURGH   MELBOURNE   AUCKLAND
HONG KONG   SINGAPORE   KUALA LUMPUR   NEW DELHI
IBADAN   NAIROBI   JOHANNESBURG
EXETER (NH)   KINGSTON   PORT OF SPAIN

First published 1981

British Library Cataloguing in Publication Data

Dukore, Bernard F.
   The theatre of Peter Barnes.
   1. Barnes, Peter *1931* – Criticism and interpretation
   I. Title
   822'.914   PR6052.A668

   ISBN 0-435-18280-3

Library of Congress Cataloging in Publication Data

Catalog Card No.: 81-81246
   Dukore, Bernard F.
   4. The Theatre of Peter Barnes.
Exeter, NH: Heinemann Educational Books
   153P   8107   £5.50   810320

Printed and bound in Great Britain by
Biddles Ltd, Guildford and King's Lynn

To Margi and Joan

Contents

Prefatory Note

It is a pleasure to express my indebtedness to James Mellen, whose invitation to join him at *Leonardo's Last Supper* and *Noonday Demons* over eleven years ago introduced me to Peter Barnes' plays, and whose invitation to see *Frontiers of Farce* over four years ago introduced me to Barnes' adaptations. Not only for agreeing to be interviewed and for having checked my German and French translations am I grateful to Martin Esslin, I am also grateful for the day he pressed me to read *The Bewitched*. As he predicted, it convinced me of Barnes' stature. It also led me to a book shop to acquire his other published works and made me decide to write about him sometime. I therefore especially thank Albert Wertheim, whose invitation to contribute a chapter to a book on contemporary British dramatists ended my procrastination and prodded me to propose Barnes; that chapter became the genesis of this book, and Wertheim is probably its 'onlie begetter'.

I am indebted to the Humanities Research Centre of the Australian National University, whose award of a Visiting Fellowship provided the time and opportunity to complete a first draft of this book. Happily, I give thanks to Ian Donaldson, its Director, for reading portions of that draft; I particularly value his comments on Jacobean drama. I am certainly grateful to the perceptions of Margaret Mitchell Dukore, who read first and later drafts. In addition, I thank Timothy West for consenting to be interviewed, Jeremy Boulton of the British Film Institute for arranging a showing of the film *Leonardo's Last Supper*, and Ian Todd for providing information on the court ruling of the libel case that involved *The Ruling Class*.

Last, but definitely not least, I thank the subject of this book, Peter Barnes, for his generosity in making his unpublished manuscripts available and for his patience in the face of numerous and probably silly questions by an American visitor who resides almost two oceans away. Without his cooperation, my task would have been impossible. As one says here, *Mahalo nui loa!*

Kaneohe, Hawaii, USA

I | *The Barnes Controversy*

In his Introduction to *The Ruling Class*, Peter Barnes' first full-length play to be produced in England and his first play to be published, Harold Hobson, then theatre critic of London's *Sunday Times* and dean of English theatre critics, declares, 'The most exciting thing that can happen to a dramatic critic is when he is suddenly and unexpectedly faced with the explosive blaze of an entirely new talent of a very high order.' Judiciously, he adds, 'This happens very rarely.' When such an event does happen, however, it may 'prove a turning point in the drama. . . .' In twenty years of professional theatre-going, only four events suddenly and unexpectedly excited him in this manner: the English productions of Samuel Beckett's *Waiting for Godot* in 1955, of John Osborne's *Look Back in Anger* in 1956, of Harold Pinter's *The Birthday Party* in 1958, and of Peter Barnes' *The Ruling Class* in 1968.[1]

Time and critical consensus have confirmed Hobson's assessment of *Waiting for Godot*, whose author is Irish and who is more than a generation older than the other dramatists, who are English and of the same generation: born in 1929, 1930, and 1931, respectively. Today, Osborne's early promise seems largely unfulfilled; despite the historical importance of *Look Back in Anger*, its author now appears less prominent than he did. However, Hobson's assessment of the talent of Pinter and Barnes remains valid. Both playwrights have grown in stature. In terms of originality, distinctiveness, theatrical vitality, and intellectual power, they tower above all other contemporary English dramatists.

Yet how different they are. Unlike Pinter's drama, which is not politically oriented, Barnes' drama is permeated by class hatred and by a loathing of the social, economic, and religious bastions of Western society. Although both are theatrical, each employs the stage differently from the other. Whereas Pinter's art is intense and contractive, like that of Beckett, whom he reveres, Barnes' is full-blown and expansive, like that of Ben Jonson, whom he reveres. Pinter's proscenium-arch stage is an enclosed, confined space, often suggestive of a tomb. Barnes' is a music-hall show-place, frequently evocative of the amusement-park atmosphere of the pier at the seaside resort Clacton-on-Sea, where he spent much of his youth.[2]

Harold Hobson's judgment that *The Ruling Class* places Barnes in the company of Beckett, and my contention that Barnes and Pinter are the playwriting giants of their generation in England, are critical views that, at present, do not have widespread support. As Barnes himself recognizes, 'The people who like my work like it fanatically, but the reverse is true, and those who don't like it vastly outnumber the people who do.'[3]

From the start, critical controversy has surrounded his drama. When *The Ruling Class* transferred from Nottingham to London, Hobson praised it extravagantly, as did Ronald Bryden, who called it 'one of those pivotal plays . . . in which you can feel the theatre changing direction, a new taste coming into being.' Bryden predicted, 'People who don't care for verbal fantasy and coruscation, for the spectacle of intelligence revelling in its own display, won't warm to Barnes' style.'[4] Among those who did not warm to it, Hilary Spurling off-handedly dismissed 'most of it' as 'too boring to go into' and Milton Shulman patronized it as 'sporadically witty' with 'a patina of profundity which is essentially shallow and glib.'[5]

After the double-bill *Leonardo's Last Supper* and *Noonday Demons* opened in December 1969, Irving Wardle maintained that they 'confirm Mr Barnes as one of the most original and biting comic writers working in Britain.'[6] Not everyone found such confirmation. 'Certainly devastating,' said Peter Lewis of the 'knee-in-groin humour and sudden bursts of wildly inappropriate popular songs,' yet: 'Whether they mean very much is another matter.'[7]

When Ronald Bryden, who had stopped play-reviewing and started play-reading for the Royal Shakespeare Company, completed his second reading of *The Bewitched*, he sent a memorandum to the RSC's Artistic Director, Trevor Nunn: 'I think this is a work of genius' ('Introduction,' *The Bewitched*, p. viii). Unaware of Bryden's memo, Martin Esslin echoed it in his review of the RSC's production: '*The Bewitched* is a masterpiece, a work of true genius . . . one of the major works in our modern classical canon.'[8] As with Barnes' earlier plays, there was critical controversy. Whereas one reviewer called the first-act climax 'magnificent' and 'perhaps the most astonishing feat of historical imagination, strictly founded in poetic truth, and of irrefutable political significance, that the theatre has ever shown,'[9] another called it 'spectacular, but confusing.'[10] Going still further, other reviewers condemned the play as a work of 'coarse and meretricious vulgarity' and 'a monumental and tasteless bore.'[11]

With *Laughter!*—to date, Barnes' most recent original play to be performed—critical opinion continued to be divided. Irving Wardle of *The Times* was jubilant:

> Nothing is more exciting in the theatre than a moment of genuine stylistic change: when the old dramatic categories crack apart under pressure of a new experience and one sees a playwright not merely writing a play but reinventing what a play ought to be. . . .
> I got [this] sensation from the opening of Peter Barnes' new play which declares war on the one element that does most to keep the theatre in business.[12]

Others found no occasion for excitement. Particularly devastating for a play entitled *Laughter!* was the title of one such review: 'It's Not Funny.'[13] Michael Billington, a frequently perceptive reviewer, suggested a reason for what he considered a failure: 'Charles Marowitz's production is heavy as lead. . . .'[14]

What of critics who did not write under pressure of newspaper or magazine deadlines, but who had more time to offer more considered judgments? Among such critics as well, response was divided as to Barnes' merits. To Katharine J. Worth, for example, *The Ruling Class* was 'a striking achievement' and to Jonathan Hammond, Barnes' dramatic corpus 'combines savagery, precision and wit . . . with a clarity about the basic political causes of the sickness in our modern society that makes him a worthy follower of Jonson, and one of the most significant, as well as one of the most entertaining, British playwrights of the day.'[15] According to Arnold P. Hinchliffe, however, *The Ruling Class* was 'intellectually contrived' and Barnes' work was insignificant.[16]

There is little point in multiplying quotations that demonstrate similar conflicting views. Unquestionably, Barnes' drama has provoked critical controversy. His own observation, quoted earlier, seems accurate. Among his critical admirers and detractors, few respond in a moderate manner to his work. My own view, expressed in the second paragraph of this chapter, places me among his immoderate admirers. If it did not, there would be no reason for going to the effort of producing a book about his theatre. Analysis and evaluation, both of which are the obligations of a critic, form an apparently circular road. Because of initial analysis, one evaluates; despite efforts to be objective, such evaluation underlies the composition of subsequent analysis. Although this book aims at analysis, with as much objectivity as is possible, its underlying viewpoint is that Peter Barnes is one of the major figures of contemporary drama. I hope it demonstrates why. I hope, too, that it leads the reader to examine or re-examine Barnes' plays and form his own conclusions.

Although *The Ruling Class* did not spring Minerva-like from the head of an Olympian author, the approach to this book is not entirely chronological. After a biographical chapter, it analyses, seriatim and chronologically, Barnes' mature plays, which begin with *The Ruling Class* and continue through his most recent, the unpublished *Red Noses, Black Death*. Following this analysis is a study of his distinctive theatrical style. The next chapter explores his early plays, most of which have been produced but none published; following, as it does, the study of his mature plays, it aims to reveal the progress which led him to his distinctive style. In addition to, and between, writing his original plays, Barnes has edited and adapted works by Jacobean and non-English writers. A chapter will analyse these and try to relate them to his own plays. A concluding chapter suggests Barnes' position in modern English drama.

2 | *Biography and Survey*

A cockney, Peter Barnes was born on 10 January 1931 in the East End of London, off Bow Road, within the sound of the bells of Bow Church. His parents, Freddy (who died while Barnes was in his twenties) and Martha, also had a younger child, a daughter named Germaine. Barnes' mother is Jewish; his father was Church of England. To marry Martha, Freddy converted to Judaism— apparently a strictly ceremonial action, since it became a family joke. According to his mother, says Barnes, his father 'slipped the Rabbi £5 to get him through.' As Barnes recalls, 'Neither cared much for religion. In any case, the Second World War made certain I had no religious upbringing: I was evacuated to the country.' Nevertheless, he is interested in both religion and God, a distinction he carefully makes, though he adds, 'Whether He or She is interested in me, I have my doubts.' To Barnes, questions of God, creation, and human existence are major creative problems with which a writer should try to deal.

Before the Second World War, his working-class parents left London for Clacton-on-Sea. In this seaside resort in Essex, with an amusement park that included ferris wheels and similar attractions, he spent most of his youth. In Clacton-on-Sea, his parents 'ran amusement stalls on the pier: rolling balls into holes, darts, games of chance where you won prizes instead of money.' When the war broke out, he was sent to Gloucestershire, where his family soon joined him. During the war, his father worked in a munitions factory. 'My war was spent in the country,' says Barnes. 'The curious thing was that I spent part of it in London, where I stayed with an aunt, during vacations, because I liked London so much, despite all the dangers, the bombings. I just used to think of coming up to town.' In town, he would have what might be called movie orgies, going to one after another. 'I was mad on movies,' he recalls, 'even when I was young.' After the war, his family returned to Clacton-on-Sea, where his parents had a restaurant, then a catering business.

Barnes attended a secondary school, then a grammar school. At seventeen he passed a civil service examination and left school for a position in the Greater London Council. From 1949 to 1950, he served in the Royal Air Force and was stationed with a radar unit in England. Upon completion of his military service, he returned to the GLC, which had an in-house, glossy, monthly magazine. Still 'mad on movies,' Barnes persuaded the editors to let him, without remuneration, write film criticism for it. Because the GLC had thousands of employees, the magazine had a large circulation. For this reason, film exhibitors were anxious to have young Barnes review their movies. He received press tickets for virtually every film shown in London.

In the early 1950s, he resigned from the GLC to become a free-lance film critic. His reviews appeared in *Films and Filming* and other cinema magazines. In 1956, at twenty-five, he became a Story Editor for Warwick Films. In this position, he read new novels as well as scripts that were submitted, made synopses of everything he read, and recommended whether or not Warwick Films should purchase film rights. On 14 October 1961, he married Charlotte Beck, a Viennese whom he had met at the British Film Institute, where she worked as a secretary.

In 1958 he wrote his first screenplay, *Violent Moment*, adapted from a short story he 'just happened to find.' Other screenplays followed: *The White Trap* (1959), *Breakout* (1959; not to be confused with the Charles Bronson film of the same title, made over a dozen years later), *The Professionals* (1960; not to be confused with the Richard Brooks film of the same title, made half a dozen years later), and *Off-Beat* (1961). With Frank Launder, he shared screenwriting credit for *Ring of Spies* (1964; also released as *Ring of Treason*); and with Norman Panama and Larry Gelbart, screenwriting credit for *Not with My Wife You Don't* (1966; starring George C. Scott and Tony Curtis).

In 1960,[1] he wrote *The Man with a Feather in His Hat*, which British ABC, a commercial television station that has since amalgamated with Thames Television, broadcast as an episode of Armchair Mystery Theatre. This drama (to be discussed in Chapter 5), as well as his screenplays, Barnes regards as 'assignment work, craft work. One knows what the producers want and one gives them the best that one can, knowing the specifications one has been handed.' Barnes does not denigrate such work. To the contrary, he takes pride in his craft. However, he contrasts it with what he calls 'the other work, for which there are no specifications other than what I want to write,' a description which upon more careful consideration he changes to 'work that I am compelled to write.'

Because the writer of films and television plays usually has less influence than the director, producer, or star, Barnes turned to the stage, where he could express his own ideas with integrity and without having to fashion a script to order. Only after he did so did he realize that the theatre was his true medium, for he thought in terms of the living, three-dimensional stage.

Between his film assignments, he wrote his early, unassigned stage works. His first play, *The Time of the Barracudas*, was produced in 1963 in San Francisco and Los Angeles, starring Laurence Harvey and Elaine Stritch. Although Barnes hoped the West Coast production would be followed by a New York run, the play failed and closed in California. On 20 June 1965, under the direction of Charles Marowitz, his next play, *Sclerosis*, a one-act political satire about Britain and Cyprus, opened at the Traverse Theatre, Edinburgh. Although it transferred to London's Aldwych Theatre on 27 June for a single Sunday night performance, no one considered a regular run because stage censorship was still in effect. In 1966, he wrote another full-length play, *Clap Hands, Here Comes Charlie*, which interested numerous actors, including Richard Harris and Jason Robards. Yet a production did not materialize. Only after his next play, which was successful, did he receive the opportunity to have it performed, but he realized that to agree to this 'would have been going backwards. I withdrew it.' Barnes has not changed his mind. He regards *Clap Hands, Here Comes Charlie* as an apprentice play, whose production he still refuses to permit unless the conditions are right.

In 1967 Martin Esslin was a member of the British Arts Council's Play-Reading Subcommittee, one of whose purposes was to award, on the basis of scripts submitted to it, bursaries (grants) to playwrights. One day, Stuart Burge, also a member of the subcommittee and at that time Director of the Nottingham Playhouse, came to him with a script he had received and said of its author, 'This man's a bloody genius!' After Esslin read it, he told Burge, 'You're right. He *is* a bloody genius!' Although some members of the subcommittee disagreed, Barnes received a bursary—and more. 'I'll produce it in Nottingham,' declared Burge. 'I'll translate it into German,' said Esslin. Each was as good as his word. The play was *The Ruling Class*. Directed by Burge, it opened in Nottingham on 6 November 1968, then transferred to London on 26 February 1969. In Esslin's translation, it was subsequently produced throughout Germany.[2] In

England, it received acclaim from important critics and won two prestigious playwriting prizes: the John Whiting Award in 1968, which Barnes shared with Edward Bond for *Narrow Road to the Deep North*, and the *Evening Standard* Award in 1969.

His next work consisted of two one-act plays, *Leonardo's Last Supper* and *Noonday Demons*, which were first presented in London, directed by Charles Marowitz, at the Open Space Theatre, on 4 December 1969.[3] Following this double bill was another full-length play, *The Bewitched*, first presented by the Royal Shakespeare Company, under the direction of Terry Hands, at the Aldwych Theatre, on 7 May 1974. Charles Marowitz directed his next play, *Laughter!*, which premiered at the Royal Court Theatre on 25 January 1978. In September 1978, he completed his most recent play, *Red Noses, Black Death*.

Barnes writes these plays in the Reading Room of the British Museum. Daily, from 9.30 to 5.00, he says, 'I go there and then I do my day.' In the Reading Room, he has access to 'all the books. I can always refer to anything I want.' Two further advantages of working there are perhaps paradoxical. 'The terrible thing about writing is that it is such a lonely job. On the other hand, you need to be isolated; you don't want to be disturbed.' In the British Museum's Reading Room, 'I'm cut off from disturbances.' However, 'if you look up, you see other people, so you're not isolated.'

'All the books.' Barnes refers not only to works which provide inspiration or source material for his own plays, he also refers to Jacobean drama and to literary and theatrical studies of them. After he left school—or as Americans would phrase it, after he became a high-school drop-out—Barnes became intensely interested in Jacobean drama, particularly the comedies of Ben Jonson. Immersing himself in these plays, he studied them, the literature about them, and the period in which they were written. In short, he became a self-educated expert in them. Part of his absorption in Jonsonian comedy is a reaction against the national bardolatry. When he compares Jonson and Shakespeare, the latter falls short. As he puts it in a discussion on Jonson, 'Some of Shakespeare is so over-complicated I swear three-quarters of the audience don't know what the hell's going on. They sit there because it's culturally acceptable. There's a terrible snobbery about Shakespeare which there isn't about Jonson.'[4] Some of his antipathy toward Shakespeare, he admits privately, is his aversion to the sort of person who dreams, and achieves the dream, of being able to write 'William Shakespeare, Gent.' About Jonson, he asserted in 1972, Jonson's quatricentennial year, 'I'm an absolute fanatic; he's one of the greatest playwrights in the world; and we're lucky to have such a playwright writing in English. And of course we disgracefully neglect him. One is at a loss for words that there it is, the four hundredth anniversary and not a production worthy of the name is shown anywhere.'[5] With Jonsonian excess, he slashes away at the anti-Jonsonianism of respectable figures, for instance: *The Devil is an Ass* 'is one of the plays that time-server John Dryden called Jonson's dotage. I need hardly add, our vacuum-packed academics never disputed the verdict and the play is not included in the British Theatre's woefully narrow classic repertoire.' Perhaps wistfully, and with a nod in the direction of W. C. Fields, he says of his beloved Ben, 'A playwright who can kill an actor, quarrel violently with his set designer, insult the King, beat up a fellow-dramatist, refuse a knighthood and drink Shakespeare into the ground can't be bad.'[6]

In Jonson, Barnes senses a kindred spirit. Does Barnes allude to himself when he describes his Jacobean antecedent? 'Fortunately Jonson was no gentleman but an apprentice bricklayer, who had the luck not to go to university and be corrupted by literature. For though saturated in literature, he never sacrificed theatrical qualities or the study of character to it.'[7] Whether or not Barnes is conscious of the fact, the description fits him. Like Jonson, his background is working class. Like Jonson, he does not sacrifice theatrical effect or characterization to literary qualities. Like him, he did not go to a university, yet like him, he is saturated in literature. Although both have been immersed in the classics, Jonson's immersion was in the classics of ancient Greece and Rome. Barnes' is in those of his own country in Elizabethan and Jacobean times. Like Jonson's plays, Barnes' contain references to theatre, to his own plays, and to popular culture. Like Jonson, Barnes has experienced failure in the commercial theatre. Whereas Barnes writes films in order to earn relatively large sums of money, Jonson wrote masques—which, as Barnes points out, 'were the equivalent of . . . films.'[8]

Saturation in the drama of Jonson and his fellows has influenced the language, characterization, and structure of Barnes' mature plays. Furthermore, it has led him to develop, alongside his playwriting career, another career, which combines his self-created scholarship and his practical experience in play production. He has edited four Jonsonian comedies for present-day production: *The Alchemist* (the Nottingham Playhouse production, directed by Stuart Burge, opened at the National Theatre at the Old Vic on 9 February 1970; Barnes revised it for the Royal Shakespeare Company, whose production opened at The Other Place, Stratford-on-Avon, on 23 May 1977, then transferred to the Aldwych Theatre, London, on

14 December), *Volpone* (prepared in 1976, but not yet produced), *Bartholomew Fair* (produced at the Roundhouse, in London, on 3 August 1978), and *The Silent Woman* (prepared in 1979, but not yet produced). In addition, he has edited for radio Thomas Middleton's *A Chaste Maid in Cheapside*, which the BBC broadcast on 24 June 1979.

With some plays, however, he extends his role as editor into that of collaborator. He has taken two plays by John Marston, *Antonio and Mellida* and *Antonio's Revenge*, and combined them into a single play, which he calls *Antonio*. The BBC produced his radio version in 1977; his revision for the stage opened at the Nottingham Playhouse on 20 September 1979. Although the title page calls it an adaptation, Barnes more precisely regards it as 'half-and-half, really, probably more editing than adaptation. It's nowhere near anything like the work I did on *The Devil is an Ass.*' On 14 March 1973, his adaptation of this Jonsonian comedy opened at the Nottingham Playhouse; he later revised it for the Birmingham Repertory Company, which performed it at the Edinburgh Festival and, on 2 May 1977, brought it to London for a run at the National's Lyttleton Theatre. *Eastwood Ho!* (which Martin Esslin commissioned for BBC radio, where it was broadcast in October 1973), is also appropriately described as an adaptation; and Barnes has added his name to those of Jonson, Chapman and Marston as co-author.

Barnes has performed similar tasks on works not originally written in English. In 1970, he adapted Frank Wedekind's *Earth Spirit* and *Pandora's Box* for performance in a single evening, under the title *Lulu*. Like *Antonio*, his *Lulu* is an imaginative textual and directorial rendering for modern English-speaking audiences. It opened in Nottingham on 7 October 1970, then in London on 8 December. Although Barnes speaks no German, his wife Charlotte, who does, provided a literal translation, with a full gloss, which he then turned into colloquial English. Another rendering of the German was a programme of cabaret songs, poems, and songs from plays by Wedekind and Bertolt Brecht. First performed at the Royal Court Theatre Upstairs in Easter 1976 under the title *For All Those Who Get Desperate*, it was revised for radio performance and broadcast by the BBC on 20 December 1978 as *The Two Hangmen: Brecht and Wedekind*. For this, Barnes collaborated with Estelle Schmidt, who provided literal translations which he rewrote as colloquial English.

His next adaptation from foreign languages was the twin-bill *Frontiers of Farce*, which comprised Wedekind's *The Singer* and Georges Feydeau's *The Purging*. It opened at the Old Vic on 11 October 1976. In 1978, he prepared a radio version of *Eulogy of*

Baldness, written about 400 AD by Synesius of Cyrene. The BBC broadcast it on 23 February 1980. He has also adapted Christian Dietrich Grabbe's *Don Juan and Faust* (completed 1979, but not yet performed) and has begun work on an adaptation of Feydeau's *Le Bourgeon,* which he calls *The Sprout* (1979). Most recently, he created and directed a Wedekind cabaret review, called *The Devil Himself,* which opened at the Lyric Theatre, Hammersmith, on 28 April 1980; he has edited Thomas Otway's *The Soldier's Fortune* and its sequel *The Atheist,* in a two-part version under the former title, recorded by BBC radio in 1980; and he has written *Barnes' People: Seven Monologues (Rosa, Glory, The Jumping Mimuses of Byzantium, The End of the World and After, Confessions of a Primary Terrestrial Mental Receiver and Communicator: NUM III Mark 2, Yesterday's News,* and *The Theory and Practice of Belly Dancing)* for BBC radio.

Barnes' absorption in the theatre includes not only playwriting, editing, and adapting, it also includes, as the last sentence indicates, directing. In collaboration with Stuart Burge, he co-directed *Lulu* and *The Devil is an Ass;* and with Geoffrey Reeves, *Antonio.* By himself, he directed *Frontiers of Farce* and his acting edition of *Bartholomew Fair.* His reasons for turning to direction are entirely practical. First, 'it takes so long after you write a play to get it on.' As his own director, he can expedite a production. Furthermore, 'I feel that if the playwright isn't actually working in the medium in which he's writing, he can lose a sense of that medium.'

The movement from the cinema to the stage is not the usual one for a writer to take. Although Barnes is by no means uninterested in writing films, the success of *The Ruling Class* changed his situation. For a long while, film producers did not offer him the opportunity to write screenplays. 'They figured I wouldn't be interested,' he explains. When *The Ruling Class* was filmed in 1971, Barnes wrote the screenplay. However, he disclaims responsibility for it.

> Actually, it was done for Keep Films, which was Jules Buck and Peter O'Toole. I delivered the script. I think it was about 130 pages on the first draft. I said, 'Well, all we've got to do is to cut ten to fifteen pages out of this and we should be in pretty good shape.' But O'Toole read it and said, 'Where's that speech?' and 'I don't think you should have cut that scene because this had a great speech of mine in it.' So the second draft was about 140 pages, which was absolutely ludicrous. However, it was his company.

Barnes knew that if he as screenwriter refused to restore speeches or scenes, O'Toole as co-producer and star actor would have them restored anyhow. As a craftsman, he therefore did the work he was assigned, turned in the script, and refrained from seeing the movie. In 1972, he himself directed a film of *Leonardo's Last Supper*. He did not adapt it for the different medium. The small cuts in the text are deletions he might also have made for a stage production. Through different camera shots and angles, and through editing, he achieved cinematic variety. Because the money ran out, as he puts it, he was unable to complete the editing and the shooting of credits until 1977, when the British Film Institute provided money to do so. That year, the BFI showed it at the London Film Festival.

3 | *The Major Plays*

The Ruling Class

The title of Barnes' first major play—like those of all his plays—indicates its subject matter. *The Ruling Class* satirizes the nature of that class, its values and viciousness, its perversions and pernicious charm, the different means it employs to maintain its dominant position. Extolling his country at the start of the play, the thirteenth Earl of Gurney hails 'what England means to her sons and daughters,' who are ruled 'not by . . . skill/But by sheer presence' (p. 3). The existence of a privileged, ruling class depends upon the existence of unprivileged, ruled classes; authority require submission and the maintenance of the *status quo*. Is not such a society lunatic? In this play, its leading exponent is insane. Does it not pervert humanity? The madman's father, whose address has just been quoted, relaxes by wearing a three-cornered hat, a tutu ballet skirt, and a sword in its scabbard, then obtains sexual thrills by placing his head in a noose, praising the empire, and pretending to hang himself. Does it consider itself in a godly position in relationship to the rest of society? Its chief character, the fourteenth Earl of Gurney, imagines himself to be God. Does the perpetuation of the ruling class intimidate and kill members of the lower classes, and subdue possible revolt? In person and by proxy—through the law and the law's administrators—the play's peers do so. Are the urbane words it uses to impose upon the masses and bolster its own self-esteem gibberish? Barnes has one member of the ruling class misquote Shakespeare and another provide what purports to be an explanation of a man eating grass, the nature of snow, the possibility of a rooster laying an egg, and the subjectivity of space and time in terms of a once-popular nonsense song, 'Mairzy Doats,' whose lyrics, which really describe banal and loosely related phenomena—'mares eat oats and does eat oats and little lambs eat ivy' (p. 21)—stress the nonsensicality of what they supposedly elucidate.

In a Prologue, the thirteenth Earl of Gurney, speaking before the Society of St. George (patron saint of England), apostrophizes the class hierarchies that constitute the essence of England and toasts the nation. In his capacity of judge—and hanging judge, at that: 'If you've once put on the black cap,' says he, 'everything else tastes like wax fruit' (p. 5)—he links the ruling class to the nation's legal system. Because three of his four sons are dead and the fourth, Jack, is for an undisclosed reason not discussed openly, the Earl intends to engender a new heir by marrying a commoner, Grace Shelley, mistress (the play later discloses) of his brother Sir Charles, who recommends her as 'good breeding stock. Family foals well. Sires mostly.' (p. 5). Before he does so, he relaxes by means of the bisexual attire and rope already alluded to. 'A man must have his visions,' he declares, particularly if that man is 'an English judge and peer of the realm'; envisioning 'six vestal virgins smoking cigars' and an army unit marching in formation, he stands, noose round his neck, on a pair of steps. '*With a lustful gurgle he steps off. But this time he knocks over the steps*' (p. 7). Accidentally, the hanging judge hangs himself.

At his funeral, the play proper begins. Because the burial service is conducted by his relative, a Bishop, Barnes links institutionalized religion as well as the law to the ruling class (another relative, the business magnate Sir Charles, links the nation's economy to this class). Through satiric reductiveness, Barnes mocks class and clergy. At first, the Bishop is '*an imposing figure*' since he is '*magnificently dressed in red cope, surplice, embroidered stole and mitre*' while '*A great church organ thunders out "The Dead March from Saul".*' When he disrobes after the service, he '*has shrunk to a small, bald-headed, asthmatic old man in dog-collar and gaiters*' (p. 11).

Upon the arrival of Jack, the deceased's only living son, to whom the thirteenth Earl has bequeathed the vast bulk of his property and wealth, and who has inherited his title, it becomes clear why his name has been mentioned infrequently and furtively. The fourteenth Earl of Gurney, about whom *The Ruling Class* revolves, believes he is God. He received the revelation of his divinity on 25 August—the birthday, Barnes admits he knew, of mad Ludwig of Bavaria. Jack's delusion that he is God relates directly to the syndrome of the ruling class. As his psychiatrist, Dr Herder, explains, 'he's suffering from delusions of *grandeur*. In reality he's an Earl, an English aristocrat, a peer of the realm, a member of the ruling class. Naturally, he's come to believe there's only one person grander than that—the Lord God Almighty Himself' (p. 20). Underscoring Barnes' attitude toward the nature of the English aristocracy, Jack explains that his revelation occurred outside a public urinal. Further emphasizing this attitude is Jack's explanation of how he knows he is God: 'When I pray to Him I find I'm talking to myself' (p. 22). Just as the ruling class regards itself as the ruler of the world, so does mad Jack regard himself as the 'ruler of the Universe' (p. 18). His lunacy is an extension of the lunacy of his class—a movement, as it were, from 'my lord' to 'my Lord.' Significantly, for it suggests the subordination of religion to the secular power structure, the man who believes himself to be God leaves his spiritual meditations on a mountain top to rejoin society as an earl.

Significantly, too, for it reveals the extent to which the ruling class has intimidated members of the lower classes to serve it, the butler Tucker, despite his having inherited twenty thousand pounds from the thirteenth Earl, remains to serve the fourteenth. Why does he do so? 'Fear and habit,' he admits. 'You get into the habit of serving. Born a servant, see, son of a servant. Family of servants. From a nation of servants. Very first thing an Englishman does, straight from his mother's womb is touch his forelock.' Although he calls himself an 'Anarchist-Trotskyist-Communist-Revolutionary,' he serves the peerage (p. 27). His rebellion consists solely of verbal sarcasm, and he becomes devoted to the welfare of the fourteenth Earl. As his name hints, the butler is *tuckered*, his rebelliousness too exhausted to manifest itself effectively.

Disliking the name Jack, the new Earl prefers to be addressed by 'Any of the nine billion names of God,' such as 'the God of Love,' 'J.C.,' 'the Holy Flying Roller,' and 'the Naz' (pp. 18, 24, 54). Although the ruling class employs religion to maintain its powers, J.C.'s relatives—including the Bishop—fear he may take seriously the teachings of Jesus. 'Pomp and riches, pride and property will have to be lopped off,' urges J.C. 'All men are brothers. Love makes all equal. The mighty must bow down before the pricks of the louse-ridden rogues.' Such an announcement disturbs Sir Charles Gurney far more than Jack's delusion that he is God. To call for the destruction of property and for human equality is proof, according to Sir Charles, who is *'trembling with rage'* at J.C.'s declaration, that 'he's not only *mad*, he's *Bolshie!*' (pp. 24—25). No matter that J.C. calls the lower classes 'louse-ridden rogues,' no matter that he continues to employ a butler, who brings him tea and toasted muffins while he meditates on a huge cross—both revelatory of his essentially aristocratic nature—the very reference to social equality and the abolition of property is subversive.

Even genuine belief in a God of Love may be subversive, as Mrs Piggot-Jones and Mrs Treadwell demonstrate when they attempt to persuade J.C. to speak at their church social on 'any topic of general interest. Hanging, Immigration, the Stranglehold of the Unions.' The last title suggests that the ladies expect the speech to support the ruling class's position. To them, these subjects are therefore non-political. When J.C. says, 'You can't kick the natives in the back streets of Calcutta any more,' they rightly fear he is not joking. When he insists, 'God is love' and admonishes them to love each other as he loves them, they utter cries of fear and flee (pp. 31–33).

As Dr Herder explains, the fourteenth Earl not only believes he is God, he also 'suffers from the delusion that the world we live in is based on the fact that God is love' (p. 36). Should he see what the world is really like, he will be cured. According to J.C., he is married to Marguerite Gautier, and when his cousin Dinsdale shows him a copy of Dumas *fils'* play *The Lady of the Camelias* in an effort to prove that Marguerite, its heroine, is fictitious, J.C. triumphantly describes it as his wife's biography. J.C.'s delusion in this regard inspires Sir Charles to palm off his mistress Grace Shelley (who was to have married J.C.'s father) as Marguerite, have her marry J.C. and deliver a son, have J.C. certified insane, and then become the boy's legal guardian. In a magnificent *coup de théâtre* that follows J.C.'s arguments with Dinsdale and his mother (Sir Charles's wife, Lady Claire) as to whether Marguerite really exists, Grace appears, as arranged by Sir Charles, costumed as the Lady of the Camelias, singing the 'Drinking Song' from Verdi's *La Traviata* (which is based on *The Lady of the Camelias*). The ruling class uses show business to achieve its ends.

J.C. marries Grace. On their wedding night, he enters the bedroom clad in white pyjamas, riding a one-wheel bicycle, and commenting, 'It's the only way to travel.' But he immediatly jumps off and announces, 'God loves you, God wants you, God needs you. Let's to bed.' Only his head is unhinged. As Grace says the next day, 'there's nothing wrong with the rest of his anatomy' (pp. 59–60).

To Dr Herder's *post facto* objections, Sir Charles blandly remarks, 'You said he needed a harsh dose of reality. You can't have a harsher dose of the stuff than marriage' (p. 61). The ruling class can handle someone like Herder, too. He has submitted an application for a research grant, to conduct experiments on the brains of rats, to a foundation on whose board Sir Charles sits, and Lady Claire seduces him. Funding for scientific research and sex are among the weapons in the ruling class's arsenal. But the Gurneys had not counted on Herder's pride. Although he and Claire seduced each other for ulterior motives—he to fund his rat experiments, she to prevent him from causing trouble—he insists, 'I don't like being made a fool of' (p. 62) and determines to cure J.C. He does not realize that regardless of whether he succeeds, the ruling class is bound to triumph. Since he aims to make people adjust to the society in which they live, the psychiatrist serves the interests of the ruling class. If he cures J.C. by ridding him of the delusion that the world is based on the idea that God is love, then the fourteenth Earl will truly take his place as a member of the peerage. If he fails, Sir Charles will render the fourteenth Earl harmless and will assume his place by proxy, all the while raising J.C.'s son to take that place as the fifteenth Earl when J.C. dies.

Because 'it's impossible for two objects to occupy the same space at the same time' (p. 64), Herder confronts J.C. with a rival madman, McKyle, who—far from considering himself a prince of peace—regards himself as the Old Testament God of Vengeance. 'I made the world in mae image,' asserts McKyle. 'I'm a holy terror. Sae that accoonts fer the bloody mess it's in' (p. 68). Herder presses the rival claimants: 'If one of you is God, the other must be somebody else.' While J.C. and McKyle argue, Dinsdale enters with the 'Super news' that since an old member of parliament is dying, a by-election will occur, and he implies that his victory is certain (p. 67). As the God of Vengeance defeats the God of Love, one hears *'the distant sound of a single slap and a baby begins to cry faintly.'* J.C. declares, 'My name's Jack'—an acceptance that Herder had earlier indicated would herald his return to normality—whereupon Sir Charles enters carrying a bundle and announcing, 'It's a *boy!*' As the former J.C. repeats his real name, *'The baby starts to cry'* (p. 70).

But the fourteenth Earl of Gurney—whose behaviour, as Dr Herder puts it with an irony of which he is unaware, 'is nearer the acceptable norm' (p. 74)—substitutes one form of madness for another. The second act begins with the music 'Oh for the Wings of a Dove'; soon, a pistol shot rings out; next, a dead dove lies at Jack's feet. The God of Murder replaces the God of Love. When Jack jokingly remarks that a cousin who considered himself Christ would not be a political asset to Dinsdale, who hopes to win a seat in the House of Commons, Dinsdale—referring to Edward Heath, then the Prime Minister—responds, 'I don't know. The Tory Leader's the son of a carpenter, after all.' Jack is surprised: 'Lord Salisbury's a carpenter's son?' (p. 75). His reference to the Marquis of Salisbury, a Conservative Prime Minister of the previous century, hints what he shortly confirms, that he believes he is living in 1888, when the ruling class held far greater power than today. Announcing that 'the day of vengeance is in my heart! Hats off for the God of Justice, the God of Love is dead,' he declares himself to be 'Jack, not the Good Shepherd, not the Prince of Peace. . . . I'm . . . Jack the Ripper!' (p. 86). A more appropriate symbol of the ruling class than J.C., and (according to some theories) an aristocrat who might even have some connections to royalty, Jack the Ripper is, as Ronald Bryden observes, 'that legendary English executioner of lowborn vice. . . .'[1]

Meanwhile, Sir Charles, proceeding with his plan to have the fourteenth Earl declared insane and himself appointed guardian of Jack's son, invites the Master in Lunacy to examine Jack. While Master Truscott admits that his main concern is not sanity and insanity but rather 'property and its proper administration' (p. 82), an interest that would seem to serve Sir Charles's purposes admirably, Sir Charles has not counted on the old-boy system. When, during the interview between Truscott and Jack, Jack unexpectedly sings the Eton Boating Song, and Truscott more unexpectedly joins him, it becomes apparent that they had been schoolmates. Of course, claims Truscott, 'the fact that we're both Etonians can have no possible influence on my recommendation.' Although he confesses, 'Etonians aren't exactly noted for their grey matter,' he insists, 'I've always found them perfectly adjusted to society.' What firmly convinces him of his former schoolmate's sanity is Jack's unequivocal declaration of the principles of his class: 'Our country's being destroyed before our e-e-eyes. You're MOCKED in the Strand if you speak of patriotism and the old Queen. Discipline's gone. They're sapping the foundations of our society with their adultery and fornication! . . . The barbarians are waiting outside with their chaos, anarchy, homosexuality and worse!' (p. 83). Truscott pronounces Jack fully recovered.

Whereas the God of Love horrified Mrs Piggot-Jones and Mrs Treadwell, the God of Ruling Class Justice wins their devotion. 'Why, the Hangman holds society together,' says Jack. To this, the ladies *'nod vigorously.'* Emboldened by their assent, Jack goes further: 'Bring back fear. In the old days the Executioner kept the forelock-touching ranks in order.' After he calls for a return to such good old days, when 'The punishment for blaspheming was to be broken on the wheel,' the ladies register overwhelming approval. As Jack summarizes, 'We understand each other perfectly. But that's only to be expected. Breeding speaks to breeding' (pp. 89–90).

Unlike Claire, who regards the professed ideals of the ruling class as notions she can either uphold or ignore as she pleases, Jack takes them seriously. When she tries to seduce him, that part of him which is Jack the Ripper emerges. Imagining her to be a lower-class whore, he stabs her to death. Then, as he frames the butler for the crime, he thereby subdues subversion. The police discover works by Lenin and Mao Tse-Tung in Tucker's library. When the butler pleads for help from his master, Jack remorselessly accuses him of the deed and provides the police with the motives: envy, hate, and revenge. Impressed by such inspirational behaviour, one of the awe-stricken policemen, whose job it is to protect the interests of the ruling class, gushes: 'My lord, I'd just like to say what a pleasure it's been meeting you. . . . You've shown me what *noblesse oblige* really means' (p. 104).

Devastated by Claire's death, Dr Herder questions whether he has indeed cured the fourteenth Earl. Jack points out, 'Behaviour which would be considered insanity in a tradesman is looked on as mild eccentricity in a lord' (p. 106). Using the psychiatrist's weapons against him, Jack forces Herder to admit that since the evidence confirms he is normal, Herder's belief that he is guilty of murder is paranoiac. Herder goes mad.

Revered by the Bishop, adored by his wife, and worshipped by Dinsdale, Jack assumes leadership of the Gurneys and reduces Sir Charles to a shaking, greying, feeble, impotent old man. In the House of Lords, Jack's maiden speech, a rousing invocation of his class's values—with its call for rule by fear and manipulation of the weak, lower classes by the strong, upper classes—arouses spontaneous shouts of enthusiasm from all the peers present. Finally, alone with his lower-class wife—'good breeding stock,' as his father had called her—he kills her. And why not? She has done her job for him by providing a male heir. What remains is merely sex, which Jack the Ripper punishes by death. The God of Ruling Class Justice has no need of the aptly named Grace, which J.C. admired, for 'It means a gift of faith' (p. 45).

Although Jack is mad, he is not essentially different from the other peers. The play is named after his class, not after him. His skirt-and-sword wearing father is also looney. As Tucker says, Jack is 'a nut-case all right, but then so are most of these titled flea-bags. Rich nobs and privileged arse-holes can afford to be bonkers. . . . Life's made too easy for 'em. Don't have to earn a living so they can do just what they want to. Most of us'd look pretty cracked if we went round doing just what we wanted to, eh, sir?' (p. 37). While Jack's final speech—which calls for flogging, bludgeoning, mutilation, and hanging the lower classes when the social order requires such measures—is shocking, he is not the only member of the peerage to hold such views. Immediately preceding his speech, other lords express similar sentiments, such as 'In order to protect the public the criminal must be treated as an animal' (p. 113). Earlier, Dinsdale had announced that the basis of his electoral campaign was 'the reintroduction of the death penalty' (p. 89). With himself in the House of Commons and his cousin Jack in the House of Lords, they will 'work as a team,' for 'We think alike on lots of things' (p. 108). While Jack is the most prominent member of the ruling class, he is typical of them, not unique among them.

Furthermore, J.C. and Jack the Ripper are the same person, the fourteenth Earl of Gurney. Two aspects of humanity which reside in one breast, to use Goethe's phrase, they are also two methods by which the ruling class rules. The God of Love inspires meekness and humility among the populace—which is useful to and convenient for the ruling class. The God of Justice inspires fear and cowardice—which is equally useful and convenient.

In this elegantly wrought 'baroque comedy,' as Barnes subtitles *The Ruling Class*, the first act climaxes with the arrival of a newly born boy, the second with another type of birth, the arrival in society of that child's father: *'He's one of us at last!'* (p. 114). The Prologue begins with poetry derived from Shakespeare (John of Gaunt's famous speech from *Richard II*), the Epilogue with lyrics derived from musical comedy ('Along Came Bill' from *Show Boat*). The Prologue ends with an accidental death, the Epilogue with a murder. The play starts with a eulogy of its titular class, it ends with a typical action by an exemplary member of that class, the murder of a commoner, the lowly-born mother of the murderer's son. Despite her death, the class remains. As the thirteenth Earl of Gurney declares at the start of the Prologue, England's 'fabric holds, though families fly apart' (p. 3).

Leonardo's Last Supper

Whereas *The Ruling Class* provides a view of the top, *Leonardo's Last Supper* offers one further down the social ladder. Property and authority concern not only the ruling class, who have them, but also the middle class, who want them.

In *Leonardo's Last Supper*, the painter of 'The Last Supper' has a last supper—though unlike the subject of the painting, it occurs after, not before, his resurrection. When he realizes he is alive, Leonardo da Vinci *'eagerly stuffs bread into his mouth, eating wolfishly.'* Then, *'Taking the wine-flagon he throws back his head and pours wine into mouth and over his face'* (p. 23). Like Jesus, Leonardo is betrayed by his own people, fellow Florentines. Jesus' supper celebrated the Jewish feast of Passover, so named to commemorate the night before the

Israelites departed from Egypt, where they were slaves, and entered the promised land. On that night, the Angel of Death went into the homes of the Egyptians and slew their firstborn children, but he passed over the Israelites' homes and spared their firstborn. In *Leonardo's Last Supper*, no Angel flies over the Ambois charnel house that is the play's setting, but one resides within, *Angelo* Lasca, who with his wife and son kill the resurrected Leonardo so that they may acquire money to permit them to return to Florence, which to them represents a promised land and a deliverance from the poverty which enslaves them—a deliverance they explicitly compare to that of the Israelites from the Pharaoh's yoke.

The tolling of a funeral bell and the chanting of the 'Miserere' give way to '*a yell of joy,*' a singing of 'Hey troly, loly loly,' and a dance around the corpse of Leonardo da Vinci (pp. 3–4). Commissioned to bury Leonardo, the Lascas delight at the generous payment, half of which they have already received, and at the prospect of increased business once it becomes known whom they buried, since people will consider it fashionable to employ the services of those who buried the great artist. On his knees, Lasca addresses Christ in what amounts to a parody of piety. He renders prayer and thanksgiving in anti-Christian terms of financial profit and vengeance, and he speaks mercilessly while invoking divine mercy:

> Christ, my Saviour, remembered his humble servant at the last, and sent down this golden carcass for his profit. Now, now, by the grace o' our Redeemer I can go back. *Old debts, Madame, old scores honoured Sir!* Oh sweet Jesus, I'll make 'em grovel like pigs in dung! Oh Holy Virgin Mother, I'll make 'em tremble till their breeches stink from their droppings! Oh Lord o' Mercy, I'll make 'em lick pomegranate seeds out o' me arse!   [pp. 4–5]

In the midst of their jubilation, Leonardo's corpse unexpectedly rises. When he sees Lasca wearing a half-mask of a large-beaked bird (which he dons as protection against the vapours of the dead but which also suggests a scavenger), Lasca's son Alphonso costumed as a skeleton figure of Death (which he will wear in a production of *Everyman* but which hints that, like the character in the play, he will come for Leonardo), and Lasca's wife Maria dancing with her skirt up (ironically named after Mary, she is the mother of a killer, not a saviour), the revived homosexual artist exclaims, 'Two fiends, and a woman with her skirts up. It's the Sodomite's Hell' (p. 14). His outburst is ironic. Although he is in France rather than in Hell and sees a family rather than fiends, the Lascas become fiendish as they make Leonardo's new life a veritable Hell.

Because his death turns out to have been a mistaken diagnosis, the Lascas not only demand full payment for the burial, they also insist on reimbursement for their loss of trade when people learn that Leonardo is alive. Lasca regards Leonardo's gratitude as insufficient: 'Thanks won't feed us, clothe us, give us back our villa, our slaves, our hot baths. Thanks is a cheat 'less backed by hard gold and silver' (p. 24). When Leonardo offers 'the gratitude of future generations' as reward, the Lascas regard this too as insufficient. 'I'm the future,' says Alphonso, 'and I'm not grateful' (p. 26). Ape-like, crouching and with their arms dangling, the Lasca men—still attired as a scavenger-like bird and a Death-like skeleton—advance menacingly on Leonardo, while the Lasca woman *'utters little coos of happiness in the background'* (p. 27). Plunging Leonardo headfirst into a bucket of excrement, urine, and vomit, they drown him.

At the play's start, a spotlight illuminates an enlarged reproduction of Leonardo's 'Divine Proportion' and a voice hails the Renaissance: 'In an extraordinary burst of intellectual energy the human spirit recovered its freedom after centuries of political and spiritual oppression. . . . The Gothic night dissolved, making way for the birth of modern man and the achievements of our age' (p. 3). As the play demonstrates, however, artistic creativity and intellectual achievement were not all the Renaissance spawned. It also hastened the rise of capitalism and the triumph of the profit ethic. It was a time when Leonardo painted the 'Virgin of the Rock' and ''Twas a time for the man o' business. For the only question asked was "how does it profit me?" It was . . . Lasca time' (p. 18). Speaking 'in the name o' God and profit' (p. 10), Lasca serves Mammon as he invokes the Christian God. The Gothic night did not entirely dissolve. Concurrent with the 'extraordinary burst of intellectual energy,' Lasca bottled farts, whose smell, people believed, warded off the plague. If it failed to do so, he profited by burying them. Because 'wind's difficult to bottle,' Lasca next bottled excrement. Among 'the achievements of our age' which the Renaissance prepared are merchandizing techniques. A Renaissance Man, though in a different sense from Leonardo, Lasca explains how he sold the '100 per cent proof' excrement he bottled:

'Lasca's Excremental Goodness' came in three sizes. 'Lady's Own' was a tiny bottle most beautifully engraved with signs o' the Zodiac and attached to a gold necklace. 'Man's Size' was flat and decorated with the figure o' Hercules strangling a lion; it sold at six florins. Our 'Jumbo Family Jar' cost all o' ten florins, but it lasted weeks. Signor, I'd discovered the secret o' wealth. I o'ertopped those learned Alchemists. They only turned *lead* into gold.   [pp. 19–20]

Though humanity supposedly recovered from 'spiritual oppression,' religious superstition still prevailed. Proudly, Maria recounts her performance of her 'Christian duty' when she denounced a woman for having 'practised the Black Mass, spawned incubes and kissed Lucifer's arse every night' and Lasca boasts that he followed his 'Christian conscience' when he put the torch to her pyre (p. 6).

At the dawn of the modern age, a solitary intellectual and artistic genius confronts a tightly-knit, money-grubbing family. Whereas his province is life, theirs is death. Whereas he creates beauty, they create profit. 'I'm the future,' says the son, accurately. 'We're needed. You're a luxury. We're the new men you scholars prate on about. You put us in the centre o' the Universe. Men o' trade, o' money, we'll build a new heaven and a new earth by helping ourselves. . . . You're our meat, you belong to us' (pp. 26–27). After they kill him, they sing the song popularized by Nat King Cole, 'Mona Lisa.' All Leonardo means to the future Lascas of the western world is a machine-made hit song that trivializes a work of genius and profits those who market it as Lasca did his 'Excremental Goodness.' To the Lascas and those like them, Leonardo's painting might be, as the song's and the play's final line says, *just* a work of art. Leonardo's legacy is in the hands of the Lascas, whose name derives from *lascito*, legacy. Barnes admits, 'I usually take tremendous care about names.'

Leonardo's Last Supper begins with a spotlight on the artist's 'Divine Proportion', it ends with a light on the same drawing, but then the Lascas are savagely cutting and hacking away at the corpse of the man who drew it. At the play's start, a voice hails the Renaissance as 'a new birth: revival: resurrection' (p. 3); at its end, the voice speaks of death and regards Leonardo's non-resurrection with relief: 'we can safely say we shall never see his like again' (p. 28). At its start, bass voices chant the 'Miserere'; at its end, a woman's, joined by two men's, sing 'Mona Lisa.' At its start is a verbal ode to intellectual liberation; at its end, a musical embodiment of what such liberation really amounted to.

Noonday Demons

Written to be performed as the second part of a double-bill with *Leonardo's Last Supper*, *Noonday Demons* takes place in a darker age than that of the former play, the fourth century. 'Still the Devil stirs at noon,' says the hermit St Eusebius (p. 34). At that time of day, demonic powers are traditionally at their highest. To St Eusebius, an *'emaciated figure, covered with sores and dressed in a filthy loin-cloth,'* with *'long, matted hair and a grey beard clotted with dirt'* (p. 33), who for thirteen years has lived in a cave, chained, on a daily diet of seven black olives and muddy water, the demon arrives punctually. 'It's Temptation Time, folks!' he announces (p. 36), and he projects onto a giant, hard-baked mound of human excrement the lures of money, lust, and power. 'Noonday thoughts creepeth back into my soul,' says the worried Eusebius before the tempter arrives (p. 33). The play suggests that saintliness and religion are themselves demonic. The devil is not a separate character but resides within the holy hermit, who changes his voice to tempt himself.

Reinforcing the conception that religion is demonic, Barnes has a rival saint, Pior, enter the cave. Like Eusebius, Pior is chained, emaciated, covered with sores, dressed in a filthy loin-cloth, has matted hair, and is dirty. ''Tis a noonday demon!' they exclaim in unison, referring to each other (p. 42). Commanding the other to depart in the name of the Lord, each sprinkles holy water at the other and, when this tactic fails, tosses the entire contents of his bowl of holy water in the other's face.

Each saint claims the cave as his own, given him by God. Eusebius refuses to relinquish his territory: ''Tis true God's house has many mansions, but this one is occupied' (p. 45). They argue as to whom God commands to occupy the cave. 'He speaks now,' says Pior. 'List.' Cocking his head to one side, he repeats God's statement, which only he hears, that he should remain in this cave that is his dwelling place. 'I hear Him,' says Eusebius. 'My Jesus speaks.' Cocking his head to one side, he repeats the same words. 'They both canst not be God's voice,' says Eusebius, 'even if He doth move in mysterious ways. We must determine in the Light o' Truth who heard the Word o' Truth' (pp. 45–46). Their argument as to who suffered most for God ends in a stalemate. Next, they vie for the honour of having given up most for God. When Pior relates how he left his plough to follow God, Eusebius triumphantly points out that as farmers are poor, he sacrificed nothing but instead received power he never would have had as a farmer, since as a monk he can command the most highly born to kneel in prayer. On the other hand, says Eusebius, he himself gave up a life of luxury to serve the Lord as a poor hermit. *'The ringside bell clangs and* ST EUSEBIUS *raises his right arm to acknowledge his victory.'* Bitter at his defeat, Pior accuses Eusebius of having lived in the type of sin and corruption that a lifetime of suffering cannot erase. 'Yea, I am a sinner and proud o' it,' declares Eusebius, who takes the opportunity to remark that heaven rejoices more over one repentant sinner than over ninety-nine just persons who require no repentance (p. 50). Refusing to admit defeat, Pior challenges Eusebius to a levitation contest. Rising on tip-toe, each is convinced that he is levitating, but neither convinces the other. Increasingly certain that their rivals are demons sent to corrupt them, the saints wrap their chains around their fists and fight each other. With great fury, Eusebius flays Pior's face and body until they are bloody. 'Look at thy raw carcass!' he exclaims triumphantly. 'I ne'er look at my body,' says Pior smugly; ''tis vanity' (p. 54). Pior smashes a water jug over the head of Eusebius, who does not flinch. Then, he savagely beats Eusebius with his chains. To fashion a lethal glove, each wraps his loose chains around his right fist and pounds the other with it. 'Kill, kill, kill for Jesus!' cries Eusebius. 'Kill, kill, kill for Christ!' cries Pior (p. 57). Brutally pounding each other as they climb the mound of excrement, they finally reach its top, whereupon Eusebius strangles Pior with his chains. His neck broken, Pior falls to the base. Eusebius sings 'Gloria in Excelsis.' Murder results from extreme devotion to God. The murderer kills in the name of God and believes his action to be holy.

The conclusion of *Noonday Demons* parallels that of *Leonardo's Last Supper.* Early in the play, the tempter tells Eusebius that all his privations, self-inflicted humiliations, and painful efforts to reach God are meaningless, incapable of accomplishing good. They never have and never will make virtue win, justice triumph, innocence adored, equality admired, guilt despised, or evil hated. 'It's all meaningless,' he concludes, and he predicts what will happen as a result of Eusebius' sufferings: 'You'll be resurrected in the second half o' the twentieth century as a stage freak. Your agonizing abstinence'll be treated as a subject for laughter.' He will be regarded only as a figment of a playwright's grotesque imagination: '"Noonday Demons" by Peter Barnes' (p. 39). The tempter's words prove true. At the end of the play, after he kills Pior, the dead saint rises and a duplicate Eusebius joins him in a curtain call. Trembling with fear, the first Eusebius watches in horror as Pior and the second Eusebius bow. Praying to God for mercy, Eusebius receives only applause. Like 'Mona Lisa,' he becomes show biz entertainment.

Noonday Demons begins with prayer and a recitation of physical deprivations for spiritual purposes. It ends with a demonstration of the uses to which these are put.

The Bewitched

Dramatized in earlier plays, such themes as a ruling class, authority and submission, profit, torment and murder in the name of religion, and show biz reappear in new form in *The Bewitched*. True to its title, the play focuses on bewitchment by secular and religious authority, which both intentionally and unintentionally employs murder, torture, intimidation, and entertainment for the purpose of bewitching the populace. It even employs murder, torture, and intimidation *as* entertainment. Insidiously, those who bewitch are themselves bewitched, for the authorities believe in the system that gives them power. So self-deluded are some of them that they think their sheer words can turn defeat into victory. Triumphantly, a Spanish nobleman rejoices: 'Madrid celebrates the victorious fall o' Barcelona!' (p. 98). The aristocracy is bewitched by the concept of a ruling class, royalty by that of divine rule, inquisitors by the dread of heresy. The Inquisitor-General reveals that 'in the darkest watches o' the night I e'en have doubts about His Holiness, Pope Innocent XII, himself!' (p. 70).

Set at the close of the seventeenth century, *The Bewitched* revolves around Carlos II, King of Spain, last of the Hapsburgs, whose failure to beget an heir resulted in the War of the Spanish Succession, which left millions dead and wounded, and which devastated western Europe. Thus, Carlos is known for the consequences of something he did not do, whereas if he had done it, he might be unknown. In this play, church and state join to help an exemplar of absolute authority procreate. What is this person who would reproduce himself? Reigning by what he considers divine right, his empire administered by clerical and secular statesmen, the King is a stuttering, slobbering, vomiting, pants-wetting, impotent, spastic, epileptic. This, Barnes satirically suggests, is authority. Staggering about in fury, his limbs jerking spastically down the steps that lead to his throne, he refuses to acknowledge his condition and cries, 'YOOOO say IIII'm Impo-Impo-Impo*TENT TENT*? Am IIII AM?' (p 12). No one dares to respond affirmatively. The presence of such authority stifles truth. In convulsions, he insists, 'III aaaaam Spain' (p. 40). So he is, a living symbol of the folly and evil of unquestioned authority. Referring to Carlos' penis, a genuflecting courtier, who is as bewitched by the King as his social inferiors are bewitched by him, proclaims, 'Like Atlas, Sire, you balance our world on 'ts tip' (p. 23). So he does. For the future of Europe to depend on a grotesque lunatic's erection and potency—which it did—is both symptom and symbol of authority's bewitchment.

A Prologue heralds the play's themes: efforts to beget a successor to the throne, the horror and death which result, and the joy of the bewitched subjects. The old, hobbling, diseased, sore-festering Philip IV of Spain, whose son is dead, must engender a new heir so that Spain may have a King. Because he is less virile than he used to be, he conjures in his imagination a vision of his former mistress, beautiful and young, who sexually stimulates him so that he will be capable of having intercourse with the Queen. Since church as well as state demand an heir of him, *'He makes the sign of the cross over his crotch'* while voices sing the 'Magnificat' in the background (p. 6). His stimulant vanishes, the Queen appears, she and Philip enter the royal bed. A Cardinal sprinkles them with holy water, intones a Latin blessing, and makes the sign of the cross. Wheels, screws, and pistons move and thud as the bed creaks, a woman screams, a skeleton jerks upright and collapses on a bier in a heap. The screams become the cries of a woman in childbirth and the stage splits open as, from a dark, glutinous liquid within a crack, a shapeless body emerges and hauls itself onto the floor. The sound of a sharp slap is followed by the cry of a baby, then by a choir that sings 'Gloria in Excelsis.' When the body hauls itself upright, revealing itself to be the deformed Carlos II, the horrified Philip clutches his chest and collapses, dead. Funeral bells toll, Carlos mounts the throne, the bells change into joyful peals and the cries of rapturous crowds, who cheer the new King.

More grotesque than his father (as his successor will be more grotesque than he is), Carlos represents a deterioration of the essential power of authority, which thus requires increased propping by external means. Whereas age and disease enfeebled Philip and made it difficult for him to beget an heir, the impotent young Carlos finds the task impossible. His wife, Queen Ana, therefore insists, 'You casn't produce an heir wi' the usual instrument so you must use pen and ink' (p. 12). She and his mother, Mariana, vie with each other to persuade him to name their choice of successor. Charles of Austria, Ana's nephew, is her selection; José of Bavaria, the Queen Mother's great-grandson, is hers. With starvation and the plague ravaging the land, the country at war, and the treasury empty, Cardinal Pontocarrero, who presides over the Council of State, determines to prevent Philip Bourbon of France from becoming Spain's next ruler. He and the Count of Monterrey contend as to whether Charles or José should be named, but Father Motilla, the Royal Confessor, ends their dispute with the announcement that Ana is pregnant.

Although it soon becomes clear that the diagnosis was mistaken,

Ana pretends to be pregnant—partly because she hopes she will become pregnant, partly to prevent her rival mother-in-law from acquiring more influence as a result of Ana's inability to conceive a child. Because Mariana does not believe Ana is pregnant, she has Theresa, the Head Washerwoman, sniff every item of Ana's dirty laundry to detect an odour of menstrual blood. When Mariana presents Carlos with a blood-stained pair of Ana's drawers as proof that Ana has lied about her pregnancy, Ana denies the charge and claims that Mariana manufactured and planted the evidence.

To provide Spain with a royal heir is a religious duty, the churchmen believe. On the basis of a vision he has while he is being flagellated, Father Motilla persuades Almirante, a noted fornicator and begetter of bastards, to copulate with the Queen. Sneaking him into the Queen's bedchamber, Motilla warns Almirante and Ana: 'No one will interrupt whilst I'm here t' see you committed adultery in godly fashion, wi'out sin. On pain o' thy immortal souls, there casn't be one jot o' pleasure in 't' (p. 54). But before the couple can do anything, Carlos enters, followed by Mariana. In the manner of bedroom farces, with heads jutting out of bed-curtains and people hiding in wardrobes, Almirante manages to avoid detection. At her wit's end, though, Ana clutches her stomach and tells Carlos that because his mother frightened her, she lost their child.

To rouse Spain's armies, to curb internal dissent, to provide entertainment for the exploited masses, but mainly to stimulate Carlos' virility, Pontocarrero persuades the King to have the church stage a massive *auto da fé*. 'Nine months after the last *auto generale*,' he recalls, 'there was an almighty outcrop o' births.' Motilla concurs: 'The stench o' burning flesh seems but t' stir up our vile lust f' life.' Adds Pontocarrero: 'Pray 'twill stir up His Majesty' (p. 69).

People are tortured. During the *auto da fé* that is the grotesque climax of Act I—an appropriate theatrical embodiment of the grotesque folly of the fate of Europe to depend upon a cretin's potency—gagged and manacled prisoners, some half-dead, march to their pyres while pedlars hawk programmes, hot chocolate, sweet cakes, and 'Souvenirs! Crucifixes! Beads! Virgin Marys! Authentic splinters from the stakes! Only two ducats!' (p. 80). People are burned alive and even dead (a skeleton is exhumed for the purpose). While a doctor examines Carlos' crotch with a magnifying glass, screams rend the air, the red wax of an effigy bubbles and flows like blood, and flames light the sky. Then, as a choir sings 'Hallelujah! Hallelujah! Hallelujah!' an eight-foot phallus sprouts from between Carlos' feet and, carried by a priest, impales the Queen (pp. 83–84).

Despite the sufferings and executions, Carlos fails to impregnate Ana. After Mariana dies of cancer, the King—finally persuaded to name a successor—selects his mother's choice, José of Bavaria. Shortly after he does so, however, comes news that José is dead. Wavering between Philip Bourbon and Charles of Austria, Carlos blames Ana for their inability to produce an heir of their own. Father Froylan, the new Royal Confessor, then mentions the unmentionable. He tells Carlos he is impotent. Although such a charge would ordinarily result in Froylan's torture and execution, the Royal Confessor provides an extraordinary interpretation of Carlos' impotence: witchcraft. Therefore, he explains, 'The fault's not in thee, Sire. . . . You're bewitched, Sire' (p. 112). He receives confirmation of this view from the possessed nuns of Cangas Convent, whose demons he tries to exorcise. When he demands the names of those who bewitched Carlos, the nuns chant a litany of virtually the entire Court. In a sense, they are correct. Propped by courtiers and statesmen who support secular and religious authority, the King *is* bewitched by such authority, as are these pillars and the populace.

Once more, the torture chambers fill with victims, for Froylan jails everyone suspected of being under diabolical influence. With him comes Theresa, the Head Washerwoman, who sniffs out witches and warlocks as formerly she sniffed laundry for menstrual blood. Whereas previously she searched for blood that had been shed, she now causes blood to be shed. So crowded are the torture chambers that the Chief Torturer complains of overwork and demands of Father Froylan, who tortures to root out witchcraft, and the Inquisitor-General, who tortures to root out heresy, 'Holy Fathers, you must gi' me a policy decision! We casn't save the immortal souls o' *both* witches and heretics. We haven't the equipment or men' (p. 127).

Despite the massive scale of torture and murder, Carlos' condition does not improve. Pontocarrero presses Carlos to decide upon a successor. To counteract Froylan, he asserts that Carlos is not bewitched but possessed—that is, influenced not by demonic powers outside his body but by a demon who has entered it. Even so, the King is not himself at fault. As the Inquisitor-General puts it, 'The cause's in you, Sire, though you're not the cause' (p. 129). In one sense, he is correct, for Carlos is himself the creation of blind submission to authority. In another sense, he is wrong, for while Carlos was created by such obedience, he creates it in others. Bewitched or possessed? Determined to be potent by any means, Carlos confounds the rival factions by insisting he is both bewitched *and* possessed, as indeed he is: influenced by and also incorporating authority. Since the King of Spain is possessed of authority, no one dares to contradict him. He is the bewitched bewitcher and the possessed demon.

The bewitched victims of authority reject neither the cause of their sufferings nor the established rituals that maintain them. Visiting the torture chamber in the first act, Carlos accidentally moves the rack handle. A prisoner screams in pain and gasps, ''Twas a great honour, Your Majesty' (p. 73). Visiting it in the second act, he hears courtiers declare, 'God be praised. My life-long friendship wi' the Queen's not broken, though my ten fingers are' and 'E'en in the House o' Pain my rank and privileges were observed. My body's fire-wracked, my mouth blood-filled, but I cry out, "God save the King!"' (p. 139).

One reason they submit is that authority relieves them of choice and provides certainty, frightful though that certainty may be. As the Inquisitor-General maintains, 'authority and submission're the twin poles on which Jehovah turns the world. . . . Oh man needs belief not reason! . . . We hunger f' the blessings o' blind ignorance, Lord!' (pp. 130–131). In a rare moment of post-epileptic lucidity, Carlos perceives the horrors and irrationality of a world where some starve while others have surfeit, where masses are poor while merchants amass wealth. He concludes that 'Authority's a poor provider./No blessings come from 't./No man born shouldst ha' t' wield 't./Authority's the Basilisk' and as long as one man commands and another obeys, it will ruin the world (pp. 137–138). But when he offers to renounce his crown and vacate his throne, his tortured, bewitched subjects cry in terror and flee. Without authority, the bewitched believe, in the words of the possessed nuns, 'Blind chance rules the world!' (pp. 115–116).

Yet it is authority that creates chaos, not the absence of authority. At the end of the play, Carlos—still impotent—is dying. With Spain's populace starving, its provinces in revolt, its enemies joined and ready to pounce, Pontocarrero presents him with a Will, ready for signature, which names Charles of Austria as his heir. Carlos acts upon the logic of authority and the *status quo*, not upon that of rational scepticism and humanity. Although he and his councillors recognize that to name Philip Bourbon of France as his successor will plunge Europe into a ruinous, bloody war, he commands that Charles' name be deleted and replaced by Philip's. Based on his premises, his reason is sound: 'Only France's strong enough t' hold our Empire together.' When Carlos says that he is Spain, he is right. The sole logical decision made by this cretin derives from and aims to maintain what he incarnates. Although the logic of this decision 'makes all that's gone afore meaningless,' Carlos' will is done. As he recognizes, the result of the authority he personifies is that 'The Lord o' Unreason rules and we stand alone at the mercy o' Chance. The empty Universe's deaf t' our voice, indifferent t' our hopes, crimes and sufferings. . . . My reign's a glorious monument t' futility' (p. 145).

Carlos is exemplary, not unique. According to the Queen's brother, 'all the Catholic crowned heads o' Europe've been possessed f' years' (p. 133). The Epilogue shows Philip V, Carlos' Bourbon successor, to be '*another freak, with massive legs and arms, bloated stomach and a small elephant's trunk hanging down over his chest in place of a nose.*' His face is that of a grinning imbecile. Although Pontocarrero's voice calls Philip's ascension a moment of hope rather than despair, of life rather than death, and the dawn of the age of reason, the recollection of Carlos' prediction of the slaughter and devastation of the War of the Spanish Succession, made shortly before the end of the previous scene, together with the vision of a monstrosity even more grotesque than Carlos, derides these assertions. As Philip's subjects cry, 'God save the King' (p. 149), a prayer similar to the one still heard in the England of Queen Elizabeth II, Barnes makes clear that the generations after Carlos' are as bewitched as his.

The Prologue to *The Bewitched* begins with the tolling of a funeral bell and a voice that speaks of a dying king; its action revolves around the conception of an heir; it ends with that king's death and the ascension of the heir, a deformed idiot. The Epilogue to the play has the same voice announce 'our ending's not despair but hope. Not death but life' and others proclaim 'The King shall live forever' (p. 149); its action revolves around the ascension of a new king, a freak even more deformed than the new king of the Prologue; it ends with the projection of his face, that of a grinning imbecile. The action of the play and the new character of the Epilogue mock the Epilogue's opening words. With such a future, the end is not hope but despair, and a life that is deadly.

Laughter!

Laughter! dramatizes themes of earlier plays in an entirely new manner. In *Tsar*, the first of its thematically related one-act plays, Ivan the Terrible embodies the authority of a ruling class. In *Auschwitz*, the second, the Nazis do. The subjects of both Ivan and Hitler are bewitched by authority. A courtier explains why he worships the tyrannous Tsar: 'You're God's anointed. You've the authority o' blood, Sire, authority that rests on the past. It gi'es our world a permanence which men need. . . . You gi'e us certainty, Sire, which is better than goodness' (p. 10). According to a functionary at Auschwitz, 'The German people've always preferred strong government to self-government. . . . We're tormented by choice.' As in *Noonday Demons* and *The Bewitched*, Tsar derides the value of suffering for God. Religion serves the state. 'Christ's crucified's a pledge o' God's pardon,' says Ivan, who notes, 'his hands nailed flat casn't strike me' (p. 3). The play emphasizes the similarities between Christianity and secular tyranny. 'I cried out, "Holy Father, Lord God Almighty, I sleered [slew] my son!"' exclaims Ivan. '"Me too," He answered' (p. 22). In Nazi Germany, the state and its leader have replaced religion and the deity. 'The State doesn't acknowledge God exists,' says one functionary. 'If he did, I'm certain Adolf Hitler'd be notified before anyone else.' According to another, 'National Socialism [is] Catholicism with the Christianity left out' (pp. 34–35).

The major emphasis of *Laughter!* links with a theme raised in *Noonday Demons* and, particularly, *The Bewitched*. In addition to trying to make Carlos potent, the *auto da fé* aims, through torture and murder, to entertain the populace—thereby distracting them and preventing them from doing anything about their exploitation by secular and religious authorities. In the torture scenes, Barnes— providing entertainment for his own audience—draws laughs from suffering. *Laughter!* goes further. Making his audiences laugh, Barnes also prods them into recognizing why they should not have laughed. 'Audiences,' says he, 'English audiences particularly, don't like being attacked. *Laughter!* is an attack. It's deliberately worked out to disturb. All my plays are extreme, but this was going across boundaries, into uncharted territory—for me, anyway.'

Laughter! is chiefly about the nature of its title. Framing *Tsar* and *Auschwitz* is a Prologue, which is a comic attack on laughter by a character called the Author, and an Epilogue whose action is the murder, both comic and horrifying, of two comedians who are concentration camp inmates.

Barnes' text might derive from a passage in Jonathan Swift's Preface to *The Battle of the Books,* one with which he admits familiarity and of which he says, 'I absolutely agree': 'Satire is a sort of glass wherein beholders do generally discover everybody's face but their own; which is the chief reason for that kind reception it meets with in the world. . . .'[2] In the Prologue to *Laughter!* the character named Author asserts that 'Comedy itself is the enemy. Laughter . . . cures nothing except our consciences and so ends by making the nightmare worse. A sense of humour's no remedy for evil.' Laughter 'softens our hatred. An excuse to change nothing, for nothing needs changing when it's all a joke. . . . Laughter's too feeble a weapon against the barbarities of life. A balm for battles lost, standard equipment for the losing side; the powerful have no need of it.' He demands we 'root out comedy' (p. 2). During his impassioned jeremiad, a custard pie hits his face, a carnation in his buttonhole squirts water at it, and his trousers fall down. The slapstick comedy provides a demonstration of how laughter diverts us from ideas that should engage our attention. The more we respond to the comedy, the less we respond to the Author's argument. His statement, less a thematic summary than a challenge based on a recognition of the limitations of the satirist's art, is more extreme than Barnes' own view. Through the Author, Barnes raises questions rather than provides answers.

According to conventional opinion, says Barnes in his own person, 'laughter alleviates suffering and makes us bear our miserable lot with equanimity and a little more grace than we would if we didn't laugh.' But he believes one should examine this view.

> There is a strong argument that laughter, far from alleviating, only increases the suffering, in the sense that if we laugh, then we don't change the miseries and the injustices. Hatred is sometimes more remedial in alleviating injustice than a sense of humour. It's too easy for comedians and satirists to say, 'I'm making fun of it; therefore, I'm doing some good because I'm helping to change it.'

Although this might possibly be the case, he adds, 'I think you must think it through before you embark on it as if it were definitely. Because you are a comic writer, it doesn't mean that you don't have to examine your position as an artist.' In a published interview on the subject, he provides an example of the social ineffectiveness of satiric comedy. If satire accomplished all its proponents claim, then '*The Government Inspector* should have washed away forever the meanness of bureaucracy. But it hasn't.'[3]

In *Tsar*, set in Russia of the late sixteenth century, Barnes derives laughter from the atrocities of the despotic Ivan. Some minutes after he spears the courtier Shibanov's foot to the floor, Ivan asks why he is moving in a circle. 'My foot's still nailed t' the floor, Sire.' Ivan furiously demands, '*(pulling out the staff)* Must I do everything?' When he insists Shibanov tell him the truth, the wounded courtier replies, 'I canst only speak the Tsar's truth, Sire, not real truth, truth's truth.' Once, but no longer, he was like Seneca and Socrates, who died for telling truth's truth. Then, 'I had ethics.' 'I don't care if you had carbuncles,' says Ivan. 'Tell me truth's truth.' But Shibanov fears death if he does that. 'Prince Reprin once spake truth's truth t' my face,' Ivan tells him. 'I'd like t' meet him, Sire,' ssys the courtier, 'and shake his hand.' Comments the Tsar: 'I'm not going t' the trouble o' having him dug up jus' so you canst shake his hand' (pp. 13–14).

At the start of the play, Ivan stands before Odoevsky—who is seated, with heavy weights attached to his feet, impaled on a wooden stake which, covered with congealed blood, is driven through his body—and has the audacity to claim that his own spiritual suffering is worse than Odoevsky's physical suffering. Pleading for sympathy from the man he is barbarously torturing, Ivan explains that because Odoevsky only betrayed an earthly ruler whereas Ivan betrayed God himself, Odoevsky's punishment is slight, merely a stake driven through his body. He should therefore 'smile, your chastizer's human, not divine, who gi'es his victims, *mercy*. Smile, my son, that Christ stakes me not you! You buy forgiveness cheap. . . . My pain's infinite, yours has a stop. Oh, some men're lucky!' Odoevsky's response is to scream with pain (p. 4). Although Ivan claims he wants to rid himself of the burden of rule, he bestows his crown on Semeon, a man incapable of ruling, a man whose attempts to reign only remind everyone of the more authoritative Ivan, whom they insist on obeying. Each implores the other to relieve him of the responsibility of ruling. 'Only save me!' cries Semeon. 'Only let me be saved!' cries Ivan. 'Uuuuuuuuhhrr eee,' screams Odoevsky (p. 7), in effect mocking Ivan's professed desire. That Ivan's desire not to rule is insincere is clearly revealed when his son, the Tsarevitch, demands he relinquish the throne to him. Attempting to demonstrate his ability to succeed his father, the Tsarevitch describes his military prowess and his proficiency at murder. All Ivan is willing to concede is that 'at times you remind me o' me when I was young.' Although the young man is not as devious, malignant, or cruel as Ivan was, 'in *some* ways you remind me o' me' (p. 15). When Ivan complains that the crown crushes him 'wi' power's pain,' the Tsarevitch urges Ivan to yield it to him. 'I keep it t' save you,' insists Ivan, but when the Tsarevitch tries to snatch the crown, Ivan hits him with the iron tip of a staff and, as he falls, continues to spear him until he dies (pp. 20–21). At the end of *Tsar*, a voice explains, 'The title "Terrible" was due to an unfortunate mistranslation; it was more accurately "Ivan the Awe-Inspiring"' (p. 26). Barnes' point is not academic. Both translations are appropriate, the play demonstrates, for Ivan's terrors are what inspire awe.

Whereas *Tsar* derives comedy from individual despotism, *Auschwitz* focuses on impersonal slaughter. In a transitional scene between the plays, Ivan is visited by Samael, who is otherwise known as 'The Angel who wrestled with Jacob at Penial,' 'The Wind that Stinks,' and, simply, 'Death.' He is dressed in the style of the future: a *'double-breasted, blue serge suit, starched collar, waistcoat and stainless-steel framed spectacles'* (pp. 21–22). Upon learning his identity, Ivan prays in Latin. 'I appreciate your using a dead tongue,' says Samael, 'but I prefer tomorrow's language today: non-operating deductions, contingent, liabilities, functional obsolescence.' In the manner of a dispassionate professional judgment, he observes that Ivan 'made death too personal, arbitrary, a matter of chance: too much like life.' In the future, he foresees with pleasure, people will institutionalize death, 'take the passion out of killing, turn men into numbers and the slaughter'll be so vast no one mind'll grasp it, no heart'll break 'cause of it. Ah, what an age that'll be. How confidently they'll march on to extinction' (pp. 23–24). His description befits *Auschwitz*. Although Ivan, clinging to life as he did to his crown, defeats Samael in battle, Ivan is human. As Samael predicts before the battle, 'You can't avoid general deterioration of the total equipment' and 'someday the day must come when the day won't' (p. 24). Ivan dies. All that remains is a mistranslation of his name and a statue covered with bird-droppings.

Auschwitz is set in the German concentration camp of that name, which is used as a symbol of how most people blind themselves to and thereby perpetuate its and other horrors. Audaciously, Barnes manipulates the spectators' responses to make them recognize, by the end of the play, their kinship to the functionaries who administer Auschwitz, and therefore their guilt as well.

These functionaries, a group of civil servants, tell jokes to help them bear—but not to change—their lot under Hitler's Third Reich, such as: 'Coming to work this morning, I stopped to pull in my belt. Some idiot asked me what I was doing. I said, "Having breakfast"' (p. 29). Engaged in bureaucratic rivalry with Gottleb, the quintessential Nazi, who heads another department, Viktor Cranach and the people in his department, Else and Stroop, include among the beginning duties of their day a search for one of Gottleb's bugging devices, which they find and destroy. Suddenly interrupting their conversation, Cranach *'sniffs suspiciously.'* He flings open the door to catch Gottleb, who wears a Hitler moustache, crouching, obviously having been listening at the keyhole (pp. 35–36). They try to outmanoeuvre each other with rival memoranda, each designed to discredit the other's actions. When Wochner, a black marketeer, enters to deliver goods to Cranach and those who work for him,

Gottleb appears to have the upper hand, but Wochner reveals that he has some merchandise for Gottleb as well.

Gottleb tries another tactic. As Cranach and his co-workers get more and more drunk from the wine purchased from Wochner, Gottleb tries to persuade them they should become friends. Lulling them into a false sense of security, he goads them into telling anti-Nazi jokes, even though Cranach recognizes that such jokes are criminal offences. *'Giggling,'* Stroop relates what Mrs Goering told her husband at their wedding reception: 'Why've you got on your tuxedo and medals Herman, this isn't a first night.' Else remarks, 'The only virgin left in Berlin is the angel on top of the victory column—Goebbels can't climb that high.' Cranach tops these with an anti-Hitler joke: 'what do you call someone who sticks his finger up the Führer's arse?!' The answer: 'a brain surgeon!' (pp. 54–55). Whereas most jokes about leaders of the Third Reich carry penalties of five to fifteen years' hard labour, anti-Hitler jokes bear a mandatory death penalty. Producing a small tape-recording machine, Gottleb swears he will have Cranach sentenced and hanged by the end of the week.

Fortunately for Cranach, the myth of German efficiency proves mythic in another sense of the word. The machine fails to work. When Gottleb plays back the tape, all that emerges is *'a cacaphony of high-pitched screeches, muffled squawks and clicks'* (p. 56). Gottleb tries to bribe Else and Stroop to testify they heard Cranach tell the joke. Cranach, however, offers them something more valuable than the perquisites, higher salaries, rank, and pension promised by Gottleb. He gives 'security.' Gottleb is 'not one of us. He isn't safe!' (p. 59). Turning against Gottleb, Else and Stroop assert that he, not Cranach, told that joke. But Gottleb is not yet ready to admit defeat.

While he tries and fails to turn the workers in Cranach's department against Cranach, spectators sympathize with the functionaries, people like themselves, and become hostile to the ruthless Nazi zealot. At the start of the play, they laugh at Cranach's bureaucratic jargon, such as: 'Component CP3(m) described in regulation E(5) serving as Class I or Class II appliances and so constructed as to comply with relevant requirements of regulations L2(4) and (6), L8(4) and (7)' (p. 28). After Gottleb fails to sway the civil servants, he determines to make them face the reality behind the jargon, which are specifications of the concrete chimneys of the Auschwitz crematoria. He forces them to recognize what underlies bureaucratic terminology:

Future cases of death must be given consecutive Roman numbers with consecutive subsidiary Arabic numbers, Numerical I/1 to I/185. If you could see the dead roasted behind Roman numerals I/1 to Roman numeral XXX/185 you'd run chicken-shitless, but you haven't the imagination. Even if you read of six million dead, your imagination wouldn't make you see a single dead man. But I'll make you see six million! I'm going to split your minds to the sights, sounds and smells of Auschwitz.   [p. 61]

He tells of block commanders using newly-born babies as footballs, slave labour, starvation diets, injections of poison, axe-murders, and Zyklon B crystals gassing the inmates. As he describes further atrocities, upstage filing cabinets—which hold and conceal records that substantiate such facts—open to reveal Nazi Sanitation Men mutilating bodies and scavenging the gold teeth of gassed corpses. Spectators see what underlay their laughter. In reality, the civil servants have known what they were doing—'Deaths and paragraph fifteen isn't any of our business' (p. 38)—but they have shut their minds to it. To Gottleb, who has become the spectators' enemy as well as the civil servants', the functionaries protest their inability to prevent the atrocities of Auschwitz: 'I can't fight 'em. . . . This isn't the time to say "no." I've just taken out a second mortgage!'; 'But what can I do? I'm only one woman'; and 'You can't expect me to say "no". . . . I'm retiring next year. I'd lose my gold watch!' (pp. 64–65). Having previously manipulated the spectators' sympathies toward ordinary, apparently decent people at the mercy of a Nazi beast, Barnes turns the spectators against these people. To keep their minds closed to their knowledge, the functionaries replace Gottleb's descriptive language with neutral language. Fighting Gottleb with bureaucratese, which divorces meaning from words, they shut their minds to Auschwitz's horrors. As Cranach says, 'hard facts leave nothing to the imagination. We're trained to kill imagination before it kills us. So close mind's door, shut out the light there. Concentrate on what's real, what's concrete. Concentrate and repeat: Component CP(3)m, described in regulation E(5) serving as Class I or Class II appliances shall be so constructed as to comply with relevant requirements of regulations L2(4) and (6), L8(4) and (7).' As Else and Stroop repeat the regulations—which no longer provoke laughter—the filing cabinets close to seal off the sights and sounds of Auschwitz. Although Gottleb cries, 'You can't shut it out, not word play, dream play, I've been there! *It's real!*' he cries in vain (p. 66). The man whose name, as Barnes admits, derives from *God* and *to live* only momentarily vivifies death, and Viktor Cranach, whose given name, Barnes also admits, forecasts his victory, triumphs.

The civil servants exult in their defeat of the Nazi fanatic: 'We may not be much, but we're better than Gottleb. This time it didn't end with the worst in human nature triumphant, meanness exalted, goodness mocked.' Proudly, Cranach prophesies that Gottleb's defeat will make future generations recognize that those who really ran Auschwitz were 'ordinary people, people who liked people, people like them, you, me, us.' With these banalities, Barnes convicts the audience. Those with whom we empathized are worse than the Nazi Gottleb, who does not blind himself to the truth about Auschwitz, as people 'like . . . us' have done, as we 'like them' still do. Driving home his point, Barnes audaciously follows this statement with the victorious trio of ordinary people turning to the audience, singing 'The Brotherhood of Man' (from *How to Succeed in Business Without Really Trying*), and requesting the spectators to join them in song (p. 68).

In an Epilogue, two hollow-eyed concentration camp inmates do a dance and patter number, with such gags as 'Bernie Litvinoff. . . . Drunk a whole bottle of varnish. Awful sight, but a beautiful finish' and 'According to the latest statistics, one man dies in this camp everytime I breathe.' 'Have you tried toothpaste?' (p. 69). Gassed during their act, they die while telling jokes. As they expire, one recalls the words of the Author in the Prologue: 'In the face of . . . Ivan the Terrible . . . or Auschwitz, what good is laughter?' (p. 2).

The Prologue to *Laughter!* contains a comic attack on laughter and a call for its liquidation. Its Epilogue contains two joke-telling comedians who are liquidated. In context, their comic patter is savage as well as funny. In answer to the question, 'Did the audience laugh at the jokes in the Epilogue?' Barnes replies, 'On the good nights, they didn't.'

Red Noses, Black Death

To date Barnes' greatest and most complex work, *Red Noses, Black Death* represents both the culmination of his previous original plays and a new direction, in that it suggests the basis of positive action to eliminate the social evils he satirizes. As in *The Ruling Class*, *Red Noses, Black Death* demonstrates how rulers retain their power and privileges at the expense of the ruled. As in *Leonardo's Last Supper*, culture is marketed for the masses. As in *Noonday Demons*, religion is a diabolical force that accomplishes no social good and that drives some zealots to self-mutilation. As in *The Bewitched*, people prefer bewitchment by authority to the terrifying responsibility of freedom. 'Tell us lies even if they're not true,' a commoner begs a helpless doctor, and another commoner demands, 'Give us something even if it's nothing' (I,v). Recalling the earlier play, *Red Noses, Black Death* has Pope Clement VI say, 'Submission and belief [are] the twin poles of the world' (II,iv). Recalling *Laughter!* a character in the later play asserts that the abandonment of goodness is 'a small price to pay to remove the terrible necessity of choice from mankind' (I,x).

Chiefly, according to Barnes, *Red Noses, Black Death* derives from the Prologue to its immediate predecessor, *Laughter!* 'It dramatizes a situation in which people use laughter. Does it help to alleviate the suffering that goes on around them, or does it make it worse?' Examining the hypothesis of the Author in *Laughter! Red Noses, Black Death* asks, in Barnes' words, 'Can we ever get laughter from comedy which doesn't accept the miseries of life but actually helps to change them? Without laughter, the world will probably be grey. The laughter we have now helps perpetuate the *status quo*. Laughter linked with revolution might be the best of both worlds.' Only half-jokingly, he maintains that this most recent play, set in Europe in the mid-fourteenth century during the plague, 'is really about the birth of show biz.' In *Red Noses, Black Death*, Barnes makes theatre people his central figures. Although one should be careful not to identify a dramatist too closely with a character, even—as in *Laughter!*—a character called the Author, Father Flote, the protagonist of *Red Noses, Black Death*, comes by the end of the play to a realization similar to that of Barnes, who admits, 'A lot of what he goes through is a process I have undergone in writing comedy. I've theorized about it, but he lives it as a created character.'

The fourteenth century was a time of death on a vast scale. 'One-third of Christendom lies under sod,' says Father Flote in 1348, only a year after the outbreak of the plague (Prologue). It was a time of chaos and anarchy, for death struck randomly. Neither youth nor physical strength could withstand it: children might die and the aged live, the strong fall and the weak stand. Goodness, wealth, and trappings of power were no proof against it. From Pope to peasant, everyone was terrified. 'Men've seen death treat all men equal,' says an Archbishop. 'Authority's gone, no place for Christ' (I,iii). Not only did people wonder, 'If there's life after death, why bother to die?' (I,i), they also considered, 'Is there life before death?' (II,ii). Gone was the authority of secular experts, who themselves recognized it had no basis to begin with. As a doctor laments, 'I prescribe wine and they die, no wine and they die, abstinence and they die, debauchery and they die, cold meat and they die, hot meat and they die, sleep on the right side and they die, left side ditto. I've a hundred percent record of failure' (I,ii). With the perceptions that the Black Death levelled all human beings and that conventional authority was powerless, it was a time of enormous revolutionary potential.

Three major groups contend to influence the populace. Although each is necessary, each is insufficient as a force for social improvement.

Lamenting that 'Men casn't live in this misery, die in this despair,' Father Flote—inspired by God, he believes—forms the Red Noses, a religious 'brotherhood of joy, Christ's Clowns, God's zanies,' designed to 'cheer the hearts of men with gibs, jibes, and jabber jinks; masques and other merriments' (I,iii). Each member wears a symbol of the order, a clown's red nose. Trying to lighten the dying moments of a plague-stricken lawyer, the red-nosed priest jokes, 'Is it true lawyers believe all men innocent till proved penniless?' The man laughs and dies. To a young woman, he relates, 'Old Dubois told the marriage broker he wouldn't marry the girl without a sample of her sexual powers. "No samples," said the girl, "but references he can have!"' The woman smiles and dies (I,i).

Opposing the Red Noses are the Black Ravens, former galley slaves freed to bury corpses, whose possessions they loot and whose plague pus they bottle and sell to the superstitious, who believe it will protect them. Aiming to destroy the existing order, they ask the poor to join them in killing the rich. 'The world's dying only to be born again,' they insist, and 'Plague-time heralds a new dawn' (I,ii). 'Spit on the fat bellies,' they urge. 'Spit and take their fine places' (I,v). They dream of 'a different ordered world . . . [with] no property, no money' (II,v). However, they understand hatred, not how to implement their egalitarian vision. As one of them later confesses, 'I broke the eggs but I didn't know how to make the omelette' (II,v).

Whereas the Black Ravens would change the world with blows directed against the wealthy and powerful, the Flagellants would change it with blows directed against themselves. The Master Flagellant would like to be 'a true Vicar of Christ who fed the hungry, clothed the naked and helped the oppressed' (Prologue). Calling the Pope 'a sucking dog-leech' who sells religion for profit, the Flagellants aim to 'appeal-to God direct. We need no mitred prelates to intercede for us. No man needs to go to Avignon [where the papal seat has moved] nor Hell to find Pope or Devil. Both lodge in his own breast!' (I,vi). But its leader recognizes afterward, 'We flagellants embraced pain when we should've been trying to eliminate it' (II,vi).

While the Black Ravens represent a type of anarchistic socialism, the prostitutes—a group less thematically prominent than the other three—represent a type of trade unionism. Since wealth is useless against the plague, the gold merchants believe that money has lost its value and want to indulge in a grand debauch before they die. The prostitutes take advantage of this unbusinesslike attitude. Because their commodity is in greater demand than ever, their guild strictly regulates prices, which it raises: 'Twenty-two denari for the missionary position,' 'Fifteen denari for a one-handed put,' 'Thirty f' blowing the grousel,' 'Fifty gold nobles for an all-night special.' According to Camille, 'We're certified free of all infection, plague clap, blue-boar or worse. . . . The Whore's Guild has to keep up standards with so many fiery young wag-tails on the game not knowing their arses from their elbows. That's why Whore Inspectors're out every night checking on performances. If yer want a-la-carte humping yer have to pay for it.' 'We'll pay for it with pleasure,' says a gold merchant, to which she responds, 'With pleasure it'll cost you more.' When a non-member wants to join the orgy, the prostitutes prevent her: 'Not 'less you've got a fully paid up Guild card, you can't' (I,vi). With such views, the social order does not change in essence; it merely replaces those in charge. Those previously exploited now exploit their former exploiters, but exploitation persists. In a reversal of the usual situation, the trade unionists control the businessmen. As Bernard Shaw says, 'Trade Unionism is not Socialism. It is the Capitalism of the Proletariat.'[4] Unlike the Black Ravens, the Whore's Guild does not seek to alter the system; it seeks greater wages from it.

Like the prostitutes, and in contrast to both the Black Ravens and the Flagellants, the Red Noses do not aim to change the *status quo*. Rather, they wish to instil in the dying enough hope that, as Flote puts it, 'the shit [will] start t' smell good' (Prologue). Their compassionate mirth diverts people from such facts as 'Ten percent of the population of Auxerre dies of starvation every year without plague help' and 'Free men're made bondsmen, dress in tatters, whilst their fields're enclosed and stolen by landlords' (I,v). Thus, the Red Noses perpetuate social conditions that constitute a plague comparable to the Black Death.

And they are more effective than any other group. Vying with the Black Ravens and the Flagellants, it is they who influence the populace. Their comedy even diverts the gold merchants and prevents them from copulating with the prostitutes ('Can't do it. The rhythm's gone. Lost the beat'), though—since both serve the same larger society—they do not do so for long: 'Did you say *aaa-ooh-*

ahh? That's good. *(Jerking violently up and down)Aaa-ooh-ahh*'s a better beat than *huhh-huhh. Aaa-ooh-ahh*'s the carnal beat, my bawds!' (I,vi).

With their increased power, the Red Noses attract more members: Le Grue, a blind juggler ('Le Grue must be to juggling what Attila the Hun is to needlework'); a stuttering stand-up comic, introduced as 'Pierre "I-suffered-for-my-art-now-it's-your-turn" Frapper' ('Someone should throw a shoe at him and forget to take out their foot'); and the dancing Boutros Brothers, each with one good leg and a crutch for the other ('the very apotheosis of Christianity: the triumph of hope over experience'). As Father Flote says of all these performers, 'Failing to be good, they succeeded in being completely bad' (I,viii). Thus, they produce laughter.

To determine whether he should sanction the Red Noses, Pope Clement VI summons Flote to Avignon. Employing a variant of the conventional justification of laughter, Father Toulon urges the Pope to disband the Red Noses: 'Flotism'd encourage worse rebellion, Your Holiness. Laughter produces freedom. It's against all authority, ripping off the public mask to show us the idiot face beneath. St Peter and your local Tom-Turd man look equal shivering in their soiled underpants.' Testing whether laughter is more apt to encourage or discourage rebellion, the Pope questions Flote: 'Will you disband your Red-Nosed Brotherhood if I ask?' Although Flote tries to evade the issue with a string of one-line jokes, Clement VI is firm: 'Will you believe I am His true voice on earth, Christ's voice, and obey?' Flote collapses. Because he has obeyed papal authority, Clement VI recognizes that laughter, far from being an effective weapon against it, is a weapon in its arsenal. Instead of disbanding the Red Noses, he blesses them and promises to recognize them as a religious order, which he will finance. 'The Church is endangered,' he tells Flote. 'New enemies call for new methods to combat 'em. Go out, Father F, give 'em joy this Easter. Dazzle 'em, take what's left of their minds off the harsh facts of existence' (I,x).

Meanwhile, the Flagellants and the Black Ravens, who are less persuasive than the Red Noses, join to destroy their major rival. Confronting each other in a climactic scene, they all recognize that each group has something valuable: the Red Noses, the joy and laughter that should be the cornerstone of a new world, in contrast to the misery and pain of the old, and the ability to influence the masses; the Black Ravens, the conception that the populace should overthrow the ruling classes, seize power, and change the social order; the Flagellants, the idea that divinity resides within every human being. Since they also recognize that only together can they create a better world, they join in fraternal communion. 'Blow trumpets, for a new age, new world, new light, new birth!' exclaims Flote (II,iii). Because they act too late, Flote's command is inappropriate. At the scene's end comes the announcement that the plague is over. The Black Ravens' egalitarian ideas threaten authority, the Pope recognizes. He proclaims them 'anathema, hell-spawn, without protection.' In return for financial assistance, the French King agrees to support the Church in crushing the Flagellants, who endanger it not only by their 'independent manifestation of zeal,' but: 'More important, what's to become of the most profitable function of the Holy Office—selling salvation—if men can cleanse themselves of sin by self-inflicted penances? If they're getting it free from the Flagellants we'll be forced out of the salvation business.' With the normal order restored, church and state join to isolate and crush the groups which threaten them. Still, Clement VI sanctions Flote's Red Noses. 'He's helped keep unrest down to a minimum, made men more readily accept their miserable lot. Flote's proved useful. A revolution never returns' (II,iv). Warned of Flote's alliance with the Black Ravens, however, the Pope takes note.

Despite the slaughter of the Flagellants and the Black Ravens, the laughter of the radicalized Flote serves revolution, not the *status quo*. He creates an acronym for social reform through moderation: 'Slow, Lawful, Orthodox Progress: S-L-O-P, SLOP' (II,v). As before, the Pope orders Flote to obey him and to disband the Red Noses. In contrast to his earlier obedience to a papal command, Flote this time refuses to submit. 'Our humour was a way of evading truth, avoiding responsibility,' he tells the Pope. 'Our mirth was used to divert attention whilst the mighty slunk back to their palaces.' He is unable to return to such humour, as are the other members of his order. Therefore, the Pope has them killed by the cross-bows of his Iron Guards (II,ix).

Barnes' position in *Red Noses, Black Death* differs from that of the Author in *Laughter!* Laughter need not be only for losers. The later play proposes a socially productive type of laughter, and it contrasts both types. Exemplifying them are two plays-within-a-play, twin climaxes of the play's two acts. In the first act, a parody of *Everyman* demonstrates the laughter that is for losers. In the second, a parody of a nativity play shows revolutionary laughter.

The *Everyman* parody diverts people's minds from the reality of death. Everyman's baby throws a spoonful of porridge in Death's face and hits Death with his rattle. Death agrees to let Everyman bring a companion—'if you can find a friend dumb 'nough.'

Although Everyman and Death play dice for Everyman's life, Everyman asks, 'Shall we make it truly interesting and play for money as well?' (I,xi).

By contrast, the nativity parody subversively derides secular and religious authority. 'What do you do?' asks Herod. The answer: 'Nothing. I'm a nobleman.' One of the three Kings tells the infant Jesus, 'remember in Thy coming years of triumph KINGS paid you tribute. We bend knee to you so your followers'll bend knee to us after.' Mary declares, 'I *have* been a virgin and a mother. Not both at once, of course.' A character announces, 'In a stable the infant Jesus chose to lie. Amongst the poor who never die. How can they die, they've never lived.' Another quotes a psalm (137) out of context to justify the slaughter of the innocents: 'Happy shall he be that taketh and dasheth thy little ones against the stones' (II,ix). From gags to bleak humour, such jokes, subversive of authority, are potentially revolutionary.

The stage spectators' responses to the parodies—which in such plays-within-a-play cue the real spectators' responses—differ from each other. Of the *Everyman* parody, a Black Raven complains, 'They haven't shown the world as 'tis or how we can change it. 'Tisn't real enough.' The audience boos him and a prostitute cries, 'let 'em play' (I,xi). Of the nativity parody, an Archbishop complains, 'We were promised soothing syrup and see what they give us!' This time, the prostitute concurs: 'It isn't funny!' Flote removes his red nose. To the targets of his revolutionary jokes, he agrees, the nativity play is not comic: ''Tisn't funny when they feed us lies. . . . 'Tisn't funny now inequality's in the world, naming rich and poor, mine and thine. 'Tisn't funny when power rules. 'Tisn't funny till we throw out the old rubbish and gold and silver rust. Then it'll be funny' (II,ix). After the *Everyman* parody, nature's plague comes—as Death does in the play—for one actor. After the nativity parody, the Pope, who represents the plague of secular and religious authority, slaughters—as Herod does the innocents—all the actors.

Because unsympathetic forces of reaction destroy sympathetic characters who exemplify progress, the play contains a note of despair. But *Red Noses, Black Death* is a composition of more notes than one. The nativity performance and the actors' defiance of authority after it constitute hopeful notes. So does an Epilogue, in which voices of the dead -Red Noses echo passages from earlier scenes—not only quips, such as 'Don't eat so fast, Le Grue. It's the first time I've seen anyone get sparks from a spoon,' but also thematic statements, such as 'I see hatred of authority as our first duty' and 'Every jest should be a small revolution. We come to ding down dignity and make a new world. All forms of rebellion must come together.' Moreover, Flote makes a new statement: 'A world ruled by seriousness alone is an old world, a grave, grave-yard world. Mirth makes the green sap shout and the wilderbeast run mad. Not mirth born of anxiety and fear but [mirth] announcing the dawn-day of freedom.' When Toulon complains that the dialogue was supposed to be a résumé but Flote had never said that, he replies that he should have. As the Red Noses prepare to meet their maker, they declare, 'We want to find out how He came to make such a botch job of everything' and 'God's up for judgment.' Revolutionists die, but the idea of revolution lives, joined by laughter.

The Prologue to *Red Noses, Black Death* begins with a man seated on the edge of a grave, meditating on death and on God. It ends after his death, meditating on that graveyard world, as he prepares to meet God. In the Prologue, laughter is born, and with it the Red Noses. In the Epilogue, after the Red Noses have died, laughter is reborn, but it is a different type of laughter. In the Prologue, Flote aims to make laughter help unfortunate people bear their lot. In the Epilogue, he affirms his desire to make laughter help them change their lot.

4 | *Barnes' Theatrical Style*

'Every play is a problem of language,' says Barnes in his Introduction to *Leonardo's Last Supper* and *Noonday Demons*. For each of these plays, he sought 'a live theatrical language which had the feel of a historical period (Renaissance and AD 395), yet could be understood by a contemporary audience,' an 'artificial vernacular' with 'historical weight yet . . . flexible enough to incorporate modern songs and jokes. For such deliberate anachronisms can only work fully if they spring out of an acceptable period texture. So I pillaged; everything from Elizabethan argot to the Bible' (p. ix). In *Leonardo's Last Supper*, Lasca remembers, 'Those gotch-gutted curs drove me out o' Florence. Ten years in this French wilderness; ten years o' eating snails and garlic—they rot the gut and maketh the breath stink' (p. 4). In *Noonday Demons*, with an authentic-sounding texture of a different period, Eusebius attests, 'I drinketh muddy water and for-glotten seven black olives daily for sustenance' and says of a nude woman, 'She bygyle none, 'cept to belch, belke and bolke thro' heart's pity' (pp. 34, 38). Pior recalls, 'A grimliche country; petrified like my heart, dead like my body' (p. 44).

Barnes' language is invented, different for each play and character. The 'gotch-gutted curs' of Lasca would be as inappropriate in the mouth of Eusebius or Pior as Eusebius' 'for-glotten' and 'bygyle' or Pior's 'grimliche' would be in Lasca's, or as the language of either of the saints would be in the mouth of the other. Indeed, they would be inappropriate for any character in Barnes' other plays. In *The Bewitched*, for example, one character promises, 'Ne'er fear, if she's pinked I'll smell 't out, Ma'am' (p. 34). In *Tsar*, Ivan calls man 'a two-eyed, two-balled dawish freak whose seared soul's more foul than his sinsoiled carcass' (p. 4) and he insists, 'I wasn't garred t' command' (p. 6). 'These hands've stabbed, slashed, and clubbed fair flesh into two groats' worth of dead meat. Yet these hands're delicate enough to carve a doll's head and carry a fart to a privy,' says a character in *Red Noses, Black Death* (II,iii), where Barnes has another character refer to 'a very perfect gentle knight' (II,iii, a phrase pillaged from Chaucer's *Canterbury Tales*). He imitates the language of mystery plays, when Mary says of the infant Jesus, 'Lookee, look how he merrys, my sweeting laughs. Oh, he's a prince, divine' (II,ix). As these examples indicate, Barnes' language is, as he himself states, 'not tape-recorded dialogue. It's usually a language which I've invented. It's not a language that anybody speaks. It's a language for actors. It is a carefully constructed new language. For each play it's a slightly different language, and for each character it's a different language. It is a stylized language.'

The 'artificial vernacular' and 'carefully constructed new language' of a playwright immersed in Jacobean drama has a Jacobean flavour, indeed a Jonsonian flavour. He admits Jonson's influence on his work.[1] Not only his period plays, but also his works that are set in modern times have striking imagery and extravagance that are Jacobean. 'You'll be nicked down to your bloody membrane, Mary,' says Jack in *The Ruling Class*. 'You want two seconds of DRIPPING sin to fertilize sodomized idiots' (p. 94). In his maiden speech before the House of Lords, Jack proclaims—boldly heaping up concretely brutal images—'My Lords, these are grave times, killing times. Stars collapse, universes shrink daily, but the natural order is still crime—guilt—punishment. Without pause. There is no love without fear. By His hand, sword, pike and grappling-hook, God, the Crowbar of the World, flays, stabs, bludgeons, mutilates' (pp. 113–114). ''A a cloud-topping man,' says Lasca in *Leonardo's Last Supper*—in what falsely promises to be the start of an ethereal passage yet actually begins a series of antitheses—'But now he's wrapped in cool crêpe. His mind was the light o' the world, they saith, but his flesh'll rot, red, green and black, just the same' (p. 13). 'Lord, I suppeth up sin as 't were water,' says King Philip of Spain in *The Bewitched*, and he adds, with baroque excess, 'My lust corrupts the age. Troops o' virgins passed under me; ripe lips bathed in rancid grease, pink bodies smelling o' perfume and sweet waters t' cover the stench from their wrinkled thighs and armpits. And f' these delights I'm damned' (pp. 4–5). With vividly Jacobean imagery, Queen Ana declares, 'I've dog-headed, web-fingered nightmares' (p. 45). With a passion for language and a privy vulgarity that recalls the Jacobeans, Barnes has Tsar Ivan tell Odoevsky, 'Your punishment's but a stake riven up through backarse, cleavage where fartleberries cluster. Doest feel thy anus split, rectum cleifed, pancreas lanced on a point, tripes born out in blood and piss-water?' (pp. 3–4) and then tell Semeon, 'Yet see how they'll jump t' swim seas o' vomit, wade nostril-deep through snot rivers, sleer [slay] wives and daughters, condemn their souls t' Hellpit on my orders' (p. 9). Brutally and rhythmically, Gottleb demands that the functionaries see the Auschwitz inmates 'packed, buttock to buttock, gazing up at the waterless douches, wondering why the floor has no drainage runnels.' From above, Zyklon B crystals pour 'through false shower heads, fake ventilators. What visions, what frenzies, the screaming, coughing, staggering, vomiting, bleeding, breath paralysed, lungs slowly ruptured' (p. 63). In *Red Noses, Black Death*, the nun Marguerite employs striking imagery as she laments, 'My life's full of low ceilings, walls set at angles' (I,vii) and a Count commands himself, with a multiplicity of phrases, linguistic relish, coarseness, and rhythmic, formal coherence that are Jacobean:

> Don't move muscle, eyelid. Stay rock-still. Ants bite, birds nest in my hair, mongrels piss up 'gainst me but I don't move. Move and you die. Plague worms attack anything that moves. I eat, drink, shit at night so they don't see me move. When I was scholar and arse-licker at the Papal Court I shot up the greasy pole, bowed, sneezed, carried out orders. Now the afflictions of the hour make the greatest sit on the ground. [I,ix]

Into the period texture of his Jacobean linguistic style, he inserts, as he says, modern jokes. Lasca hums the 'Dies Irae,' then comments, 'Always been one o' my favourites' (*Leonardo*, p. 5). In *Noonday Demons*, the tempter announces, 'Great news. NO Easter this year. They found the body!' (p. 35). He says Eusebius has 'B.O.' (p. 36) and 'I'll believe in miracles the day you take a bath' (p. 39). *The Bewitched* defines a priest as 'a man too lazy t' work and too frightened t' steal' (p. 30). This play contains such exchanges as: ''Tis true His Majesty's behaviour's become passing strange. He wants t' build a bridge on the Jarama River.' 'There's nothing wrong wi' wanting t' build a bridge on the Jarama.' 'Lengthways?' (p. 17). Tsar Ivan recalls his court jester's quip, 'In Holy Russia we never hang a man wi' a moustache. We use a rope' (p. 19). When he hears the screams of a soul in torture, he comments, 'They don't write songs like that anymore' (p. 20). Complaining that he is stuck behind a desk, Gottleb would rather work 'in the field,' for—as he says in post-World War II slang—'the gas-chambers of Auschwitz . . . is where it's happening' (p. 60). Between the black-marketeer and a female civil servant is a series of jokes which, though of the same general period, are from the world of vaudeville rather than that of a bureaucratic office:

> WOCHNER: Fräulein, I'm looking for a wife—anybody's wife.
> What would it take to make you fall in love with me?
> ELSE: A magician. My father said, work hard and be a good
> girl. You can always change your mind when you're older. Now
> I'm older and it's too late. I've reached the age where I'm
> beginning to find sex a pain in the arse.
> WOCHNER: That means you're doing it the wrong way. [p. 42]

Such one-liners form part of the texture of *Auschwitz*. *Red Noses, Black Death*, a play with many characters who are comedians, contains modern gags in abundance. An actor punningly calms an actress with stage fright, 'you'll get a warm hand on your opening' (I,xi). It contains one-liners—'A doctor felt our purse and said there was no hope,' 'People are dying this year who've never died before,' 'I've seen better specimens in glass jars' (I,v,viii,ix)—and two-line exchanges: 'What would you call a priest found consorting with a lusting, wanton nun?' 'Lucky' (I,x); 'How shall I sing it?' 'Under an assumed name' (II,iii).

In addition to modern jokes, Barnes inserts into his period texture meaningless words and phrases of his own invention. 'Must get my grunch thoughts in order,' says Jack (*Ruling Class*, p. 111), the adjective suggestive of crunching grunts. 'Cow-elephants kneel' (*Bewitched*, p. 138) evokes bulky, mighty beings in obeisance. Such words and phrases as 'rabbit suckers' (*Leonardo*, p. 69), 'Buss-beggar' (*Bewitched*, p. 10), and 'Hairless, pig-gelders' (*Red Noses*, II,ix) connote archaic expletives, but they mean nothing (is it possible, for example, for one to suck rabbits?).

The textural authenticity of Barnes' plays is more than a matter of language. As he says of *Leonardo's Last Supper* and *Noonday Demons*, 'I can vouch for the authenticity of the facts in these plays—except the biggest' (Leonardo's resurrection).

> Mother Midnight could have been found guilty of witchcraft the moment she swore she was not a witch; the goldsmiths did beat out gold along the Canto di Vacchereccia; the Chancellor of Hungary did have a billygoat tied to his sickbed to absorb the plague; the desert saints did live on black olives, dry bread and muddy water, practised elevation and 'even' elongation and watered dry sticks in the desert. And, yes, according to the records, the smell from privies was supposed to be a protection from the plague. [Introduction, p. ix]

The Bewitched reflects the seventeenth-century attribution of impotence to bewitchment by diabolical forces. When Dr Bravo describes his 'traditional methods,' his adjective is accurate: 'drawing eight ounces o' blood from his left shoulder and administering a sneezing powder o' hellbore t' purge the brain and crushed cowslips t' strengthen 't. Plaster o' pitch and pigeon dung was put on his feet, cat-fat on his chest and a draught o' vinegar and wormwood forced down his throat' (p. 16). Many of Gottleb's party-line statements in *Auschwitz*, says Barnes, derive from Nazi propaganda. Gottleb's claim, 'Whenever I hear noble sentiments I reach for my wallet to see if it's been lifted' (p. 59), recalls Herman Goering's remark about reaching for his revolver when he hears the word *culture*. As Barnes says, most of the gags in the Epilogue to *Laughter!* are authentic concentration camp jokes. The Red Noses' whirling, staggering, and falling in order to determine which direction to go come from the practice of St Francis and his disciples. The Flagellants and the Black Ravens derive from actual groups, as does the Red Noses:

> A particularly interesting feature of the Middle Ages are the ecclesiastical fraternities which were founded to combat the fear of death—for instance, 'The Company of the Fool' of Aarau [in Switzerland] under the patronage of the plague St Sebastian and the Virgin Mary. Unfortunately no details concerning them have been preserved, and we know only that on the outbreak of great epidemics they cheered the hearts of the people by public masquerades and processions.[2]

Although Barnes' Red Noses have a different patron saint, theirs is appropriate, for St Genesius is the patron saint of actors. 'The more bizarre the fact,' says Barnes, 'the more certain one can be that it happened, sometime, to someone' (Introduction, *Leonardo*, p. ix). This includes the speeches on the restoration of flogging and hanging in *The Ruling Class*, which he took from the 1960s House of Lords debate on capital punishment. It also includes the confrontation of the rival messiahs, whom Dr Herder tells, 'If one of you is God, the other must be somebody else' (p. 67). This situation, the author makes no attempt to hide, comes from an actual experiment in Ypsilanti, Michigan. In 1959, Dr Milton Rokeach brought together three men, each of whom claimed to be Christ. Among Dr Rokeach's goals was to discover how 'their delusional systems of belief and their behaviour might change if they were confronted with the ultimate contradiction conceivable for human beings: more than one person claiming the same identity.'[3] Unlike the resolution in the play, the rival Christs of Ypsilanti did not change their delusions. Despite their deadlock, they sought 'ways to live with one another in peace rather than destroy one another.'[4] Not only did Barnes take his idea from this experiment, he also took details. Although none of the Michigan Christs was an Electric Messiah, as McKyle calls himself, one of them said he would 'shake off so many hundred units of electronic duping imposition.'[5] The real-life mental patient referred to 'negative insinuendo,' which he defined as 'insinuation toward innuendo. The implication of reincarnation through negativism.'[6] J.C. too refers to 'negative insinuendo,' with a similar definition: 'insinuation towards innuendo, brought on by increased negativism out of a negative reaction to your father's positivism' (pp. 46–47). As Barnes concludes, 'Nothing a writer can imagine is as surrealistic as the reality. Everything has happened.' (Introduction, *Leonardo*, p. ix).

Barnes' pillage—of literature as well as life—is not haphazard. His linguistic thefts conform to his themes and situations. Largely because of the apt and original use to which he puts his plunder, of both classical literature and contemporary popular culture, he transforms it into his own property. Let us first deal with the former, his allusions to and use of classical literature and traditional music.

In *The Ruling Class*, in three successive speeches by Jack, which total less than a page, Barnes juxtaposes William Blake's *Preface to Milton* (Jack is horrified that 'England's green and pleasant' land has abolished the death penalty), Shakespeare's *Troilus and Cressida* (the social discords that follow the elimination of fear, as Jack says; of degree, as Ulysses says in his speech on order), and Browning's *Pippa Passes* (only with an executioner, according to Jack, does one know that God's in his heaven and all's right with the world) (pp. 89–90). If one recognizes none of these sources, however, one still perceives archaic linguistic resonances that suggest tradition buttresses Jack's views.

At the start of the play, Barnes parodies, misquotes, jumbles the order, and thereby transforms John of Gaunt's famous praise of England (*Richard II*) into a condemnation—unintended by the speaker, the thirteenth Earl of Gurney—of the basis of English society: a 'teeming womb of privilege' (not 'of royal kings'), whose shores protect it from the turbulence of 'foreign anarchy' (not 'envious siege')—no doubt the revolutions of 1789 and 1917 (p. 3). Important, too, these lines derive from Gaunt's *dying* words, since the entire Prologue—which ends in death—is a compendium of allusions associated with death, including the donning of a black cap (worn by English judges when they passed the death sentence),[7] the last words of Sidney Carton in Dickens' *A Tale of Two Cities* ('It is a far, far better thing I do,' etc.), a paraphrase of Claudius after he discovers Hamlet has killed Polonius ('Desperate diseases need desperate remedies'), the last words of Viscount Palmerston in 1865 ('Die my dear doctor? That's the last thing I shall do'), and those of the Bishop of Worcester ('Be of good cheer, Master Ridley, and play the man') (pp. 5–7). Even if one fails to recognize any of these sources, the archaic mode of some passages suggests moribund tradition (Gaunt and Worcester); death is sometimes implicit (Claudius), sometimes explicit (Palmerston), sometimes visual (the speaker climbs to a noose before he quotes Dickens, places it over his head after).

Barnes is particularly devastating when he does not tamper with the original. At the thirteenth Earl's funeral, his relatives sing 'All Things Bright and Beautiful,' that familiar set of Victorian pieties in praise of social stratification, for it declares that God himself orders the different estates of the rich man in his castle, the poor at the gate.

Literary and Biblical allusions pepper *The Bewitched*. When Philip IV is erotically stimulated by the sexy young woman of his imagination, he observes, '*It quivers*. 'Tis not as hard as a ram's horn, nor as stout as Hercules but 'twill serve' (p. 6). Whether or not one recognizes the reference to *Romeo and Juliet* (Mercutio's comment on his death wound, ''tis not so deep as a well, nor so wide as a church-door; but 'tis enough, 'twill serve'),[8] the statement is funny. Also, it is both ironic and appropriate. Whereas Romeo and Juliet are young, romantic lovers, Philip is decrepit and unromantic; yet by the end of the scene—which begins with a funeral bell—Philip will be, in Mercutio's words, 'a grave man.' 'What's Bavaria t' me, or me t' Bavaria, eh?' asks a Spanish grandee (p. 19), an allusion to Hamlet, who asks these questions about Hecuba. More concerned with his prerogatives than with the future of Spain, José of Bavaria, who might succeed Carlos, means as little to him as Hecuba does to the actor about whom Hamlet asks his question. Urging a Spanish nobleman to copulate with the Queen in order to give Spain an heir, a priest hurries him on: 'What's t' be done must be done quickly' (p. 54). The reference to Macbeth's 'If it were done when 'tis done, then 'twere well/It were done quickly' is ironic, for Macbeth refers to death, the priest to conception. It is also apt, for in both instances a man would take the place of a king (one in bed, the other on the throne). The Queen's parrot cries, 'O impotence, where is thy sting?' (p. 85), which parodies 'O death,' etc. (1 *Corinthians*, 15:55). Though ironic—the parrot addresses the absence of *le petit mort* in words that evoke *le grand mort*—the allusion becomes apt at the close of the scene, when the Queen Mother strangles the parrot. 'How can I rule when God's gi'en up the ghost?' asks Carlos (p. 95), punning on *Luke*, 23:46, where Jesus 'gave up the ghost.'

A single speech by Carlos links several references. 'I'll wound the earth,' he cries, suggesting chiefly *Tamburlaine*, Part Two ('draw thy sword/And wound the earth'), also *Paradise Lost* ('Earth felt the wound'); 'Storm the vault o' heaven,' evoking *King Lear* ('That heaven's vault should crack'); 'Resistance t' tyrants is obedience t' God,' paraphrasing John Bradshaw, one of the killers of Carlos' namesake, England's Charles I. Recognize them or not, one perceives a rage that encompasses the cosmos, and rebellion as well.

As in *The Ruling Class*, Barnes devastates when he does not tamper with the original. At the end of the second-act torture scene, after the Inquisitor-General prays for royal authority and submission to it, a chorus of blood-stained courtiers in chains sing an actual hymn, 'Praise my soul, the King of heaven,' whose lines include 'Well our feeble frame he knows' and 'Sun and moon, bow down before him' (p. 131), all appropriate to Barnes' themes of torture and submission to authority.

In his next full-length play,[9] *Red Noses, Black Death*, he employs such music as a Latin hymn ('Jesu, Corona Virginum'), a flagellant's chant ('Pain, pain, pain'), lyrics based on a traditional sixteenth-century street song ('Now If You Do Not Pleasure Me'), and a song based on Thomas Nashe's poem 'From Summer's Last Will and Testament'—an appropriate title for a play about the black death. When Father Flote says ''tis a joy . . . [to] pluck folk's hair and make 'em swear by God' (I,i), he aptly refers to *Nehemiah*, 13:25, a passage which includes smiting people as well. Pope Clement VI's admonition, 'Remember St Augustine's prayer, "Make me a good man, Lord, but not yet"' (I,x) does derive from the *Confessions* ('Give me chastity and continence, but not just now'). The name Bembo, one of the Red Noses, no doubt derives from the Cardinal mentioned by Volpone when he is disguised as a performer.

In 'The Second Coming,' Yeats writes, 'Things fall apart; the centre cannot hold.' In *Red Noses, Black Death*, a character observes that with the plague more than the centre cannot hold: 'The rim and centre's breaking' (I,iii). The phrase 'the old moulds crack' (I,x) recalls *King Lear* ('Crack nature's molds'), and in both plays the universe seems torn asunder. 'We must be ready to seize the day,' says a Black Raven (I,ii), an apt allusion to the *Odes* of Horace, who follows this admonition with 'put no trust in the morrow.' When a character refers to a court jester's bells as 'All Tintinnabula' (I,vii), the phrase echoes Poe's *Bells*. In the poem, the bells foretell 'a world of merriment,' but soon their turbulence tells 'a tale of terror' and outpours 'a horror.' Though at the start of the poem the bells seem delightfully to be 'jingling and tinkling,' at the end they are 'moaning and groaning.' In the play, the tinkling bells of the Red Noses seem merry, but horror soon unfolds and despite their tinkling, they cannot disguise the moans and groans of the dying.

During the Black Death, prostitutes raised prices, for money was valueless to those who might die and death decreased supply while it increased demand. When the plague ends, prostitutes—about to marry and give what they once sold—lament, 'we've dwindled to wives' (II,v). The allusion is to Congreve's *The Way of the World*, where Millament, having set forth conditions under which she would marry Mirabell, says, 'I may by degrees dwindle into a wife.' In one respect, the reference is ironic. Whereas Millament will retain her independence, the prostitutes will lose theirs. As they recognize, they are rushing to their chains. In another respect, the allusion is apt. *This*, Barnes hints, and not Millament's contract, is the way of the world.

While most of Barnes' references to popular culture are anachronistic—only *The Ruling Class* is set in the present and *Auschwitz* in the recent past—they are what Bernard Shaw, in his notes to *Caesar and Cleopatra*, calls *apparent* anachronisms, for they mock the notion that mankind has progressed since the play's historical period. Although Barnes is unfamiliar with the play, he subscribes to Shaw's statement, 'The notion that there has been any . . . Progress since Caesar's time (less than twenty centuries) is too absurd for discussion. All the savagery, barbarism, dark ages and the rest of it of which we have any record as existing in the past, exists at the present moment.'[10]

Songs, particularly from musicals, constitute one of the major aspects of popular culture that Barnes' plays reflect.[11] 'I'm steeped in music hall,' he says.[12] He is also steeped in film musicals and in American popular songs and singers. As mentioned earlier, a rendition of 'Mona Lisa' ends *Leonardo's Last Supper*. Many of Barnes' popular music references—part of his background, whose lyrics and melodies his memory holds but whose sources it does not always contain—are less easily ascertainable. He does remember that 'Sniff Sniff Sniff,' sung by the Head Washerwoman and Father Froylan in *The Bewitched* as they search laundry for a whiff of menstrual blood, derives from 'Dig, Dig, Dig for Your Dinner,' sung by Gene Kelly and Phil Silvers in the movie *Summer Stock* (released in England as *If You Feel Like Singing*), and that 'The Show Must Go On,' sung by the Red Noses, comes from the Rita Hayworth film *Cover Girl*, where Phil Silvers repeats the title over and over again. Other sources, he simply does not remember. Indicative of the difficulties involved in locating them is a statement that precedes the text of *The Bewitched*: 'It has not been possible in all cases to trace the copyright holders of lyrics. The publishers would be glad to hear from any such unacknowledged copyright holder' (p. vi).

Twice in *The Ruling Class*, Mrs Piggot-Jones and Mrs Treadwell join the fourteenth Earl in a song-and-dance, and on both occasions the lyrics support thematic lines. In the first act, J.C. leads them in 'The Varsity Drag,' from the musical *Good News*. In the play's context, the lyrics acquire new emphasis: obedience to authority. Whether you are dumb or wise, you can pass if you answer the professor's call to go down on your heels, up on your toes, and so forth. In the second act, their rendition of the American Negro spiritual 'Dry Bones' follows a demand to break the bones of those who disobey authority. Whereas the original song has bones connected, Jack (before the ladies join him in song) demands they be disconnected.

In *Leonardo's Last Supper*, the Lascas—overjoyed that their commission to bury the great painter will deliver them from misery in France and return them in riches to their beloved Florence— '*exultantly*' sing, in their charnel house, of the Lord's having delivered David from the slaughter-house, Daniel from the lion's den, the Israelites from the Pharaoh's decree, and now 'You delivered us' (p. 5)—another American Negro spiritual, which Phil Harris recorded as 'The Preacher and the Bear.' In *Noonday Demons*, the tempter aptly sings Gershwin's ''S wonderful, 's marvellous, 's awful nice— paradise!' (p. 35) and the fourth-century hermits sing 'Monks,' a parody of 'Kids,' from the musical *Bye Bye, Birdie*. Barnes' alteration of the lyrics is appropriate to the saints, each of whom believes the other is less worthy than himself, and to his play's anti-religious theme. Whereas the musical's father complains that no one can *understand* anything kids say, Barnes' hermits sing that no one can *believe* anything monks say. The kids are 'Noisy, crazy, *sloppy*, lazy, loafers,' the monks 'Noisy, crazy, *lusty*, lazy loafers.' While kids 'do just what they want to do!' monks 'say anything—even if it isn't true!' (p. 48).

Having failed to produce a child, and having caused torture and death in their efforts to do so, Carlos and Ana of *The Bewitched* sing a satiric version of 'Lucky in Love,' from *Good News*. In the song, 'bad luck scatters every time I'm with you,' but in the play, 'Good luck scattered when I first looked at you' (p. 94). Perhaps the most audacious use of popular music in this play occurs at the end of the first-act torture scene, when the company steps forward to sing 'That's Entertainment,' which is appropriate as well as ironic, since the *auto da fé* that is to culminate the torture aims to entertain the populace. However, Barnes alters the lyrics to conform to his own satiric purposes. The company sings of 'The ache when they're burnt at the stake/Or the thrill when you're in at the kill' and of 'The liar who is thrown on the pyre/By the priest, who will make him deceased/F' the faith o' the whole Christian race/Lord Thy world is a stage./Thy stage is a world o' entertainment.'[13] About halfway through the run, says Barnes, and while the play's text was in galley, the composer objected to the satiric lyrics. Although Barnes might have claimed the traditional rights of parody, he instead changed the song to 'John Brown's Body,' which the published text carries. In it, 'We'll sing a holy chorus when they're screaming on the rack./We try to make them Christians but they all get cardiacs' and 'To keep the public happy is the object of the show./They need the entertainment and it helps the status quo./Men cannot live by bread alone/But now we have to blow./'Cos the show is on the road' (pp. 76–77)—a version whose lyrics may be more thematically pointed, but, perhaps paradoxically, are less stinging than the lyrics to a tune whose title, 'That's Entertainment,' one immediately recognizes as savagely ironic.

The song that concludes *Laughter!* is devastating in its irony. The dying Auschwitz inmates tell jokes as they dance to the tune of 'The Sunny Side of the Street.' In death, these victims of Nazism will leave their worries on the doorstep, and conditions will be sweeter on the other side of life's street.

In *Red Noses, Black Death*, Flote sings 'Life Is Just a Bowl of Cherries' to people dying of the plague. True to the Red Noses' function, to take people's minds off serious matters, it urges them not to take life seriously (if they did, they might revolt against the *status quo*) and it tells the poor that they cannot lose what they never owned. 'I survive!' exclaims an Archbishop, then: 'I'm here because I'm here' (II,iv). This familiar lyric, endlessly repeated, to the tune of 'Auld Lang Syne,' is appropriate. Tautological rather than explanatory, it is for that reason meaningless, and there is no meaning in his or anyone's survival during the Black Death, where chance dictated who would live or die. When a nun who has joined the Red Noses laments the death of the jester who is her beloved, the company dons its red noses to sing 'Red Noses for a Blue Lady,' which like 'Red Roses for a Blue Lady' aims to 'chase her blues away.' The comedians sing: 'We put on red noses for a blue lady./Wear them for the bravest girl around./We all here made a bet./We'd help that girl forget./That dear sweet dead man five feet underground' (II,i).

Not every reference to popular culture is a song. In *The Ruling Class*, J.C.'s concerns extend unto the least of mankind, including Mr Moto and the Cisco Kid, of Hollywood B-movies. When the butler is arrested for murder, the event recalls that cliché of detective novels and films, 'The butler done it.' As he removes a handkerchief to wipe his eyes, '*a half-dozen spoons fall out of his pocket with a clutter*' (p. 102)—an allusion to the movie *Animal Crackers*, in which, when police are about to arrest Harpo Marx in a society matron's home, silverware falls from his sleeve. Appropriate to the contradictory identities of his mad master—first the God of Love, then Jack the Ripper—the butler responds to Jack's command with a misquotation of a nursery rhyme, 'Yes, sir, no, sir, three bags full' (p. 89). Well before Eusebius has a vision of the future, his tempter employs the language of the future: he recites clichés of microphone testing, 'Able Charle Baker testing 1, 2, 3, 4,' and calls his projections on the mound of dung 'B-picture temptations' (pp. 35–36). In *The Bewitched*, the advice of court-jester father to court-jester son—'Thy only call is t' entertain. . . . If thou has a message, sent 't by messenger' (p. 14)—derives from advice attributed to comic playwright George S. Kaufman, 'If you have a message, use Western Union.' Suggesting the later work about an English King, Shibanov tells Ivan the Terrible and his son, 'You're my now and future Tsars' (p. 16). Referring to a series of Hollywood movies whose titles changed yearly, Gottleb describes the Nazi Sanitation Men tearing at the mouths of the gassed victims of Auschwitz: 'They're extracting gold teeth from the corpses. That's why they're called the "Gold-diggers of 1942"' (p. 64). *Red Noses, Black Death* contains numerous such allusions. 'Join us on this pilgrimage,' suggests the Master Flagellant, who adds, 'a hundred thousand lemmings can't be wrong!' (Prologue)—a reference to the popular saying of World War I about fifty million Frenchmen who went in swarms to their death and who, like the medieval multitudes, could indeed be wrong. Adapting the well-known observation about the army, Barnes has the cynical Clement VI admit, 'Christianity is a system designed by geniuses for execution by idiots' (II,iv). When the blind Le Grue declares himself, against his conscious will, for he knows the consequence is death, on the side of the rebellious Flote and against the Church, he employs the exit line of B-movie star Mantan Moreland, whose roles included that of Charlie Chan's chauffeur, 'Feet, do your stuff' (the original line, invented by Moreland, was 'Feets', etc.). Like Moreland, the frightened Le Grue wants to leave but does not. As with Barnes' allusions to literature, the dialogue is funny if one does not recognize the reference, funnier if one does.

Language and references to literature and popular culture are only part of the extravagant theatricality of Barnes' plays, which are often comic as well as spectacular. In *The Ruling Class*, as policemen arrest and carry out the stiff, horizontal butler, he sings the 'Internationale,' tips his hat to a lady, then sings 'I'm Only a Strolling Vagabond.' Her aptly theatrical comment is: 'What an exit!' (pp. 103–104). Jack's execution of Claire is an enactment of one by Jack the Ripper. Playing up to him as a prostitute would, Claire speaks in a cockney accent and kisses him on the mouth. When she does so, the set changes. The drawing room stands in the middle of a nineteenth-century slum street. She removes his jacket, waistcoat, and shirt. Stripped to the waist, he permits her to caress him and as he kisses her, he plunges a knife into her stomach. While Leonardo talks of his artistic works, the Lasca family, indifferent to such matters, perform a juggling act. The noonday demon projects onto the mound of excrement a pile of gold, which turns the mound yellow; then, a ten-foot image of a pink naked lady; finally, an equally tall image of a Pope, in purple regalia. In *The Bewitched*, as the royal family howl and hiss with increasing rage, the lights flicker faster and grow brighter until, at an intense flash, the family emits a loud cry and falls into epileptic fits. His head rotating, his tongue lolling, and his limbs thrashing wildly, Carlos whirls. As her body jerks up and down, Ana tears her dress and excitedly hits her crotch. Mariana's teeth bared in a fixed grin, she kicks convulsively and clutches her hair. The parrot screeches. Looking unconcerned, two attendants walk to them, place sticks between their jaws, and return to their places. The royal family's convulsions end. The lights fade to a spot on the trio, who are *'now in a state of post-epileptic automation.* CARLOS *rips off his breeches and* ANA *pulls up her dress. As he throws himself passionately on top of her,* MARIANA *rocks back and forth moaning a lullaby and the* PARROT *screeches mockingly. Spot out'* (p. 13). Later, a despairing Carlos cries, *'There is no God,'* whereupon:

> *Thunder, a streak of lightning and a great voice booms:*
> GOD'S VOICE: YES THERE IS.
> CARLOS: I've prayed t' you. Where's my son?
> *Another streak of lightning.*
> GOD'S VOICE *(wearily)*: NO SON—ONLY LIGHTNING.
> *Thunder, another streak of lightning and* CARLOS *collapses.*   [pp. 63–64]

The last phrase has dual implications: no son for Carlos, no saviour for mankind; instead, only lightning to scourge human beings. As Ivan unsuccessfully tries to persuade Semeon to remain Tsar, an invisible force pulls Semeon backward, until he is spreadeagled against an upstage wall, which sucks him in and swallows him. In *Auschwitz*, while Else recalls attending afternoon dances when she was a girl, the lights dim slightly, there is an illusion of swaying Chinese lanterns overhead, and she and Stroop waltz to the humming of Cranach and Gottleb. A play about theatre people, *Red Noses, Black Death* is filled with theatrical elements. A rope uncoils from above the stage and a Black Raven, cawing loudly, slides down it; a gold merchant opens his oversized, golden codpiece and money falls out; a female leper unwraps bandages around her face to reveal a rusty metal frame shaped like a face; fearful of contracting the plague, the Pope receives visitors who enter not his room but an antechamber, where they see him in a huge magnifying mirror and kiss its reflection of his ring. A superbly theatrical *tour-de-force* combines language, sounds, song, banners, and the movement of objects. Rather than kill each other, the Black Ravens, Flagellants, and Red Noses agree to let God determine the victor. The Ravens unfold their banner, a black raven against a red background; the Flagellants theirs, a crucified Christ; the Noses theirs, an angel and St Genesius. Releasing a black balloon, a Raven cries *'Caw-caw-caw'* and enunciates his creed. Releasing a red one, a Flagellant cries *'Ahhh-ahhh-ahhh'* and declares his. Releasing a blue one, Flote laughs *'Haaa-haaa-haaa'* and states his. Boos from above follow each speech. Then, Flote recognizes that jokes should be revolutionary and that the three groups should join to create a better world. As the leaders link hands, the black, red, and blue balloons—now tied together— descend, accompanied by applause from above the stage. Everyone sings, 'Join together, that's the plan. It's the secret. Man helps man. . . . Join together. Go, go, go. Change conditions. Here below' (II,iii).

Barnes' theatricality includes the theatre conscious of itself as theatre. If the doctor does not wish to hear about Claire's death, says Jack, 'Then kindly leave the stage' (*Ruling Class*, p. 106). The noonday demon explicitly refers to that play and its author. In *Red Noses, Black Death*, a First Attendant, recognizing that he has the buboes which are signs of the plague, knows where to assign blame: 'All the fault of *writers*—cock-pimping scribblers. . . . Always writing stories where some characters're important and others jus' disposable stock—First Attendant, Second Peasant, Third Guard.' But before he can explain why a First Attendant is as important as anyone else, he dies (I,iii). Part of the theatrical self-consciousness of this play is self-theft, i.e., repeated gags and effects from Barnes' earlier plays, such as: 'You'll never be the man your Mother was' (*Demons*, p. 39; II,ix) and the Master Flagellant breaking a paper butterfly, which screams (I,vi), as in *Auschwitz*, where Cranach pulls the cord of an electric bugging device *'and there is a faint cry of pain from far off'* (p. 30). Expressionism is among Barnes' theatrical devices. Instead of stating that J.C. changes from an apostle of goodness into a pillar of respectability that masks institutionalized evil, the author has a hairy, eight-foot beast, dressed like a Victorian gentleman, shake J.C. violently until he states his name is Jack. Hyde subdues Jekyll. Barnes does not explain that the ruling class is outmoded and monstrous; he shows members of the House of Lords to be skull-faced, cobweb-covered, bloated-bellied, goitered men smothered in dust, seated beside a skeleton.[14] Instead of stating that the devil is taking possession of Eusebius, Barnes expresses it theatrically: *'As his body jerks and his voice gabbles there is a sound of a troop of horses approaching at speed. Simultaneously as they thunder over the roof of the cave, a wall of heat and light shoots in from the entrance like a sudden blast from an open furnace.* ST EUSEBIUS *goes limp and falls forward at the waist.'* He then speaks in the tempter's voice (p. 35). To express that Queen Ana of Spain is not pregnant, Barnes has a patriarch, during her account of a dream about her baptised child, pour blood over her and a baby in christening clothes. To indicate that the Queen Mother has cancer, he has her gasp in agony as a carbuncled, wheezing, old man places a silver crab-brooch on one of her breasts, which he squeezes. Later, she cries in pain as the same man stabs her above the brooch. Expressive of Ivan's fear that danger lurks everywhere, a giant axe chases a seven-foot tree, then interrupts the chase to attack him. To demonstrate what underlies the splendour of the Catholic church, Barnes has Father Flote observe *'a richly gowned religious procession in cope and mitre . . . led by a mongoloid* THURIFER, *giggling insanely and splashing holy water over a Dwarf behind him, staggering under the weight of a large Cross.'* Following them are a 'BOY CARDINAL *whose mitre keeps slipping over his face, and two half-paralysed* DEACONS. *The lurching procession exits gibbering . . . as the choir sings triumphantly "Exultant caelum laudibus"'* (I,ix). With the black death over and Europe returned to what the Pope calls 'normality,' Barnes demonstrates what such normality really is: as the Pope leaves, he is greated by applause mixed with wolf-like howling (II,iv).

Barnes, who acknowledges his debt to Antonin Artaud, tries—as Artaud would have it—to make language approximate cries or screams, and become inarticulate sounds that convey meaning. Ivan the Terrible says and does as much: 'Suffering beyond the reach o' language. *KK arrrxx ccrrrrr aaaaakk AAAARRR*' (pp. 21–22). During their frenzied argument, the language of Spain's royal family bursts into pure sounds:

> ANA: Toads gnaw thy flesh and the little devils laugh *hee-hee-hee*, they laugh *hee-hee-hee*.
> MARIANA: I hear thy screams *aaarrhh*, mercy, mercy *aaarhh aaarhh*.
> CARLOS: Sssssins sssins sssssss.
> *The lights flicker.*
> ANA *(prowling like an animal)*: Laughing *hee-hee-hee-heeeee-heeeee*.
> MARIANA *(jerking her head like a bird)*: *Aaarrhh-aaarrhh-aaarrhh*.
> CARLOS *(wriggling like a snake)*: *Sssss-sssssss*.
> *They howl and hiss with increasing fury. . . .*   [p. 13]

Demanding wolves rather than men, the language of Pope Clement VI itself turns vulpine: 'But where are the wolves who'll serve? *Arrwaaa. (He howls like a wolf.)* Where are the wolves? *Arrwaaa*' (I,x). An entire scene of *The Ruling Class* (II,x) expresses emotion through inarticulate sounds. Hunching his shoulder and dragging his left leg, like Richard III, Jack emits sounds *'from back of throat'*: 'Graaa gruuuuuuaaKK,' etc. Then, *'face contorted with rage'* and *'As if bringing up phlegm, the cries now come from the pit of the stomach'*: Arrk-ar-rk ARR ARR k-k-k-k, YIT YIT TRUGHUUGH ARK KKKK,' etc. (p. 112).

Unlike Artaud, however, Barnes is a comic writer who parodies his own technique, as in *Noonday Demons*: 'And I, I spake unto them, sweetly in the language o' angels. "Eeeeeepphh-Singggeeee-Yaaaanngg" I said. And they answered, "Eeeeeepphh-Singggeeee-Yaaaanngg" to you too' (p. 35). Through sounds, the Nazi Gottleb imitates Hitler's brutal, hysterical speech. In *Red Noses, Black Death*, a prostitute imitates different animals fornicating, then recapitulates in sequence: 'Pigs grunt *zzz-zzz*, vultures groan inside dead carcasses *uuuuur*, frogs ride twenty-days at a time *huhh huhh*. *Zzzz-zzz uu rr uurrr huhh-huhh*' (I,vi) and several characters engage in dialogue by means of sounds:

> GREZ: Once we cried *ahhhh ahhh*; now we shout *arrrra arrrrgrr arrrrkkk*.
> FLOTE: *Haaa-haa-haa?*
> GREZ: No. *Arrrrxx arrrggk grrrxx.*
> 1ST FLAGELLANT ⎱
> 2ND FLAGELLANT ⎰ *Arrrgggk, grrrrrr, rrrkkk.*   [II,vi]

Like that demanded by Artaud, Barnes' theatre visually and aurally depicts the cruelty of existence. In *The Ruling Class*, Jack reduces Dr Herder to a state of idiocy by proving, as he flails at the doctor with his cane, that his own behaviour is normal. In *The Bewitched*, characters inflict bodily pain through force of will: 'PONTOCARRERO *lets out a grunt of pain*' and 'MOTILLA*'s face contorts in agony. Neck muscles tighten, faces turn white with strain,*' until: '*Suddenly blood pours from* MOTILLA*'s mouth and nose. It gushes down the front of his white habit, but he never takes his eyes off* PONTOCARRERO. *There is a sickening "crack" as a bone snaps and* PONTOCARRERO*'s arm is broken. It is quickly followed by another "crack" as his right leg is smashed too*' (p. 102). Ivan the Terrible and Samael (Death) fight in 'Kung Fu' style. Punching and kicking savagely, '*they never actually touch each other, though we hear the sounds of their blows unnaturally loud*' (p. 25). A Nazi's pincers tear at the mouth of a corpse at Auschwitz, '*accompanied by a loud, wrenching sound*' (p. 64). During the Black Death, the Black Ravens demonstrate the cruelty of existence. They squeeze pus from corpses' plague-boils into bottles, slit open a corpse's stomach and watch the black blood run out, and slide a recently deceased woman offstage to fornicate with her corpse.

Again unlike Artaud, the comic Barnes mocks cruelty. When the terrified butler, accused of killing Lady Claire, pleads for help from the nobleman he faithfully served, Jack responds brutally: 'If thy hand offends thee, cut if off. Tuck, Tuck, you rot the air with your sexual filth. And there's an innocent baby upstairs. It was you, spawned out of envy, hate, revenge. *You* killed her. *Oh, Dan, Dan, you dirty old man. (Lifts* TUCKER *up bodily by his armpits and drops him in front of* BROCKETT.) Take him away, Inspector' (p. 103). In a torture scene of *The Bewitched*, the chief torturer reprimands a prisoner: 'You're been *bleeding* again! We spend the night cleaning up your mess and you start t' bleed all over the place. (*The* PRISONER *groans.)* That's no excuse' (pp. 68–69). When the impaled Odoevsky utters a blood-curdling scream, Tsar Ivan comments, ''Tis easy f' you t' say that' (p. 4). The Master Flagellant cries, '(*stabbing himself with increasing fury):* Become all fire this Easter, God's purifying flame. Beaten! Tortured! Saved! *(He slashes his throat by mistake; realizing what he has done, he clamps his hands over his windpipe and gurgles) Uuuuuggggggrr*' (I,vi).

Like Bertolt Brecht—whose influence, Barnes asserts, pervades contemporary drama—he writes in order to change the world. Fittingly, he paraphrases Brecht (*Saint Joan of the Stockyards*): 'The phrase, when you leave, leave a better world behind you, I think is very apposite for any artist. The world changes with the speed of a glacier moving down a mountainside, an inch or so every two or three hundred years. I think the artist's job is to clear away some of the stones that hinder the advance of the glacier.' Although he distrusts parties of both right and left, he inclines toward socialism and anarchism. Class hatred permeates his plays, he agrees, and he explains, 'Class hatred's there because class is a total force in England, and in a different way in most western societies. To say that one's blinkered because one hates class distinctions is to get the problem arse upwards, in the sense that only by hating it do we try to get rid of it; you don't get rid of it any other way than by attacking it.' Class distinctions and extreme inequalities of wealth constitute 'blocks towards a better relationship between man and man, barriers between people. Permanent authority is a canker for the leader and the led.' His ideal is a situation 'which would throw up people who would handle problems as they arise, and then join the rest. That's idealistic, given the situation as it is today, but everything's changeable: the world is changeable, human beings are changeable, human nature is changeable.'

As the analysis of his plays in the previous chapter indicates, Barnes opposes class stratification, exploitation, capitalism, and institutionalized religion. The very title *The Ruling Class* tells which side he is on. Among the thirteenth Earl's bequests is 'Three thousand pounds to the Bankers Beneficent Society Ltd' (p. 15). Maria calls poverty a disease worse than the plague and Lasca candidly admits, 'honesty's one thing and trading's something else again' (*Leonardo*, p. 20). In *The Bewitched*, a Spanish grandee sees the fall of Barcelona in terms of money— 'My Government bonds! 'Tis the dark night o' the soul' (p. 95)—and Barnes shows what underlies the trappings of wealth: 'I've the most exquisite taste in Europe,' says an Archbishop, whereupon '*The rich wall-drapes are pulled down to reveal grey panels covered with filth and graffiti*' (p. 100). Paraphrasing Biblical passages—the same Brecht does in *Saint Joan of the Stockyards*[15]— and thereby turning them to his own use, which resembles Brecht's, Barnes has Tsar Ivan declare, ''Tis nature's iron law: those that have shall be gi'en' (p. 13). Stressing the link between business and war, Barnes has a black marketeer offer the Auschwitz functionaries:

> Confiscated wedding rings. Gold. For you, thirteen marks, and I'm not making a pfennig profit. Twelve? Ten? Any offers? Here's a novelty that's selling well. Very risqué. Hammer-and-sickle badges. Every one guaranteed taken by hand from the body of a dead Russian soldier. Look their blood's still on some of them. There's a human tragedy in each one of these badges. I'm practically giving them away.   [p. 42]

In *Red Noses, Black Death*, a gold merchant recites his guild's motto: 'We live by the golden rule, those that have the gold make the rules'

(I,vi) and the Pope admits that the church's important work is not to conduct services but to collect taxes and draft laws.

As Brecht does, Barnes writes on a panoramic scale, and his disorientation techniques, to be more fully discussed shortly, resemble Brecht's *Verfremdungseffekt* (Alienation Effect, as it is usually translated, but perhaps more accurately, Reorientation Device). Their chief differences are that Barnes makes more frequent use of jokes to disorient and permit social evaluation, and that his transformational techniques operate swiftly, usually as comic diversion, so that the spectator evaluates speeches or actions just after the sudden, frequently comic shifts in theatrical mode, rather than—as with Brecht—prepares to examine them as a new mode is introduced.

Like Brecht, Barnes refuses to permit easy empathy, but disorients and reorients the spectator to maintain his objectivity. Immediately after the shocking scene in which Jack brutally stabs Claire, the butler enters, singing 'Come Into the Garden, Maud,' sees the corpse, and shouts, *'(Gleefully)* One less! One less! Praise the Lord. *Hallelujah'* (*Ruling Class*, p. 95). St Eusebius shudders as he examines a gaping sore on his arm:

> Maggots! A mass o' crawling maggots. Begone out from me! (*He squeezes the pus and waves his arm, shaking the maggots onto the ground; he suddenly stops.*) 'Thou shalt not judge.' I agulten thee Lord, forgivest Thou me. These blind worms are Thy creatures too. (*He bends down searching for the maggots.*) Come back little ones. 'Twas a mistake. The Devil moved me to throw thee out. Come back. (*He whistles.*) Here boys, here, here.   [*Demons*, p. 34]

The shift to a contemporary manner, abruptly ending whatever empathy the spectator may have had, reorients him toward the diseased saint. In *The Bewitched*, as a council of state argues as to whether to stage an *auto da fé*, tableaux show a torture wheel with a prisoner strapped to it, an open Iron Maiden, and a prisoner spreadeagled on a rack. As they appear, one grandee complains that an *auto da fé* would cost the aristocrats too much and another counters that in Spain the *auto* 'is more than jus' a national pastime, 'tis a true folk art' (p. 67). The comic dialogue permits the spectators to evaluate the shocking sights rather than only sympathize with the victims. 'Oh Lord I casn't think o' all the suffering in the world,' says Tsar Ivan, and he unexpectedly adds, 'so I don't' (p. 18). Away on business, a solid citizen returns to Lyons to discover that because the plague struck the city during his absence, an ordinance was passed to authorize the executioner to kill anyone who tries to enter the city. Donning a woman's wig and a dress, rouging his cheeks and lips, the businessman utters his last words before the executioner does his duty: 'See—I die like a man' (I,ix). When the Master Flagellant recognizes that he and his followers should have tried to eliminate pain, not embrace it, one of them comments, 'Now he tells us!' (II,vi). About to be shot by a cross-bow, Flote stands on his head for his execution. These shifts from horror or seriousness to comedy are devices that, Brecht-like, reorient the spectator toward the dramatic action.

Barnes' most distinctive artistic signature, which previous examinations of language and of Brecht-related techniques suggest, consists of disorienting and reorienting transformations from one theatrical mode to another.[16] Swiftly, lightly, and with precision, actors switch from intellectual discourse, to period argot, to poetry, to modern slang, to rhetoric, to musical comedy, to ritual, to dance, to opera, to slapstick—thereby creating what Barnes calls 'a comic theatre of contrasting moods and opposites, where everything is simultaneously tragic and ridiculous' (Introduction, *Leonardo*, p. ix). Entertainingly, he juggles the audience's moods and enables them to examine critically, detached and with a smile, the social values and attitudes he scrutinizes. 'I suppose,' he says, 'that's my trade mark. But turning on a sixpence is what the theatre's about.' *Turning on a sixpence:* 'That means switching everything round—within a sentence, for example—changing conventions, changing ideas, changing attitudes. One doesn't need a scene to establish that there's been a change. One can shift the actor to it in a twinkling of an eye. Within one sentence one should be able to change an approach and the means to express it.' To the actor—according to Timothy West, who played Ivan and Gottleb in the original production of *Laughter!*— these transformations are 'a great attraction,' for 'You can suddenly be anything you like.' He admires such 'cheek, daring, energy. It means enormous stretching of the actor's resources.' Someone once asked Barnes, West recalls, 'Why, in every play you write, do people have to sing, fight, dance, climb up trees, impale each other with swords, skate, swim?' The author's response: 'I think it's more fun for the actors.'[17] To the audience—according to the critic Irving Wardle—it results in 'a triple-piled extravaganza that brings in vaudeville routines, Italian opera, melodramatic mock-heroics, and a glittering fusillade of good jokes.'[18] Perhaps in homage to Ben Jonson, Barnes refers to his distinctive theatrical style, or trade mark, not as Barnesian but as 'Barnesonian' (Introduction, *Leonardo*, p. x).

In *The Ruling Class*, J.C. switches instantaneously from a looney conundrum ('Could a rooster forget he was a rooster and lay an egg?'), to a non-word whose meaning lies in its sound (*'Whroom'*), to pseudo-philosophical discourse ('Space and time only exist within the walls of my brain'), to a popular song with nonsense lyrics ('Mairzy Doats'), to Biblical language ('I am the Lord Jesus,' etc.), to an imitation of American night-club entertainer Ted Lewis ('Is everybody happy?') (p. 21). Within seconds, the revived Leonardo da Vinci goes from today's slang ('The verdict is in'), to prayer ('Jesu, I'm alive'), to a jig and a whoop of joy, to intellectual discourse ('The evidence proves I'm in the land of the living in the bosom of a natural family. I recognize the species: genus homo sapiens. Bipedal primate mammals. Erect bodies, short arms, large thumbs, developed brains with a capacity for articulate speech and abstract reasoning'), to a parody of 'Molly Malone' ('Alive-alive O, alive-alive O, singing pasta and pizza alive-alive O') (p. 22). In *Noonday Demons,* St Eusebius—also within seconds—prays in Latin ('In nómine Patris, et Filii, et Spíritus Sancti'), speaks an archaic idiom ('Bler-eyed, mole-eyed, my sight dimmeth and my flesh turns to pumice stone'), talks in tongues, chants a prayer, gabbles in Latin, switches from his *'old, crabbed, dry voice'* to the tempter's, which is *'lighter in tone, glib and edged with a Cockney whine,'* sings a modern song (Gershwin's *''S wonderful'*), rattles off vaudeville-like gags ('Oedipus loves Mum, Electra loves Dad, Leda loves Swans'), and then—holding a dialogue with himself—switches back and forth between his usual voice and the demon's (pp. 34–35). In *The Bewitched,* Ana switches from poetry which calls for universal love ('Oh men, Oh women, Oh fields, Oh sky, Oh sun,/Christ comes t' gather up our flower o' love!') to a song with joyous lyrics in American Negro slang (Gershwin's 'Clap Yo' Hands') (p. 138). Within three pages, Tsar Ivan the Terrible dances Cossack-style, jumping and *écarting* with joyful cries; speaks in archaic diction ('My leming lufsom boy. I leif you more than life'); hears the screams of a skeleton of a man he tortured and killed, and cracks a joke in modern diction ('They don't write songs like that anymore'); goes into convulsions as he tries to strangle himself; delivers a running gag to the audience ('Root it out!'); murders his son by repeatedly spearing him; employs inarticulate sounds to convey emotion; and sings two arias from Gluck's opera *Orfeo and Eurydice* (pp. 20–22). In *Auschwitz,* Gottleb swiftly passes from sarcastic gags ('this office is only held together by the laws of inertia'), to business jargon ('tenders for appliances CP 3(m) described in regulation E(5) Amt D wants the contract to be given to Krupps AG'), to argument, to automation (whipping out one official memorandum after another), to a bridge game, to the same running joke as Ivan's ('Root it out!') (pp. 38–39).

In a single, short speech, the red-nosed Flote orates ('We shall kindle a torch to blaze through eternity'), rationally explains the ease with which one may become a clown, utters a wordless sound, jerks his body violently, then *'immediately converts his jerkings into a soft shoe shuffle'* (I,iv). A major reason for the success of so daring a mixture of modes is their analogical appropriateness. J.C.'s changing forms of expression, none of which is truly rational, reveal his madness, as does the nonsense song whose lyrics he speaks. Since lucid discourse is insufficient to express Leonardo's delight at being alive, he bursts into song, whose lyrics celebrate life. Eusebius' shifting modes of speech, voice, and song demonstrate his hallucinations and his efforts to combat the demon within himself. So emotional is Ana's poetic call for universal love that she sings a song inviting everyone to join a jubilee. Ivan derives pleasure from the 'songs' or cries of his victims, and the world he creates is a hell, perhaps worse than the one into which Orfeo descends in search of Eurydice. Bureaucractic rivalry, business jargon, official memoranda, card-playing, and a runing gag—each in its own way a type of automation—are appropriate to the Nazi who automatically spouts party dogma. For a theatrical entertainer like Flote, whose life as it faces the dying is theatrical, 'turning on a sixpence' is, to adapt Barnes' phrase, what theatre and a theatrical life are about.

Furthermore, Barnes' transformations reflect our fragmented world, which encompasses and accommodates seriousness and laughter; the classical, the popular, and the avant-garde; Vivaldi, Frank Loesser, and the Beatles; Seneca and tap dancing; Rembrandt and Magritte. They succeed on stage partly because one is accustomed in daily life to juxtapositions of contrasting modes. Is it unusual to play a record of a Mozart quartet, then of a Broadway musical, on one's own gramophone? Is it unusual to read the comic strips of a newspaper during morning coffee, then the *Oresteia*? On television, a gripping scene in a concentration camp might suddenly shift to a commercial advertisement with an animated tuna fish who recites Shakespeare and is told that the manufacturer wants tunas who taste good, not tunas with good taste. The difference between Barnesonian transformations and diurnal transformations is that the Barnesonians are purposeful and unified, not merely random. In brief, they are art.

5 | *Early Works*

Having analysed Barnes' mature plays and their distinctive theatrical style, one is in a position to exercise hindsight and examine his development as a dramatist. These early works—the only ones available for perusal—consist of one play that he wrote for television and three that he wrote for the stage. As the second chapter indicates, only the last of these early works was not performed. So far, Barnes has permitted none of them to be published. Since the production of *The Ruling Class*, he has prohibited performances of the three stage plays.

The Man with a Feather in His Hat

Like the motion picture scripts, Barnes classifies his television play *The Man with a Feather in His Hat* among his commissioned works, written according to specifications. 'The general sort of feeling,' he says, 'was that it would be nice to do a courtroom play, with a lot of pyrotechnics, that sort of thing, and that's what I did. The story is mine, but the impulse to write it: that's different.'

A cleverly crafted artifice, *The Man with a Feather in His Hat* contains a farfetched situation, stereotyped characters (the vengeful mistress, the self-made man ashamed of his lower-class origins, the histrionic lawyer who is a courtroom spellbinder, the methodical police superintendent, and so forth), a series of reversals or twists in the plot, sufficient foreshadowing to make them seem less farfetched than they otherwise might, a sense of justice, wit, and a clever conclusion. What a courtroom play requires, the twenty-nine year old Barnes provided: a suspect to whom the evidence points, the possibility that someone else is guilty, ups and downs at the trial, shifting allegiances on the part of the spectators (who are more convinced, less convinced, or unconvinced that a character is guilty), and at least one genuine surprise (preferably, at the end). Given this genre, these are the major expectations spectators bring with them when they open the novel, enter the theatre, or switch on the television set.

At the start is a shot of a man in a street. He wears a soft, broad-rimmed hat with a small feather on one side. His face is unseen. When he notices a man watching him from the window of a ground floor flat, the camera cuts to the flat to reveal that man, Philip Stokes, looking out of the window. Inside the flat, Stokes and his mistress, Kate Lehmann, are in the midst of an argument. Because he is about to marry, he wants to end their affair. When she tries to blackmail him for £15,000, he refuses to pay a penny. When she proposes to tell his fiancée, he is unintimidated. 'Go ahead,' he dares her. 'She's broadminded' (I).[1] When she threatens to reveal his lower-class origins, however—his father was a dustman (garbage collector) whom Stokes no longer visits—he angrily throws his drink in her face. In retaliation, she decides to sell the story to a newspaper that specializes in lurid or sensational revelations about well-known figures. She laughs, he twice cries 'I'll kill you' (I), and he throws his empty glass at the mirror, which cracks.

In the hall outside, neighbours Irene Wilson and William Barber listen to the argument. Out comes a distraught Stokes, with blood on one of his hands, knocking aside Barber as he rushes down the corridor. Entering the flat, they discover Kate Lehmann's blood-stained body, with a heavy paper-knife beside it. The camera shows the lower half of the bedroom window to be open, its curtains gently blowing to and fro by the wind—a suggestion (created by generic expectations) that someone may have left by that route.

Superintendent Gorse arrives and interrogates the witnesses. Although the evidence points to Stokes, Gorse conscientiously refrains from drawing conclusions. Because the crime is murder, he wants to be certain. At this point, a telephone call announces that the police have picked up Stokes at London airport—as, we later learn, he was about to fly to Tangiers.

Under interrogation, Stokes claims to have stood in the doorway and seen Kate, her back to him, face a man who stabbed her and fled through the open window. Stokes identifies him as wearing a belted raincoat, a tartan scarf that hid the lower part of his face, and a green hat with a small feather on its side. According to Gorse, the description bears all the marks of a story invented on the spur of the moment. However, the facts that the spectators saw this man at the start and that the title characterizes both him and the man described by Stokes make them question Gorse's conclusion.

In the next scene, a clubroom, members of the legal profession discuss the imminent retirement of Charles Canning, whom they variously describe as 'great,' 'a demagogue,' 'the most successful advocate this country's seen in decades,' a man who 'turned the Old Bailey into a three-ringed circus,' 'a colourful character in a colourless age,' 'egocentric,' 'nothing but an *actor!*' At this point, predictably but with some effectiveness, one hears a voice inquire, 'Talking about me, I trust, gentlemen?' (I). Before his retirement, Canning will take one last case. When the man who is to prosecute Stokes remarks that there is so much evidence against the accused that not even Canning could secure his acquittal, the colourful advocate indicates, as one might predict (else why introduce him?), that he has undertaken to defend Stokes.

The trial reveals that the only fingerprints on the murder weapon are the deceased's and the accused's. Pointing out that the police could find no man with a feather in his hat, the prosecutor concludes that no such intruder exists. Dramatically, Stokes—in the dock—cries out that he does.

Cross-examining Superintendent Gorse, Canning gets him to admit that since burglars usually wear gloves and try not to be detected, it is unsurprising that the man with a feather in his hat would leave no fingerprints and not be seen. When the doctor who examined the deceased says she faced the window when she was stabbed and fell backwards toward the door, Canning cannily concludes that it was impossible for the accused, who stood in the doorway, to have killed her, but not impossible for the unknown entrant to have done so.

In his examination of the two witnesses, Canning scores points with one, loses with the other. He gets Barber to admit that he does not remember Stokes' exact words to Kate and that he dislikes the accused. The other witness, however, indicates that if anyone broke ino the victim's flat she would have seen him, since he would have passed her window, which was open.

The scene shifts to a bedroom at night, with a burglar at work. A woman wakes up but before she can speak or act, a man clamps his gloved hand over her mouth and presses her onto the bed. As he leans over her, the camera shows his hat, which contains a small feather.

At the trial, she becomes a surprise witness who testifies that a man with a small feather in his hat tried to burgle her flat. A caretaker and a neighbour also saw him. The jury finds Stokes not guilty.

After the trial, the prosecutor calls it luck for Canning to have had three witnesses appear at the eleventh hour. Pressed as to whether he truly believes Stokes to be innocent, Canning admits that as a professional lawyer what interests him is not innocence or guilt but acquittal or conviction, victory or defeat. Yet he reveals dissatisfaction that future generations will attribute his victory to luck. The man previously called egocentric declares that his last case should have 'something unique. Something nobody has ever done in a court of law. Something unforgettable. Luck will play no part. It'll just be me, me, me' (III).

The scene dissolves to the Old Bailey at night, lit by the moon as it shines through a high window. Enter Stokes, who finds himself alone. Then enter Canning, who places on a table the burglar's apparel, including the hat with the feather. He admits he pretended to burgle a flat in order to win his case. When Stokes wonders why he took such a risk when the real unknown man might have appeared, Canning states that this man does not exist and that he has known all along Stokes lied. Because Stokes cannot be tried twice for the same crime, says Canning, he might as well confess. He admits he killed Kate, made up the story of the unknown man, and when the police asked for a description, remembered the man he had seen in the street shortly before the murder.

Superintendent Gorse, whom Canning invited to come to the Old Bailey, arrives in time to hear him shoot Stokes—but not until Canning has staged a theatrical trial with himself as prosecutor, judge, jury, and executioner. Canning proposes to defend himself for the murder of Stokes—an appropriate end to the career of a man described as an actor and a showman. Surrendering to Gorse, he refers to the hat—in the play's final line—as the property of a man who never existed. The television play concludes with a shot similar to one that begins it: a hat with a small feather in it.

The Time of the Barracudas

In a hunting lodge in Scotland, the setting of most of the scenes in *The Time of the Barracudas*, Barnes' first play for the stage, his two chief characters, Philip Wiere and Stella, reveal the significance of the title. Observing a large, stuffed pike, with huge jaws and teeth, in a glass case above the mantelpiece, Wiere explains that pikes are from the same family as barracudas. Their chief activity is to kill. About six feet long, half their bodies are 'taken up with a huge mouth filled with razor sharp teeth.' They are 'fast, strong, and rapacious' and they lie in wait 'to pounce on anything that moves.' Quips Stella: 'give them two legs and they'd be right at home amongst us.' Jokingly imitating two-legged barracudas, the couple flap their arms like flippers, waddle, purse their mouths, and imagine barracudas with suits and bowler hats (I,viii).

To Barnes, English businessmen are indeed barracudas. As business requires, they rapaciously pounce upon and devour their victims. The two central characters are such business people. Suggestive that business is a cruel and murderous activity, their business is murder. Efficient and businesslike, they marry, take out joint insurance policies, and kill their spouses. Because Barnes regards capitalism as a crime, he depicts criminals as businessmen, and he emphasizes their links to the business community and to capitalism in general. Spouse-murder is an extension of business, a business activity, and a symbol of capitalism. Does this sound familiar? One recalls Charlie Chaplin's 1947 motion picture *Monsieur Verdoux*, whose title character does what Barnes' two chief characters do, and for a similar thematic purpose.[2] Although Barnes regards *Monsieur Verdoux* as Chaplin's best full-length film, he was unconscious of these parallels when he wrote *The Time of the Barracudas*.

In *Mother Courage and Her Children*, Brecht shows war to be an extension of business. Unlike Brecht, who dramatizes the conduct of war in terms of the conduct of business and who also shows that normal business conduct both contributes to and is among the activities of war, Barnes (and Chaplin, too, for that matter) relies chiefly on metaphor and discussion to convey his ideas. Partly for these reasons, Brecht's work successfully embodies and demonstrates its theme, whereas the first stage play of young Barnes (like the film of the veteran Chaplin) does not.

To chide Barnes, however, is not my purpose, for *Barracudas* is an entertaining, frequently witty, theatrically deft, and well-crafted work that—if it were well directed and performed—might succeed on today's stage as a commercial entertainment and vehicle for two star actors. More important, it marks the start of 'Barnesonian' drama: major social themes, theatricality, allusions to literary and popular culture (to be discussed later), and shifts (though not yet transformational) from one theatrical mode to another. Nevertheless, in its basically traditional craftsmanship, which employs time-honoured reversals and plants (similar to those in the television play, though more polished and effective), and in its reliance on customary expectations, it is—despite its theme and adumbration of Barnesonian devices—conventional entertainment.

At the play's start, Philip Wiere addresses the real spectators as if they were members of the group the character addresses, the Cockfosters Businessmen's Association—an apt name, the play later reveals, for Wiere's business. 'The object of business,' he says, 'is to translate into practice the ideals of our age' (I,i)—a statement which, the play also reveals later, applies to Wiere himself.

His homecoming provides an image of conventional domesticity: his wife Jean darns socks as she watches television, greets him as 'my Bunny-rabbit,' and switches off the set once he appears. When he tells how ill he has been, Jean remarks, with suburban innocence, 'Nobody'd even heard of Asian flu until they started opening all those Chinese restaurants in London' (I,ii). With Dr Clayton's apearance, we discover that Wiere is not suffering from food poisoning, as he supposed, but from arsenic poisoning. Only his wife, the doctor concludes, would want to kill him, for the Wieres have a large, joint insurance policy. To make certain his diagnosis is correct, Dr Clayton has sent Wiere's enesis to a laboratory, which will report its analysis the next day. Until then, warns the doctor, Wiere should be careful of what he eats and drinks. After the doctor leaves, the scene ends as custom requires with dialogue that creates an effective blackout. 'Everything all right, darling?' 'Perfect. Just growing old, I suppose.' 'You'll never grow old, Bunny-bun. I won't let you' (I,ii). The audience does not yet know Wiere's business.

As Wiere nervously awaits Dr Clayton the next day, Jean serves him fish, which he smells suspiciously. Her efforts to cheer him result in what the audience perceives to be *double entendres*. She laughingly tells him a man 'can never please a woman completely' and says that if anything happened to him, 'I'd have my memories' (I,iii). Clayton reports that the analysis confirms his diagnosis. Only Jean could have administered the arsenic, he insists—to Wiere's disbelief. When she brings in coffee, she proposes Wiere take a certain cup, since it has more sugar than the other. To please the doctor, Wiere changes cups. Then, a scream comes from the kitchen into which Jean has gone; she appears, clutching her stomach, in the doorway; she falls.

In the next scene, at a funeral parlour, comes confirmation that she died of arsenic poisoning. Digressing into a discussion of the funeral business, Barnes has the Funeral Director and a Branch Manager complain, 'Life expectancy rising every year, pneumonia no longer fatal, smallpox stamped out, medical care for the aged. It's getting worse.' Although such quips are funny, they do not support the play's thesis, for the characters discuss business that is based on death, which differs from business as murder.

Wiere then tells the audience that he is the murderer, that his business is to kill his wives for insurance money, that Jean is his third financial coup, and that she has raised his assets to £83,000. This apparent theatricality (like the address in the first scene) is realistically motivated. Although Wiere talks to the audience, he does so by talking to himself as he admires his appearance in a mirror on the fourth wall.

At the cemetery where the funeral service is held for Jean, Wiere meets Stella, a former actress who is at the grave of her late husband. They marry and take out a joint life insurance policy for £23,000.

During their honeymoon in a Scottish hunting lodge, Wiere almost electrocutes himself as he plugs his electric razor into a socket. Later, he barely escapes death when a rockslide just misses knocking him over the edge of a mountain, where he has gone to pick flowers for Stella. With two almost fatal accidents in quick succession, he ponders. After Stella leaves the room, privately examining an official-looking letter, he unscrews the wall socket and examines the wires that might have electrocuted him, then opens her suitcase, breaks the lock of her diary, and reads dates of weddings and deaths, the amounts she received from her late husbands' estates, and their own wedding date. 'A competitor!' he exclaims. Returning to confront him, she cries, 'You bastard. You've opened my diary' (I,ix). As they face each other, the curtain falls—a 'big curtain' that is both an effective and conventional climax to the act.

Predictably, the next act begins exactly where the first ends, with the characters in the same positions. No dramatic time has elapsed. After mutual recriminations, Stella explains that her letter was from private investigators, who revealed to her what her diary revealed to him. At the same time, they learn the truth about each other. Though she suggests they enter business together, he rejects the idea since they know too much about each other and urges that they make a clean break.

Having found each other out, they indulge in the luxury of talking shop. He praises her crossing of wires in the electric socket: 'That sort of technical training is invaluable, you can pick up the humanities anytime.' Barnes then has them break the realistic convention he established earlier (motivated monologues) by recognizing the presence of the audience, addressing them, and stating that they cannot interfere, only applaud. He ends the scene with a traditionally effective curtain line. When Wiere picks up Stella, her weight makes him teeter backward and almost fall down the stairs. 'What are you trying to do?' she asks. 'Kill us both?' (II,i).

As each pretends to sleep, the other sneaks out of bed to prepare a death trap—a thin wire designed to trip him on the stairs, a banister deliberately misaligned to make her fall—but he notices the wire and she avoids failing with the banister. Continuing to pretend that nothing unusual has occurred, each prepares a new death trap, but again each avoids being killed. This time definitely, they agree to part. Off she drives—to her death, as the car goes over a cliff. As Wiere explains in a motivated monologue (talking to himself while lying on the sofa), he loosened the brakes. A cleverly crafted twist has him light a cigarette and carelessly throw the match onto the stove, which explodes, as she arranged. Another twist has him emerge alive.

In a final scene, Barnes aims to emphasize his social theme and stress the play's theatricality. In a speech as unconvincing as Chaplin's in *Monsieur Verdoux*, Wiere describes his business as 'a tough way to make a living,' and adds—surprisingly, in view of that statement and the previous action—'Businessmen like me live to a ripe old age, stinking rich in the odour of sanctity.' He next enters a box in the auditorium, where he introduces himself to a young woman, supposedly a spectator, and—describing himself as 'nothing special. Just a dull, ordinary businessman'—he escorts her onto the stage, then leads her off (II,vi).

If *The Time of the Barracudas* were not so skilfully written, it might be called an apprentice play. However, the former screenwriter and television writer had learned his craft too well for this play to be so easily dismissed. As *crafted* writing—climaxes well prepared and artfully written, a spiraling series of twists and reversals—it is apprentice only in relationship to Barnes' later plays. What are weak are those aspects which later become his strengths: the social themes (not yet soldered to the conflicts and dramatic development) and the theatricalism (which wavers uncertainly, grafted upon an old convention, instead of forming part of a unique, new convention dramatized by a sure hand). An uneasy combination of the old and the new, *Barracudas* has the weakness that results from their alliance, which is paste-board rather than integrated, as well as the strength that derives from the author's skill in treating the old, plus the wit and daring he displays in introducing the new.

Sclerosis

A technical advance from the two plays that precede it, *Sclerosis* represents tentative steps from the conventionally crafted type of play to which Barnes was accustomed. Although he does not abandon such devices as reversals, plot twists, and strong climaxes in the traditional manner, he begins to strike out in new directions.

Sclerosis is a short play whose centrepiece, its longest scene, is a savage satire written realistically. Unlike *Barracudas*, the satire is not conveyed by means of analogy but is direct—a stratagem that results in a departure from the atmosphere of gentility of the earlier work to a use of devices expressive of cruelty, a step toward the Artuad-like techniques that help characterize his mature plays. There is also a more straightforward political stance as well as a step toward the concreteness and reorientation devices that characterize Brechtian drama. Surrounding the centrepiece are two short scenes— theatricalized parentheses, as it were—which expand the social framework, permit more extensive use of non-realistic theatrical devices, employ song-and-dance as social satire, and mark the start of what are to become transformationalist devices.

Following the title page is the definition of *Sclerosis* by the *British Medical Dictionary:* 'Hardening of the tissues due to inflammation.' The Cypriot struggle for independence in the 1950s is inflammatory. In the first scene, such inflammation has led to a hardening of political lines. The second scene demonstrates the practical consequences of these politics: British forces torture Cypriot prisoners. In the final scene, the tissue is stripped of its protective covering and crumbles.

After '*a jaunty drumroll,*' the first scene opens with a spotlight hitting a large easel, '*the same as those used in Vaudeville to announce the next variety turn.*' It tells place and time: the House of Commons, 28 July 1954. Beneath a large Union Jack, a Chaplain, bible in hand, 'Pomp and Circumstance' playing in the background, prays for wisdom to unite people in Christian love and charity. A government minister appears, formally attired but with a chalk-white, featureless face. At the outset, the audience is in a different milieu from Barnes' earlier works.

As the scene continues, sounds—underscoring or counterpointing the dialogue—provide theatrical satire. The minister announces that the British Government will take a new initiative toward the development of self-government in Cyprus, then that it will not contemplate a change of sovereignty there. Spectators—but not the minister—hear a dull thud, like a distant explosion. He informs the House that England will provide for both elected and appointed officials in Cyprus, a plan he admits the leaders of the two major political parties there do not yet know, whereupon another menacing thud sounds in the background. In contrast to previous policy, he says, certain Commonwealth territories 'can *never* expect to be fully independent.' A burst of machine-gun fire erupts, followed by a scream of pain. None of the Members of Parliament reacts to the sounds. More statements like this result in explosions, smoke billowing onto the stage, and battle sounds. Finally, the noises drown out the speeches of the MPs, whose unresponsiveness to them reflects their unresponsiveness to the Cypriots. Occasionally, irrelevant phrases—such as 'Lord Beaconsfield wrote to Queen Victoria in 1878'—become audible. As an MP pontificates about sports and playing fields, the Union Jack falls limply to the floor.

Scene 2, a room in a British Army compound in Cyprus, is set realistically—though the Union Jack (to be used later as part of realistic action) remains on the floor. An officer, an enlisted man, and a police inspector on short-term service with the military reveal their system: two brutally interrogate a prisoner; the third acts in a fatherly way and tries to persuade him to give information. In their efforts to make the prisoner, Georgadis, tell the name of his contact in the EOKA (a terrorist resistance movement), the soldiers yell into his ears, punch his face, knock him off his chair, and kick him. Playing the fatherly role, Inspector Seaton requests a private word with Georgadis, whom he tells he has a son the same age and whom he advises to talk in order to save himself pain. Georgadis refuses. The soldiers then take a small metal box with a handle and two wires with metal clips, strap his arms and legs to a bed, attach the clips to his earlobes, turn the crank-handle, and watch him scream and convulsively jerk up and down. Since his screams are unpleasant, Inspector Seaton picks up the Union Jack, tears off a piece, and stuffs it in the prisoner's mouth. The soldiers then return to their electronic torture, which Barnes punctuates with bitter humour. The captain stops the enlisted man and advises, 'Turning it continuously like that dulls the patient's reflexes. He gets so he doesn't feel anything anymore. Give it to me. Let the current out in short stabs. See? Effective enough if you do it right.' With each sharp turn of the crank-handle, Georgadis jolts violently.

After more ineffective torture, the British take a tea-break, during which they comment admiringly on the prisoner's professionalism. The enlisted man kicks him, then calls him 'Officer material.' Following the tea-break, the interrogators give Georgadis an injection designed to relax him sufficiently that he will forget his surroundings and respond truthfully to their questions. This method, too, proves ineffective. Although they persuade him that Seaton is an EOKA man, his imagination creates a British patrol just as he is about to divulge his contact's name. When Seaton persists, Georgadis suspects he is an English spy. To prevent him from harming Seaton, the soldiers kick him into another room.

Enter a new prisoner, Zavos, who is middle-aged, fat, and bald. Pleading that he is a respectable businessman, he explains that he joined the EOKA to save himself from bankruptcy: 'It pays to be a patriot. If I turned against them, nobody'd buy in my little place. I'd have to sell out inside a month, if I wasn't dead.' He adds, 'It's all business, isn't it, sir?' Unlike Georgadis, Zavos is motivated by business, not patriotism. Thus, he is really at one with his British captors. They haggle until they agree on how much to pay him to become a British agent.

When he divulges the name of his EOKA contact, however, Seaton checks a file and discovers that the man is a British agent masquerading as a terrorist agent. The only way the British can deal with what Zavos has told them is to believe he lied. As the innocent man pleads, they punch him and verbally abuse him.

Imperceptibly, the lights fade and Zavos' dying groans mingle with the voices of a choir, who sing 'Land of Hope and Glory,' which rises to introduce the final scene, set like the first in the House of Commons, this time—a new vaudeville easel informs—19 February 1959. The torn Union Jack is now hoisted. In the midst of a heated debate among MPs as to whether Britain should negotiate with the Cypriot leader Archbishop Makarios, the Prime Minister—in top hat, white tie, and tails—dances on, singing 'Where Have You Been All the Day, Billy Boy,' in which the MPs join, and—without pause—he shifts his mode of utterance from song to an announcement that Great Britain, Greece, and Turkey have agreed to the formation of the Republic of Cyprus. As a minister steps forward to play 'Red Sails in the Sunset' on his violin, the Prime Minister announces amnesty for convicted prisoners, release of detainees, and return of exiles. His trousers drop, to reveal Union-Jack underpants. As, one by one, the MPs drop their trousers to reveal Union-Jack underpants, he pins medals on his own chest. When an MP mildly points out that this solution could have been achieved four years earlier, the others laugh at him, pelt him with tomatoes, and hoot 'rotter! bounder! cad!' Amid the shouts, a chorus line forms and dances off, singing.

Although the final scene is within a framework of extravagant vaudeville or music-hall satire, it represents a movement toward the Brechtian and transformational techniques characteristic of Barnes' later plays. The central scene is satiric realism, but its savagery is new to Barnes, and his attention to concrete detail takes political shape; further, it represents a step toward a more universalized dramatization of cruelty. In contrast to *The Time of the Barracudas*, *Sclerosis* has theatrically satiric elements that augment rather than clash with realistically satiric elements, and at one point a single property (the Union Jack flag) is employed in both realistic and theatrical manners, thereby unifying them. Like the first scene, the last scene contains theatricality that supports the play's satiric themes. While *Sclerosis* is relatively slight and at times heavy-handed, its political satire, bolstered by various theatrical artifices, are essays that attempt to bring together diverse theatrical techniques into what will become a new form.

Clap Hands, Here Comes Charlie

In terms of characterization, satire, allusions to literary and popular culture, facility in combining different theatrical modes, development of transformationalist techniques, and de-emphasis of conventional dramatic craft, *Clap Hands, Here Comes Charlie* represents a major step forward. Like John Osborne's *The Entertainer, Charlie* is, as Barnes asserts, 'steeped in music hall,' and its chief character, like Osborne's, is an entertainer. As in Harold Pinter's *The Caretaker*, the central character is a seedy tramp with a vague background. Unlike Pinter's Davies, however, Barnes' Charlie Ketchum lacks restraint. A colourful character, Charlie uses his teeth to pull a cork from a bottle, slops whisky into glasses, frequently tosses off such one-liners as 'It's a sore ass that never rejoices' (I,ix), and employs colourful invective, for instance, 'may your balls turn grey an' yer left penis drop off' (I,viii).

Celebrating the spirit of anarchy in conflict with bureaucratized and compartmentalized modern society, it takes an individualistic nonconformist as its major figure. Ultimately, however, the play in which the anarchic Charlie Ketchum is the linchpin fails to demonstrate convincingly that his credo is an appealing alternative to suburban values. One can excuse his disregard for property, but he is a hedonistic, egotistical slob with no regard for anyone's person—to the point that he rapes, murders, and behaves as if these were forgivable rather than indictable offences. Partly because it becomes increasingly difficult to sympathize with Charlie as Barnes seems to intend, the play's theme becomes unconvincing, the play itself little more than a star turn for an actor and an anticipation of the author's mature work.

In a Prologue, a character named Peter Barnes announces that interpretations of creative works, particularly plays, 'are usually wrong, and always beside the point.' To prevent the spectators, including critics, from misinterpreting this play—perhaps as demonstrated by the preceding paragraph—he will tell them what he is driving at. When he starts to explain, a sandbag crashes from above, landing just beside him; hands reach out from the curtain to grab his ankles; and a mallet, striking at him through a slit in the curtain, misses his head. Cursing England but recovering himself in time to read his prepared text, he announces, 'The play's meaning is crystal clear: it's this'—and a large, vaudeville-like hook whisks him offstage. Spectators hear a blow, a groan, and a thud. The Prologue prepares them for a comic, satiric, anti-England play with violence.

The play proper begins with buskers, a street band composed of Gunboat Smith, Joe Gaff, and Zacchaeus, led by Charlie, marching before the front curtain and playing the title song. After they depart, the curtain rises to show the first three in a cheap mission lodging house. One guzzles a bottle of lethal whisky; another removes *The Times* from under his vest, where he placed it for warmth; a third rolls a cigarette which goes up in flames when he lights it. Enter a television producer, Michael Aylmer, and his secretary Diana, to produce a documentary called *The Outsiders*. Diana explains that they have 'already done gypsies, schizophrenics, drug addicts.' The next show, says Aylmer, is 'about buskers, street entertainers.' He offers them ten pounds each to assist him. The trio wake up Charlie Ketchum, whose first line is 'Piss off!' Aylmer persuades the group to do their act. As they do so, they become snarled in the television equipment. Then Diana screams and flees. Charlie explains, 'Jus' stuck me hand up her knickers quick as a ferret, same as always— and look *(holds up* DIANA*'s torn panties)*. PAPER! It's *disgusting*' (I,i). Indignantly, he tears them to shreds.

Fascinated by Charlie, Aylmer wants to make a television film on him. To ensure his availability, he takes him home, to the displeasure of his wife Joan, who perceives, 'he's dangerous' (I,iii). Aylmer succeeds in filming Charlie at work. Joan's apprehension proves accurate. Charlie swills liquor, hogs food, and tries to steal their belongings. While Aylmer is away, Charlie jokingly half-seduces and half-rapes Joan, who though terrified laughs at his antics all the while. Later, Charlie looks up Diana's skirt and unsuccessfully tries to ingratiate himself with her.

While Peter Barnes, a guest of the Aylmers, pontificates his theories of the creative artist, he and the Aylmers—who package commodity entertainment for mass audiences—ignore Charlie, who performs a theatrical act with jokes and visual effects. The entertainment merchants are absorbed in themselves, not in the vital entertainment around them. Finally, Charlie does what Joan urges him to do: leave. But while the Aylmers are gone, he returns with his three cronies. In 'Piss-Pot Hall' and 'EASY STREET,' as he calls the apartment (I,xi), he drinks and destroys furniture, Zacchaeus thrusts his fist through a Picasso print, and they all ruin the library. When Joan returns and sees the wreckage, she is furious. After she gets rid of the three cronies, she hits and kicks Charlie, who she knows is responsible. Charlie hits this trendy, upper-middle-class, liberal wife on the head with a bust of Bertrand Russell. Upon his discovery that he has killed her, he telephones the *News of the World* newspaper and offers to sell them the story for a thousand pounds.

When Aylmer discovers his dead wife, he '*lets out a great keening cry of despair.*' In the background, however, is a recording of his voice, the same tape that he, his wife, and Barnes listened to in an earlier scene: 'The difference between tragedy and comedy is that comedy offers no hope. Tragedy shows a man broken by an incomprehensible fate; it presumes Man is worth breaking. Comedy offers no such sops to pride. From a seat in the Gods, everything that happens on Earth provokes laughter. . . . It's all a question of distance' (II,i). Trying to control himself, Aylmer looks at the audience, considers how funny the murder of this type of woman with this bust must seem, and decides that by gaining distance from the event, he will laugh rather than weep. He steps into the auditorium, walks up the centre aisle, and laughs—first quietly, then wildly.

Acting as his own defence attorney, the anarchic Charlie mocks the values of the society from which the court derives its authority. To protest the appearance of a witness, he dons a torn gown and plants an orange clown's wig on his head. When a police officer testifies, Charlie makes a travesty of the law and disconcerts the judge:

> KETCHUM *(up)*: I object!
> JUDGE: On what grounds?
> KETCHUM: I don't like what he's saying.
> JUDGE: Objection overruled.

After the officer speaks again:

> KETCHUM *(up)*: I don't object!
> JUDGE: Overruled.
> KETCHUM *(sitting)*: Thank you, m'Lud.
> JUDGE *(puzzled)*: Er, yes. The witness may continue.

Charlie turns the trial proceedings into a shambles:

> KETCHUM: Ain't nobody got a pot fer a piss!
>
> JUDGE *(shocked)*: You dare to ask—in a Court of Law—
>
> KETCHUM *(jiggling up and down)*: This is a law o' nature, yer Grace, beats all yer other laws every time, 's natural, treats everyone the same, rich an' poor, young an' old, heroes an' stinkers.

He rages, imitates the judge's voice, cries—as if he were summarizing his case—'*And another thing—my prick's bigger than yours!*' and sings the kitsch 'Yeomen of England.' Immune to the constraints imposed on most people by the dignity of the law, Charlie is defiant even when his life is at stake—perhaps because he perceives that no matter what he does he will be convicted. As the Judge recognizes, 'prisoners are usually aware that the administration of justice depends on their acceptance of certain standards of behaviour. Without that acceptance the system breaks down' (II,ii). Charlie prefers it to break down. As expected, the court finds him guilty and sentences him to death by hanging.

Although Charlie violates cleanliness and good taste, derides purveyors of art and entertainment (Barnes and Aylmer), murders, and mocks the law that punishes him, the liberal intellectual Aylmer is ready to defend him: 'I've campaigned for years for the abolition of capital punishment. I can't condone it now because it was my wife who was murdered. It's not a "cause" to be taken up and dropped when convenient.' But when Charlie tells him he made love to Joan, Aylmer goes wild, threatens to kill him himself, and cries, '*Hang him. Hang him. Hang him*' (II,iii).

Having demolished liberalism, Charlie next attacks religion. When the prison chaplain, Reverend Padley, advises him to be baptized, Charlie insists the ceremony be performed immediately. Padley protests he has no water, but Charlie urinates in a chamber pot, which he thrusts at the reverend. As Padley shrinks back, Charlie tells him to close his eyes and think of England, then sprinkles urine on himself and forces Padley to speak the words.

Charlie's next target is the hangman, who admits that his job would be impossible if the condemned did not accept the spirit of the occasion—as Charlie, of course, does not. At first, Charlie tries to cheat death by dressing Padley in his clothes and wearing Padley's turned-around collar, but the prison officials catch him. On the scaffold, he manages to switch places with the hangman, who is hanged in his place.

In an Epilogue, Barnes reveals that Charlie was caught and hanged. He is ushered into the office of Mr Nicolaus (i.e., Old Nick or Satan), who calls Hell a more efficient version of earth.

You could define Hell as a perfect bureaucracy. The functions and relationships of our denizens are defined and regulated by impersonal rules like any efficient business organization. The system absorbs all types, all shades of opinion, provided they're prepared to accept the rules. Most people do accept, gladly, despite what they say. Order and discipline bring a contentment that passeth all understanding. We give our souls security and an eternal peace in exchange for a worthless freedom.

By contrast, Heaven is 'an eternal chaos,' a brotherhood of free individualists who recognize no restraints, rules, or controls. 'It was this spiritual anarchy that finally drove me out. A totally misunderstood episode. *I* have always been the great traditionalist, the spirit of order and conformity. It is *God* who embodies the pure spirit of revolt.' While a soul is free to choose between them, the vast majority select Hell. Not Charlie, however, who will not curb himself in death any more than he did in life. At the end of the play, going up to Heaven on an elevator, he dances a jig and sings the title song.[3]

As asserted earlier, *Charlie* is a major technical advance from Barnes' earlier plays. Its satire stems from the created world of the play and is not thrust in via a symbol of dubious validity, as in *Barracudas*, or by means of a Prologue and Epilogue which relate to, but do not form part of, the main plot, as in *Sclerosis*. More boldly and more deftly handled, the theatricality is part of the dramatic action. For example, a spotlight picks out the hairy leg and thigh of Charlie, who enters in a silk dressing-gown and bath-slippers, nonchalantly stroking his eyebrows and singing a music-hall song; then, the other stage lights go up to show a producer tape-recording the number. In this play, the theatre is acutely conscious of itself as theatre. Enter a character named Peter Barnes, whom Charlie examines incredulously: 'Barnes? Barnes? I never seen none o' your writings, an' I know every piss-house in England' (I,ix). Parodying himself, Barnes has the bespectacled stage Barnes stammer and even has a second Barnes emerge from the audience to call the Barnes on stage an impostor. Brechtianly, the play employs film to expand the action: the buskers, led by Charlie, entertain in the streets of London. Theatricality reinforces satire. 'God save the King!' declares Charlie, who pulls a toilet chain. As the lights go out to the sound of flushing, Charlie cries, *'Help, I'm drowning!'* (I,vii)— as indeed he is, in the bureaucratized, calcified society of England. Abandoning words, Charlie employs sounds to convey meaning: 'Over the top, Parlee Vous, I was green behind the ears when *whroom bang'* (I,v). With transformational techniques, Barnes has Charlie—imprisoned, behind wire netting—utter a cry of rage when he sees Aylmer and Diana *('Arrrrrrx')*; crack an obscene joke ('Lovely pair o' top 'uns, eh? And a juicy snatch-box t' match'); then leap onto the wire, hang with one hand, and scratch himself and grunt like a chimpanzee; finally, subside with a disingenuous explanation ('Just a bit o' fun') (II,iii). In short, this play reveals Barnes more firmly in control of his medium than he was before.

Yet he has not fully developed his distinctive style. The language lacks the Jacobean qualities of his mature plays. Conventions often clash as theatricality steps beside realism rather than merges with it (as when Aylmer addresses the audience and walks through it, or when Charlie pleads with it to save him). When the conventions do not clash, it is because of a special reason: the character Charlie is an entertainer who clowns his way from one theatrical mode to another and uses transformational techniques to do so.

Foreshadowing and Progress

Of *The Man with a Feather in His Hat*, Barnes claims, 'Anything personal that got in there, got in there almost despite me. One might, if one delved very deeply, find a few personal and idiosyncratic twists, but certainly they would be few and far between.' Although they are relatively few, one does not have to delve deeply to find them. The motive for murder is characteristically Barnesonian. Kate taunts Stokes with failure to have suppressed traces of his lower-class origins in his speech: 'Watch it, Phil, your accent's showing. *'Ow* did I find out? I made it my business. You never told me *'ow* your father was still alive. Of course he's only a *'umble* dustman but he's proud of his successful son. You never go to see *'im*, though. You're embarrassed' (I). As Stokes describes his deed, 'It was a genuine English murder. It couldn't have happened anywhere else in the world. I didn't kill for any of the usual reasons—money, revenge, sex. I murdered Kate for a misplaced vowel, a dropped "h," a working-class accent' (III).

Socially satiric touches enliven this television play. When Gorse's assistant refers to Stokes' friends, Gorse interrupts, 'Self-made men don't have friends' (I). Similar is this exchange in Barnes' first stage play, *The Time of the Barracudas:* 'Do you know anyone who'd want to kill you?' 'Of course not.' 'No enemies?' 'None.' 'But you're a businessman' (I,ii). Wiere, whose business is murder, insists, 'I'm no rebel. Quite the reverse. . . . A patriotic, class-conscious, anti-Communist, white protestant, conservative. Perhaps when I've made a million I'll become a socialist and preach the brotherhood of man' (I,v). He says that the main function of the English police is not to apprehend criminals but 'to protect property. Property rights have always been more important than human rights' (II,i). Here as later, Barnes satirizes religion. At the funeral, the minister discusses religion in terms of commerce. Advised by his Bishop to 'move with the times,' he aims to 'get out and sell religion,' wants to learn 'consumer packaging,' and to attract the youth he will hold a special 'service of dedication for their motorcycles.' For this reason, he has rewritten the hymn 'Hail to the Lord's Anointed,' which he sings: 'Hurrah, for Him who's with it' (I,vi). *Sclerosis* satirizes the inhumanity and ineptitude of British government and of Britons in occupied territory. Although the satire of *Clap Hands, Here Comes Charlie* is infrequently as obvious as in the earlier plays—Charlie's outburst of rage at the spectators, 'you lot'd skin cow-turds if there was money in it!' (I,viii) is unusually explicit—it attacks England's conformist society, trendy liberalism, legal system, and religious attitudes. In the targets of his social satire, the young Barnes anticipates the mature Barnes.

None of these early works has the Jacobean flavour so characteristic of the mature plays. The television play superficially relates language to social class, but the stage plays skilfully employ language to characterize class: an upper-middle-class businessman and a former actress; parliamentarians and soldiers; tramps, television people, and an earnest playwright.

All of these early plays contain jokes, even *Feather in His Hat:* 'Er, Superintendent, do you think I'll get my name in the papers?' 'I expect so. You found the woman. She was dead and beautiful. That's always good for a half-column' (I). In *Barracudas*, Stella says of her late husbands, 'I worship the ground they're buried under' (II,ii) and Wiere calls Shakespeare's Juliet 'The Elizabethan Lolita' (I,viii). Broad humour abounds in the Prologue and Epilogue to *Sclerosis*, whose second scene, though primarily concerned with torture, contains such gags as Inspector Seaton's praise of Cypriot women, 'we don't see women like that in East Grinstead,' and Zavos' divulgence of his EOKA contact's identity: 'His name is Hector Kranidiotis.' 'How do you spell it?' 'H-E-' 'No, Kranidiotis.' As indicated, *Charlie* abounds in gags, usually spoken by Charlie. Often, they are obscene—'A fart's the cry of an imprisoned turd' (I,ix)—and sometimes hoary, such as his comment to Joan, 'You jus' wait till we get something straight between us' (I,vi). To her husband's remark, 'I read somewhere Upper Richmond is the syphilis capital of Great Britain,' Joan crisply responds: 'Surely not since you left' (I,iii).

Even in these stages of his career, Barnes displays a sense of symmetry in the opening and closing of a play: shots of the hat with a feather in the television play, direct address to the audience at the start and close of the first full-length stage play, an opening and closing scene set in the same locale in the short play, and a Prologue and Epilogue to the second full-length play.

All the stage plays demonstrate theatricalist tendencies. In *Barracudas*, the tolling of bells at a funeral, where Wiere meets Stella, turns joyous, then merges into the 'Bridal Song' from Wagner's *Lohengrin*. The first and third scenes of *Sclerosis* contain stage effects (battle noises and smoke) that punctuate realistic debate, jaunty drumrolls and placards, expressionistic make-up and song-and-dance routines. *Charlie* has a band, and its title character frequently bursts into song, sometimes augmented by costume and a dance.

In the two full-length plays, the theatre is conscious of itself as theatre—usually ineffectively, particularly in contrast to the mature plays. Wiere and Stella introduce themselves to the audience and comment on them; he enters the auditorium to claim his next wife, and he addresses the audience, usually with realistic motivation, but at times without. Like Wiere, Aylmer changes theatrical convention to address the audience and enter the auditorium. Also changing convention, Charlie addresses the audience. Effectively, however, because the play establishes the 'author' in a direct-address mode, two characters named Peter Barnes—one on stage, the other in the auditorium, argue with each other.

The human cruelty depicted in the torture scene of *Sclerosis* adumbrates the metaphysical cruelty suggested in the mature plays. Passages of *Charlie* anticipate the Artaud-like devices of having language erupt into non-verbal sounds. Learning that Charlie made love to his wife, Aylmer shrieks, '*Hang him*'; then, '*howling in fury*,' the words turn to sounds: '*Haaaa-Haaaaa-Haaaaa*' (II,iii). The play also contains passages which, like the mature plays, parody this technique, as when the second Peter Barnes, in the auditorium, shouts, 'Everybody knows I'm, I'm articulate, lucid, cool—BLOODY SUAVE and BLEEDING SOPHISTICATED. *Arrrrrx!*' (I,ix).

Literary and historical allusions begin to appear in the stage plays, though they are few, seem tentative, and (perhaps for these reasons) fail to provide the textural richness they give the mature plays. Planning to kill Stella, Wiere quotes *Romeo and Juliet:* 'But soft!

What light through yonder window breaks?/It is the east and Juliet is the sun./Arise, fair sun, and kill the envious moon' (I,viii)— doubly ironic, since his Juliet also plans to kill him. When he discourses on the importance of zeros (£50, £500, etc.) and calls zero the rock on which their civilization is founded, Stella—quoting *King Lear*—reminds him, 'nothing will come of nothing' (II,i). Paraphrasing Nelson at the Battle of Cape St Vincent, mixed with his statement at the Battle of Trafalgar, Stella holds an empty whisky bottle to her right eye and says, 'I see no signal, Hardy. Let battle commence' (II,i)—an anticipation of the life-and-death battle to come, unsignalled, between her and Wiere. Comparing himself to Julius Caesar, the character Peter Barnes paraphrases Shakespeare's play, 'I'll bestride this petty world like a colossus,' then misquotes the words of the real Caesar to give them a sexual twist: 'vidi, vice, veni' (I saw, I conquered, I came) (I,ix). Sitting on a toilet, Charlie Ketchum parodies *Hamlet:* 'T' scarper or t' stick 'ere, that's the bleeding question' (I,vii). Barnes alludes to Dickens—'Zacchaeus by name and Zacchaeus by nature' (I,i) says that character in *Charlie* ('Gamp is my name and Gamp my nature,' in *Martin Chuzzlewit*)—and to Evelyn Waugh, when Charlie sings 'There Are No Flies on Jesus' (II,iv) (in *Vile Bodies*, Mrs Melrose Ape's hymn is 'There ain't no flies on the Lamb of God'). Such allusions, however, are infrequent. Not until *The Ruling Class*, his next play, does Barnes employ them in abundance, to texture his work distinctively.

Popular songs occasionally appear in *Barracudas*. Apparently ironic, since the spectators believe Jean will kill Wiere, is her song, 'Among My Souvenirs,' whose words recollect the 'days that used to be' which are now a memory (I,iii). 'Cheek to Cheek' is the music to which Wiere and Stella dance. 'Heaven, I'm in Heaven,' he sings— an afterlife where each would like to send the other. 'I seem to find the happiness I seek,' she sings—an appearance that does not become a reality, for she fails to kill him (II,iv). In *Sclerosis*, while the Prime Minister announces the forthcoming return of exiled, detained, and convicted Cypriots, a violinist plays 'Red Sails in the Sunset,' whose unsung lyrics concern a plea to send a loved one safely home (iii), and the colour of the title is appropriate to the Cypriots who died for their country's independence. The closing chorus line sings, as it dances off, 'We hope you've liked our little show./But now we really have to go./Goodnight, goodnight, goodnight, goodnight, goodnight!' —from the stage musical *The Littlest Revue*—appropriate to this little play and an ironic statement that the torture and killings have become merely show biz entertainment (a theme the mature Barnes develops more skilfully). In addition to its title song, *Clap Hands,*

Here Comes Charlie contains numerous traditional music hall numbers, including 'Burlington Bertie from Bow' (I,v), 'Following in Father's Footsteps' (I,vi), and 'I'm Shy, Mary Ellen, I'm Shy' (I,xi). Charlie and his trio sing 'MacNamara's Band,' substituting their names for those in the song and England for Ireland—appropriate, in Barnes' view, since he believes that 'a credit to Ould England, boys, is Charlie Ketchum's band' (I,x). Charlie launches into an English song from World War II, 'Arse-'ole, arse-'ole, a soldier I will be,' whose obscene lyrics, appropriate to the irreverent Charlie, include—beside the title line—'With piss, with piss, with pistols on my knee' (II,vi). The play has such contemporary references as a Clairol shampoo advertisment, 'Only his [*her* in the original] hairdresser knows for sure' (Prologue) and grafitti on toilet walls, including 'If your legs is short and your pump is weak/You'd better stand back or you'll pee on your feet' (I,vii). Partly because *Charlie* is richer in allusions to popular culture, it is a more colourful and textured play than the others.

Although characters in *Barracudas* break into song on occasion, they have realistic motivation when they do so. For this reason, *Sclerosis* marks the start of Barnes' transformational techniques. In this play, the Prime Minister sings and dances to a traditional ballad, then without pause makes a political announcement. An entertainer, Charlie often transforms his style from conversational to song to stand-up comic delivery, but he does so as a conscious performance technique. In this respect, *The Ruling Class* becomes an immense step forward, for it not only reveals mastery of this theatrical device, it demonstrates Barnes' ability to use it for characters other than entertainers and in contexts different from music-hall entertainment *(Sclerosis)*.

The last chapter discussed Barnes' self-thefts in the context of theatrical self-consciousness. From these early stage plays, Barnes pillages not for this reason, since few spectators would be familiar with the first two and none would know the unperformed third, but because (I infer) he does not want to waste useful material. In the first, for instance, Stella accuses Wiere, 'You use . . . words to blot out reality' (II,i)—an idea that triggers a climactic scene in *Auschwitz*. The demand to be told 'truth's truth,' part of an important scene in *Tsar* (p. 13), derives from the torture scene in *Sclerosis*, where the British demand it of Zavos. The mishaps that plague the character Peter Barnes in the Prologue to *Charlie* become less lethal to the character Author in the Prologue to *Laughter!* Charlie's comment on the British legal system—'No case too small, no fee too large' (II,ii)—is repeated by the red-nosed Father Flote (II,v).

Clap Hands, Here Comes Charlie is significant in still another way. The statement of the character Peter Barnes—'I'm trying to create a comic theatre at once tragic and ridiculous, dramatic and farcical. Monologue, soliloquies, song, dance, mimes' (I,ix)—is one the author Peter Barnes says, in similar terms, in the first paragraph of his Introduction to *Leonardo's Last Supper*. Although he fails to achieve this goal in the early plays, he succeeds in the mature works, which immediately follow them and toward which they point.

6 | *Editings and Adaptations*

The Roles of Editor and Adapter

In addition to writing his own plays, Barnes has prepared acting editions of Jacobean drama. Whether the published texts of Jacobean plays are exactly the same as those originally performed is questionable. Even if they are, however, Barnes points out that after more than two centuries words, phrases, and entire passages have lost their meanings. Editing these plays to be performed today, for spectators who for the most part are not Jacobean scholars, he tries—like many directors who do not usually announce what they have done—'to make the meaning clear to a contemporary audience, but to make the changes as vivid and as poetic as the original. As I've dealt mainly with comedy, it's important that the jokes are funny and you understand them as they're being said, not with a glossary afterwards.' An obscure Jonsonian reference to 'goings-on in 1604 no doubt had them howling in their seats, but it wouldn't mean anything today unless you had notes by your side. And that's not much good because by the time you've glanced down to find the reference, the play has moved on.' To avoid this, to make the jokes immediately comprehensible and funny today, says Barnes, 'I attempt to bring the footnotes into the text.'

With plays he considers flawed, he becomes more a collaborator than an editor. These he adapts. 'It's just a matter of degree,' he says. He would not adapt such works as *The Alchemist* or *Volpone* 'because they are fully realized masterworks. But *The Devil is an Ass* is, I feel, flawed. There are certain things that I think would be helpful to make it work on the stage.' To make it work on *today's* stage, before *today's* spectators, is Barnes' major concern. In support of his position, one might cite a passage from a Jonsonian masterpiece he has edited but not adapted, *Bartholomew Fair*, an exchange between Bartholomew Cokes and Lantern Leatherhead, who is about to put on a puppet production of *Hero and Leander*. If one bears in mind the nature of Leatherhead's audience—including Cokes himself, whose very surname indicates he is a simpleton—one recognizes that Jonson is at least partly ironic. Nevertheless, the point that performers must recognize the capacities of their audiences is valid. In harmony with the spirit of the passage, Barnes makes some deletions in order to streamline it for his own audience (here, as in the following quotations, double brackets indicate Barnes' deletions; in subsequent quotations, italics indicate his additions).

> COKES: But do you play it according to the printed book? [[I have read that.]]
> LEATHERHEAD: By no means, sir.
> COKES: No? [[How then?]]
> LEATHERHEAD: [[A better way, sir.]] That is too learned and poetical for our audience. What do they know what Hellespont is? 'Guilty of true love's blood'? Or what Abydos is? Or 'the other Sestos hight'?
> COKES: Th'art i' the right, I do not know myself.   [V][1]

To be sure, not everyone shares Leatherhead's conviction as to the desirability of not playing a work 'according to the printed book' in a 'learned and poetical' manner. According to Dennis Marks, Barnes' alterations to make the dialogue of Jacobean drama comprehensible have 'reduced the level of the imagery . . . and sometimes also the verse line has been changed: the rhythms have been changed.' He asks Barnes, 'Don't you feel you run the risk of destroying that for which these plays have survived?' Barnes' response begins with another question: 'What do you mean "these plays have survived"? Survived in the British Museum or in bookshops or in academic studies? They haven't survived on the stage, unfortunately. Shakespeare survived and a couple of odd Websters have survived. Maybe *The Alchemist*, maybe *Volpone*, but certainly you can't say *The Devil is an Ass* has survived, in the sense of being put on the stage and seen by audiences.'[2] Barnes is correct. His adaptation of *The Devil is an Ass* was the first professional production of that play in over three centuries; his *Antonio* was the first professional stage production of either *Antonio and Mellida* or *Antonio's Revenge* in almost four. One might also point to a Jonsonian comedy which perhaps all literary critics acknowledge to be a masterpiece, *Bartholomew Fair*. Although it was produced more often than any other Jonsonian comedy during the Restoration, according to a scholarly work on the subject, this play 'was weighted so heavily with the brand of realism which requires notes and glossaries' that after a production in 1731, 'it was not revived for exactly one hundred ninety years.'[3] Does theatrical neglect constitute survival? With such works, the alternative to neglect on the stage seems to be editing or adaptation.

Unconvinced by this argument, Bernard Levin insists that Jacobean playwrights should not have their works edited or adapted for performance. 'If you're going to put their plays on the stage, let us, at any rate, start with their words.'[4] To him, a play which substitutes modern words for Jonson's is a play 'marred by feeble concessions to the groundlings,' and he calls Barnes' adaptation of *The Devil is an Ass* a 'mongrel work.' With a rhetorical flourish, he asks of Barnes, 'Does he not even realize . . . that "is it theatrically alive?" is *not* the only question, for there is also the matter of integrity to be considered?'[5] This attack resulted in a barrage of replies by English directors, including Trevor Nunn, Artistic Director of the Royal Shakespeare Company, which was then rehearsing Barnes' edited text of *The Alchemist*. Nunn cogently argues that to retain certain words 'may preserve verbal music . . . but . . . miss the satiric targets. When Jonson calls something "dainty," I have no way of knowing that he means "dangerous," other than by a footnote. Unless it is explained to me that "the frail card" means "the marked card," I won't know I am meeting a cheater.' What Levin's argument amounts to is that 'anything short of his fundamentalism will please only those who know no better.' To a director, Nunn maintains, 'A theatre concerned with textual fidelity and integrity at the expense of understanding is dead.'[6]

Barnes not only concurs, he goes further. According to him, Levin's type of reasoning is a manifestation of the class system.

It's a whole English approach, that the good things are only for those who can (a) afford it and (b) have the education to appreciate it, and if you can't appreciate it, then it's not for you. It's a very English barrier. It is *We* and *Them*. *We* have got the sensitivity and intellectual ability to appreciate art. *They* have not. Unless *They* have the education to appreciate it, then *They* should be barred. It is all part and parcel of an English class attitude, the right-wing, fascist attitude. It's not just political, it's also cultural and social. It's a sign of arrogance. It's divisive. It means that instead of reaching out to embrace people, people have to come to it, into an enclosed museum atmosphere. That seems to me dead. The Levins want to keep the language static as well. But language is living, art is living. It has to go out and embrace, it has to reach out to as many people as it possibly can. That doesn't mean you debase your work by doing that. It means that you're trying to stretch out and keep the gates open.

If anyone believes that his adaptations desecrate the original plays, says Barnes in what may be his most telling argument, then he is free to produce the originals. Unlike a painter, who wipes a canvas clean in order to repaint it, and thereby removes the original from existence, Barnes does not destroy all copies of the original texts and replace them with his own. Instead, he provides alternative renderings designed for present-day audiences. The originals remain available for production.

Let us examine his alternatives: first, his editings of Jacobean comedy; then, his Jacobean adaptations; finally, his adaptations of works written in languages other than English.

Jacobean Editings

The Alchemist, Volpone, Bartholomew Fair, A Chaste Maid in Cheapside, The Silent Woman

In discussing Barnes' alterations of these comedies of greed and deceit, knavery and trickery, vice and folly, a play-by-play analysis would duplicate tediously. Instead, let us examine these comedies— the fourth by Thomas Middleton, the others by Ben Jonson—in terms of Barnes' editing stratagems.

One reason Barnes cuts passages has already been suggested: today they are simply incomprehensible. Apart perhaps from Jacobean scholars, who nowadays would regret such deletions from *The Silent Woman* as names of racing horses of the period (I) or of champion bears at bear-baiting arenas (II)? Take the following passage from *The Alchemist:*

SUBTLE: And hang thyself, I care not.
FACE: Hang thee, collier,
[[And all thy pots, and pans, in picture, I will]]
Since thou hast moved me—
DOL: O, this'll o'erthrow all.
[[FACE: Write thee up bawd, in Paul's; have all thy tricks

Of cozening with a hollow coal, dust, scrapings,
Searching for things lost, with a sieve, and shears,
Erecting figures, in your rows of houses,
And taking in of shadows, with a glass,
Told in red letters: and a face, cut for thee,
Worse than Gamaliel Ratsey's.
DOL: Are you sound?
Ha' you your senses, masters?
FACE: I will have
A book, but barely reckoning thy impostures,
Shall prove a true philosopher's stone, to printers.]]   [I]

How many spectators today would know that 'in picture' means
public exposure, that criminals frequented St Paul's, that to erect
figures means to plot the position of planets, that houses are signs of
the zodiac, that red letters emphasized printed passages, that Ratsey
was a highwayman, and so forth? For *Bartholomew Fair*, one requires
a glossary to understand most of the references in such passages as
'When a quirk or a quiblin does scape thee, and thou dost not watch,
and apprehend it, and bring it afore the constable of conceit—there
now, I speak quib too—let 'em carry thee out o' the Archdeacon's
court into his kitchen, and make a Jack of thee, instead of a John'
(I).

Another reason Barnes, like most play directors, deletes passages
is to streamline the action and thus build swiftly to a climax. From
A Chaste Maid in Cheapside, he cuts many of Tim Yellowhammer's
Latin speeches but keeps enough to retain Middleton's point that
Tim is a pretentious idiot; and he deletes such extraneous characters
as a Dry Nurse (who arrives only to have Allwit tell her he called for
the Wet Nurse, who then enters) and two swindlers whose long
scene is entirely irrelevant to the play's action. From *Volpone*, he
eliminates the eunuch and hermaphrodite (for the play's action, the
dwarf and Mosca suffice). As part of this deletion, he cuts the song
of the dwarf, eunuch, and hermaphrodite early in the first act. Their
song is merely an interlude. At this early stage of the play, the
initiation of the action is more crucial. However, Barnes retains
Mosca's song about fools, which relates to the entry of Voltore
immediately thereafter. Note how, by removing the more cumber-
some and less comprehensible portions of the first-act exchange
between Corbaccio and Mosca, just before Corbaccio leaves, the
tempo quickens and the comedy becomes, for today's spectators,
much sharper and more effective:

CORBACCIO: I'll straight about it. *(Begins to go.)*
[[MOSCA *(aside)*: Rook go with you, raven!
CORBACCIO:]] I know thee honest.
MOSCA *(aside)*: You do lie, sir!
[[CORBACCIO And—
MOSCA *(aside)*: Your knowledge is no better than your ears, sir.]]
CORBACCIO: I [[do not doubt to]] *shall* be a father to thee.
[[MOSCA *(aside)*: Nor I to gull my brother of his blessing.
CORBACCIO: I may ha' my youth restored to me, why not?]]
MOSCA *(aside)*: Your worship is a precious ass!
CORBACCIO: What say'st thou?
MOSCA: I do desire your worship to make haste, sir.

Or take this streamlined passage from *The Alchemist*:

SUBTLE: What's the complexion?
FACE: Whitish.
SUBTLE: Infuse vinegar,
[[To draw his volatile substance, and his tincture:]]
And let the water in glass E be filtered,
And put into the gripe's egg. [[Lute him well;
And leave him closed in balneo.]]
FACE: I will, sir. [II]

Enough alchemical jargon and mumbo jumbo remain to keep the scene comic, but enough go to prevent it from becoming ponderous.

To be sure, no two people will agree on the merits of every cut made by a director or adapter. From *Bartholomew Fair*, for instance, I miss the response in this exchange between Winwife and Quarlous: 'Did you ever see a fellow's face more accuse him for an ass?' [['Accuse him? It confesses him one without accusing']](I). The excision from *Volpone* of a thematically key line, by the First Avocatore, strikes me as unfortunate: 'These possess wealth, as sick men possess fevers,/Which trulier may be said to possess them' (V). Yet so infrequent are such infelicities that to quarrel is to cavil.

Often, what Barnes retains is as important as what he deletes. In *The Alchemist*, he keeps Subtle's metaposcopic analysis of Drugger— with its references to thumbs, forefingers, palmistry, and horoscope— because it is *as* nonsense that the scene is funny. Funny too is Sir Amorous La Foole's piling on of references in his account of his genealogy and Morose's continued questioning of his servant who shakes his leg or his head rather than replies aloud—both in *The Silent Woman*. These scenes remain virtually intact. Since Volpone's long performance as the mountebank Scoto is a theatrical *tour-de-*

force for a star actor, it too survives almost intact. After all, why produce *Volpone* unless one wants to give the leading actor an opportunity to play this scene?

In changing the original words so that their meanings become clear to today's audiences, Barnes attempts to retain the original rhythms of the lines, for example: 'You'll to the [[gossiping]] *christening* of Mr Allwit's child?' (*A Chaste Maid in Cheapside,* II) and 'My heart/Abhors [[his knowledge. I disclaim in him]] *to know him. He's no son of mine'* (*Volpone,* IV). Unfortunately, however, such attempts are often unsuccessful. Take this passage from *The Alchemist*:

PLIANT: Truly, I shall never brook a Spaniard.
SUBTLE: No?
PLIANT: [[Never, sin' eighty-eight]] *Why, not since the Armada* could I abide 'em.   [IV]

Although Barnes' change clarifies the meaning of the passage, it does so at the expense of the poetry, whose rhythm it mutilates. In *Volpone,* Mosca explains to Voltore:

Nay more, I told his son, brought, hid him here,
Where he might hear his father pass the deed;
Being persuaded to it by this thought, sir:
That the unnaturalness, first, of the act,
[[And then]] *Of* his father's [[oft disclaiming]] *of disowning him—*
Which I did mean t' help on—would sure enrage him
To do some violence upon his parent;
[[On]] *For* which the law [[should take sufficient hold,]] *would certainly hold him;*
And you [[be stated in a double hope]] *would as certain prosecute the attempted patricide.*
And then, oh then you'd hug the double hope
Of court fees and the taking out of thy rival, Corbaccio.
My patron would'st ne'er re-state him
In his affections after such a scandal.
[[Truth be my comfort, and my conscience,]]
My only aim was to dig you a fortune
Out of these two old rotten sepulchres.   [III]

Unquestionably, Barnes' alterations would make more sense to today's audiences than the original. Also unquestionably, his poetry is not as good as Jonson's—as Barnes would no doubt be among the first to admit. Even so, line 8 utterly confounds the poetic rhythm; despite the vivid language of lines 9—13, most of them botch the iambic pentameter; and the deletion of the ironic line 14 seems a mistake.

Obviously, iambic pentameter is not Barnes' strong suit. Having made this admission, one must next ask whether this deficiency outweighs or is outweighed by advantages. Barnes' alterations do convey a feeling similar to that of the original. When spoken by an actor, certain lines might carry more of the original rhythm (though not necessarily five feet to the line) than appears on the printed page, for instance, line 9: 'And you'd as certain prosecute th'attempted patricide.' Far more important is the question of the relative value of sense and poetic rhythm. While one might choose the latter for the printed word, one might—as, to avoid equivocating, I do—select the former for the spoken word. In performance, poetic fidelity matters less than comprehension.

With Jacobean prose, Barnes is on firmer ground, for clarity and tone need not contend with regular rhythm. Thus, his *Bartholomew Fair* and *The Silent Woman* are freer of questionable renderings than the others. Few would object to his alteration of Win's statement that her mother 'is not a wise wilful widow for nothing, nor a sanctified sister *of the Puritan brotherhood* for a song' or Zeal-of-the-Land Busy's that the fair is 'no better than one of the high places *where the Israelites did worship idols*' (*Fair*, I). Nor would many object to similarly clarifying additions or changes in *The Silent Woman*, such as 'That's a more *serious* portent' (I) or a woman who is 'above fifty too, and [[partets]] *plasters herself with face powders!*' (V). In *Volpone*, Sir Politic Would-be explains (in prose) the actions of Mosca and Nano: 'Fellows to mount a bank! *That is to say, a platform.*' When, shortly thereafter, Volpone—as the mountebank Scoto—refers (also in prose) to 'the clamours of the canaglia, *that fartsy rabble,*' the adjective is not a modern imposition (as Scoto, Jonson's Volpone mentions 'turdy-facy-nasty-paty-lousy-farticle rogues'). Barnes adds phrases for comic clarity, for instance: 'Therefore now, toss your handkerchiefs, cheerfully, cheerfully, *with your sixpences tied cheerfully up i' the corner*' (II). The addition is vivid and in the spirit of the original.

At times, Barnes aims to create not a literal modern equivalent for the word or phrase but a figuratively appropriate substitute for the kind of statement a character makes and the kind of audience response it evokes. Jonson's contemporaries would be amused at the pretentiousness of Lady Politic Would-be when she follows a paraphrase of Castiglione with 'as the courtier says' (IV). To evoke the same response, Barnes finds a pretentious twentieth-century substitute: 'the divine Castiglione/Writes in "The Courtier," Book 3, Chapter 9, Paragraph 5.' When Mosca tells Voltore, 'I do beseech you, sir, you will vouchsafe/To write me i' your family' (I), he asks Voltore to make him a servant in his household when Voltore becomes Volpone's heir. This explanation would mean less to modern spectators than the changed meaning Barnes gives— 'vouchsafe/To remember me when you are rich'—which conveys the essential but not the literal sense of the original.

At least one of Barnes' editorial changes improves upon Jonson. To provide Volpone with a uniform in which he might disguise himself, Jonson has Mosca explain, 'I know one o' the Commendatori, sir, so like you,/Him will I straight make drunk, and bring you his habit' (V). Employing motivation that is in closer harmony with the play's theme, Barnes changes Mosca's explanation: '*(calling)* Nano, the Commendatori's uniform!/We have, sir, this Sergeant-at-Law's uniform,/Left here in lieu of a gambling debt:/The habit will fit you certain.'

In *A Chaste Maid in Cheapside*, a number of Barnes' alterations are necessitated by the different medium for which he adapted the play, radio. On stage, one sees a new character in costume. On radio, a new voice may confuse. Therefore, before Mistress Allwit speaks, which in the play she does immediately upon entering, Barnes has Allwit state, 'Here comes my wife' and Sir Walter Whorehound address her by name (I). In the theatre, spectators see what Middleton describes in a stage direction: two coffins brought on-stage. For radio, Barnes adds a line, so that listeners can perceive what they cannot observe: 'See these two coffins that stand there side by side.' In the theatre, spectators watch Moll and Touchwood Junior rise from these coffins. Since the radio audience cannot see them do so, Barnes adds sound—two coffin lids open, mourners cry and gasp—and dialogue: 'Look! The dead rise up.' 'They are both alive' (V).

As earlier examples indicate, Bernard Levin is wide of the mark when he asserts that a good director can, without the intervention of an adapter, make the original Jacobean language understandable to today's audiences.[7] Without doubt, Barnes' changes clarify the meaning of passages now obscure or incomprehensible. Whether he has in all instances made the changes as vivid as the original is open to question. Dennis Marks is correct when he charges that Barnes has indeed changed the verse lines and the rhythms of the originals. As suggested earlier, however, one must sometimes decide between prosaic clarity and poetic rhythm—a decision which in practice derives from a choice between page and stage. Barnes chooses the living stage.

Jacobean Adaptations

As mentioned in the second chapter, Barnes took *Eastward Ho!* by Jonson, George Chapman, and John Marston, and—adding his own name as fourth collaborator—adapted it for radio production by the BBC in 1973. 1977 saw Edinburgh and London performances of his stage adaptation of Jonson's *The Devil is an Ass*, which he revised from his adaptation presented in Nottingham in 1973. His name appears as adapter, not collaborator. In 1977, he took Marston's *Antonio and Mellida* and *Antonio's Revenge* and made them a single radio play, *Antonio*, which the BBC broadcast that year. In 1979, his revision of *Antonio* for the stage was produced at the Nottingham Playhouse. In the last two cases, we will examine his most recent renderings. Rather than study these adaptations chronologically, however, we will do so in terms of the extent of his adaptations, which, coincidentally, is the reverse order in which I have cited them.

As in his Jacobean editings, Barnes in his adaptations deletes some passages with references made incomprehensible by time and revises others in order to make them understandable. He cuts passages to streamline the action and build swiftly to a climax. He retains—even embellishes—theatrical qualities in the text. As with the editings, he demonstrates that while he has an ear for flavourful prose, he is deficient in the composition of blank verse. Between prosaic clarity and poetic rhythm, he chooses the former. Because there is no point in providing additional evidence for these conclusions, this section will stress Barnes' employment of the resources of today's theatre or (with *Eastward Ho!*) of radio—for as an adapter he is a playwright-director—to augment or replace the staging resources of the Jacobean authors, and also his substantive changes of character and plot—for, as he admits, Barnes the adapter goes further than Barnes the editor.

Antonio[8]

No evidence conclusively proves that Marston designed his two plays to form a continuous work. Since unexpected dramatic reversals occur in each, the change of attitude in Piero, Duke of Venice, between the end of the first and the beginning of the second is probably no more surprising than his change between the beginning and end of the first itself. Nevertheless, the tones of the two plays are, as Marston's titles indicate, those of romantic comedy and revenge tragedy. In the first, Piero has defeated the forces of the Duke of Genoa, Andrugio, who like his son Antonio (though separately from him) is cast ashore in Venice. Antonio persuades his beloved Mellida, Piero's daughter, to run away with him, but Piero captures her. He promises a huge reward and his endearing love to anyone who brings him Andrugio's head. Enter, to claim that reward, a helmeted man, who upon receiving confirmation that Piero will fulfill the terms of his promise, removes his helmet to reveal that he, Andrugio himself, carries Andrugio's head. Graciously, or apparently so, Piero concedes the point. When Antonio arrives in a coffin, Mellida faints, whereupon Piero wishes Antonio were still alive for her sake. Up springs Antonio to claim her. Piero embraces his prospective son-in-law. Between the first and second plays (or acts), Piero—himself again—has killed Andrugio. To revenge himself on Antonio, he dishonours his daughter and imprisons her. Andrugio's ghost demands his son avenge him. Antonio masquerades as a court fool. Mellida dies. Together with others who want revenge on Piero—including Antonio's mother Maria, whom Piero wants to marry—Antonio kills him during the course of a masque.

Whatever the literary qualities of Marston's work, its theatrical qualities are very high. Theatricality—with all the word implies by way of visual and auditory sparkle and extravagance, as well as a consciousness of theatre as theatre—is a significant feature of both parts of *Antonio*. Instead of apologizing for such qualities in the original, Barnes embroiders and augments them. If deletions for the purpose of saving time were a major goal, for example, the Prologue to the first part, which is irrelevant to the play's action, would be among the first scenes to go. In it, the actors—*'with parts in their hands, having cloaks cast over their apparel'* (so that they can shed the cloaks and reappear instantly in costume)—discuss their roles. Essentially, the Prologue, which Barnes retains, tells the audience that theatricality is the play's chief value, and it invites them to enjoy it. Barnes expands Marston's stage direction. His actors are *'sprawled about, studying their parts. Some are only half made-up, others only half-dressed in their stage costumes.'* Demonstrating how to suit the action to the word, so to speak, the actor who is to play Piero *'strides about, making regal gestures.'*

As adapter-director, Barnes adds numerous costume details. One character wears *'a scorpion mask'* (AM,V) and Andrugio's ghost *'is some eight feet high and in armour, but there are no eyes behind the vizor'* (AR,III). He describes properties: two tall standing candelabras *'are draped with a roll of rich green velvet and glittering jewels'* (AM,II).

Employing the technical resources of today's theatre, but without interrupting the play's action and without lengthening the time of performance, as lesser directors would, Barnes makes scene-changing visually exciting: *'The rostrum, which splits in half, is swung round to form two tall gold panels draped with rich banners of the golden lion of St Mark on a green background'* (AM,II) and *'An iron grille is lowered between the two banners Up Stage.* MELLIDA *appears behind it'* (AR,II)—the last suggested by Marston's note that she speaks from behind a grating.

The adapter suggests movement and business for actors. *'The courtiers dance the stately "Pavan". They talk as they parade round and change partners'* (AM,II). Whereas Marston has Antonio appear already clothed *'in a fool's habit with a little toy of a walnut shell and soap to make bubbles'* (AR,IV), Barnes has someone bring them to him, together with make-up. During his dialogue, he dons the clown's costume, then puts white make-up on his face, reddens his lips and cheeks, and circles his eyes black. Where Marston has *'Cantant,'* Barnes of course provides specific songs: 'traditional ballads of the period or a little after the period,' he says. 'I didn't write the lyrics, though I adapted certain lyrics to fit a scene or character.' Thus, for instance, he inserts Mellida's name in a song about an unhappy lover (AR,II).

The opening of the second part gives Barnes ample opportunity to demonstrate his theatrical flair. As Marston has it, Piero enters *'unbrac'd, his arms bare, smear'd in blood, a poniard in one hand, bloody, and a torch in the other,* STROTZO *following him with a cord.'* Piero calls, 'Ho, Gaspar Strotzo, bind Feliche's trunk/Unto the panting side of Mellida.' Strotzo leaves. Barnes brings the murder onstage:

> *Drum beats. Spot Up Stage Centre,* FELICHE *in his nightshirt, looking round slightly bewildered. A shirt-sleeved* PIERO *suddenly leaps out of the darkness and plunges two long daggers into his back.* FELICHE *cries out and keels over onto the floor, dead. Lights half up on the deserted court. The two banners of the Lion of St Mark are in place Up Stage but they are now a gold and deep red, not green. As* PIERO *looks at the body,* STROTZO *enters Stage Left.*
>
> PIERO: Strotzo, go hang him up to dry.
> STROTZO *picks up* FELICHE*'s body, hoists it onto his shoulders like an old sack and exits with it Up Stage Centre.* PIERO *paces.*

To create a greater sense of urgency and of activity, Barnes cuts, adds, and reassigns speeches. Marston has Piero, anxious to find the runaway lovers, address his cohorts:

> O, my sweet princes, was't not bravely found?
> Even there I found the note; even there it lay.
> I kiss the place for joy that there it lay.

This way he went; here let us make a stand
I'll keep this gate myself. O gallant youth!   [AM,III]

As Barnes adapts the sequence:

> PIERO: O my sweet princes, was not the note bravely found? I
> kiss the place for joy that there it lay.
> FOROBOSCO: All palace gates are now guarded, Sire.
> MATZAGENTE: We'll have him, ne'er fear.
> PIERO: O gallant youth!

In the final masque, Marston has the four conspirators bind Piero
and cut out his tongue (AR,V). Barnes assigns the latter activity to
Antonio. Then: *'One by one, the conspirators whip off their masks.'* As they
vex him, Piero *'writhes on the floor.'* To enhance the ritualistic aspect
of the murder, Barnes adds stage directions to his rearranged
dialogue. Not only does Antonio stab Piero, as Marston has it, but
each of the others—uttering such rearranged epithets as 'Slime of all
filth!'—also stabs him.

More substantively, Barnes changes three aspects of the plot.
Instead of having Mellida die of sorrow at the news of Antonio's
death, Barnes has Maria report she stabbed herself. Marston's final
dumb show is trite:

> *Enter at one door* CASTILIO *and* FOROBOSCO, *with halbreds, four*
> PAGES *with torches,* LUCIO *bare,* PIERO, MARIA, *and* ALBERTO *talking.*
> ALBERTO *draws out his dagger,* MARIA *her knife, aiming to menace the*
> DUKE. *Then* GALEATZO *betwixt two* SENATORS, *reading a paper to*
> *them; at which they all make semblance of loathing* PIERO, *and knit their*
> *fists at him; two* LADIES *and* NUTRICHE. *All these go softly over the*
> *stage, whilst at the other door enters the* GHOST OF ANDRUGIO, *who*
> *passeth by them tossing his torch about his head in triumph. All forsake the*
> *stage, saving* ANDRUGIO, *who, speaking, begins the Act.*   [AR,V]

He speaks first in Latin, then in English. By contrast, Barnes' dumb
show is theatrically imaginative:

> *All the Courtiers enter silently, Stage Right and Left, carrying snakes*
> *which writhe and hiss in their hands. The hissing is the only sound that can*
> *be heard as they face Up Stage.*
>
> PIERO *appears between the two banners in black and raised on blocks*
> *attached to his shoes, some three feet off the ground. He looks down on them*
> *as they slowly move towards him, gesturing furiously with the snakes, and*
> *their expressions full of hate. He roars with silent laughter at their impotence.*
> *Lights fade to a Spot on* PIERO. *Then silently the ghostly figure of*
> ANDRUGIO *in glowing white armour rises up behind him. As the* GHOST

towers above him, PIERO *crouches down into the darkness.* ANDRUGIO'S
GHOST *stands alone for a moment, then Spot Out.*

None of the ghost's speech remains.

Clearly, the adapter's major challenge is to connect the beginning
of the second play to the end of the first. To do this, Barnes employs
four methods. First, at the end of his Act I, he directs the actor who
plays Piero to say *'slowly'*—a different adverb from *'contritely'*—that
he blushes but now honours and loves his former enemy. Second,
after Piero is tricked by the revivified Antonio, whom his daughter
kisses, Barnes changes Piero's speech from an expression of happiness
('Fair son—now I'll be proud to call thee son—/Enjoy me thus. My
very breast is thine;/Possess me freely; I am wholly thine') to:

FELICHE: Prince, thou hast been cozened twice today.

PIERO *(slowly)*: Aye, cozened twice, twice.

But the cause was noble.

Fair son, my breast is thine.

The new passage stresses the cozening, suggests Piero's displeasure
at it, and brings into the picture the man he will murder at the
beginning of Act II. Third, Barnes deletes the final line of Antonio's
concluding speech: 'Here ends the comic crosses of true love;/[[O
may the passage most successful prove.]]' By removing the prediction, Barnes emphasizes the ironic aspect of the end of comic
hardships, which suggests the start of non-comic hardships. Finally,
he removes the Epilogue, which refers to 'the comedy' just enacted,
and in its place substitutes a new passage, with two segments from
the Prologue to the second play, but in reverse order:

All except PIERO *exit in all directions amid gay music and laughter.*
Lights down to a Spot on PIERO *Down Stage Centre, smiling as the*
laughter echoes and re-echoes.
Laugh on, laugh on, another soon will laugh;
Laughter perhaps that freezes on the breath.
If any spirit breathes within this round
Uncapable of weighty passion
(As from his birth being hugged in the arms
And nuzzled 'twixt the breast of happiness)
Who winks and shuts his apprehensions up
From common sense of what men were, and are,
Who would not know what men must be—let such
Hurry amain from our black-visag'd shows.
For summer's gone now and drizzling sleet
Chilleth the wan bleak cheek of the numb'd earth.
'Tis not time nor place for gay Rossaline

I'll send her hence and summon my loyal Strotzo,
In her stead; he has work to do for me.
Cozened twice you say, twice, twice in one day.
O but there's a fine, black mass o' cozening
And laughter yet to come, my blunt Feliche!
Spot out with PIERO *still smiling. Drum beat.*

No longer is the resolution of the first part unquestionably festive. Rather, it is ominous. No longer does it conclude. Rather, it threatens. True to the spirit of the original, Barnes' adaptation brilliantly merges and recreates Marston's two plays for today's theatre.

The Devil is an Ass

Late in the play, the minor devil Pug explains its title: the Devil is an ass to think he can corrupt human beings, who are far more corrupt than he. Considering what Pug has seen on earth, he exclaims: 'You talk of a university! Why, hell is/A grammar school to this!' (IV).

At the start of *The Devil is an Ass*, Pug persuades Satan to send him to earth. Satan imposes constraints upon him: he may remain only until midnight, he must make do with a readymade body (of a cutpurse just hanged at Tyburn) instead of a new one, he must use his ingenuity to obtain clothes, and he is to serve the first man he meets. Pug delights Fitzdotterel, the fool he encounters, partly because Fitzdotterel longs to meet a devil and partly because Pug agrees to work without pay. Fitzdotterel is duped by the swindler Meercraft, whose schemes include a patent to make leather from dogskin. He urges Meercraft to include him in a land reclamation fraud that will make him the Duke of Drowned Lands. When Pug tries to seduce Mrs Fitzdotterel, she—thinking her husband put him up to it as a test—informs on him. He beats Pug. She tricks Pug into arranging a meeting with Wittipol, who loves her. In revenge, Pug tells Fitzdotterel, then recognizes too late that by preventing adultery he failed to profit his master's cause. When Fitzdotterel complains that his wife is not adapting to her forthcoming position as duchess, Meercraft and his broker Engine devise a new plan to fleece him. He should send his wife to be instructed in deportment by a Spanish lady, to whom Fitzdotterel should give a gift, a ring worth fifty pounds—soon rising to sixty, then a hundred—to be obtained from Gilthead, a goldsmith who, helping Meercraft fleece him, subtracts

Meercraft's debt from the sum. Meercraft invents a court, of which his cousin Everill is Master. For a hundred pounds and a legal deed of trusteeship, it will settle a quarrel by litigation rather than have a claimant fight a duel with the party who grieved him. Immediately, Fitzdotterel pays in order to bring suit against Wittipol. To protect Mrs Fitzdotterel—whose financial ruin her husband's idiocies are hastening—Wittipol impersonates the Spanish lady at the home of Lady Tailbush, another of Meercraft's dupes, this time in a fraudulent scheme to acquire a monopoly on fucus, a cosmetic. In disguise, Wittipol persuades Fitzdotterel to name Wittipol's friend Manly, not Meercraft, as his trustee. Wittipol then reveals himself. Meanwhile, Lady Tailbush's missing steward Ambler arrives, delayed because his clothes were stolen while he was with a woman. Recognizing them on Pug, he delivers him to the law. In jail, Satan visits him, reprimands him for being a less effective devil than the person whose body he occupies, and returns Pug to Hell, where he will punish Pug for letting humans know they could outdo a devil. Meercraft persuades Fitzdotterel that what occurred was part of a plot between his wife and her lover to steal his land and that to stay clear of the law, he should pretend to be possessed by a devil. During his feigned attack comes news of Pug's mysterious disappearance from jail. Astonished that Pug really was a devil, Fitzdotterel tells the truth.

Where Jonson is theatrically vivid, Barnes does not change the text. Early in the play, for instance, Wittipol bribes Fitzdotterel with an expensive cloak to let him talk to his wife for fifteen minutes. During their conversation, Fitzdotterel stipulates, he himself must be present and they may not kiss or touch each other. Although he agrees not to interrupt Wittipol, he forbids his wife to speak. When she fails to respond to Wittipol, he deduces the reason and, placing his friend Manly in the role of himself, speaks for her to Manly. All Barnes does is to make explicit what the dialogue implies: the men take out and adjust their watches. On other occasions, Barnes embroiders the theatricality. Jonson later has Wittipol and Mrs Fitzdotterel talk to each other from facing windows of their houses; Barnes has him jump onto her balcony, then return to his when her husband appears.

A major change is the opening scene in Hell. Whereas Jonson provides one Vice, Iniquity, for Satan to show Pug, Barnes adds three more: Wrath, Vanity, and Covetousness. He gives them striking costumes and rhymed couplets in the manner of Jonson's Iniquity. After Pug suggests he take a Vice to earth with him, Satan asks which he has in mind. He proposes Wrath.

SATAN *gestures. There is the sound of a great blast of hot air. Spot Up Stage high on the giant seven foot figure of* WRATH, *in a torn bloodstained jerkin and breeches, and armlets with iron spikes on his forearms and legs. He wears a leather helmet, studded with spikes—whilst his face is elaborately painted red like a Chinese demon. He carries a rotten melon which he continously gouges.*

After such couplets as 'Be as wrathful as you would wish;/Vengeance is always such a tasty dish,' Wrath smashes the rotten melon on Pug's head. Pug wipes the pulp from his face and suggests he take Vanity instead. Though Wrath roars, Satan makes him vanish.

Murmuring sounds of approval echo in the darkness. Spot up stage right on the seven foot high LADY VANITY. *Her gown is covered with small mirrors and she has a long peacock's train. There are mirrors embedded in the halter round her neck so she can see herself whichever way she turns. There is another mirror attached to the back of her head and her face is elaborately patterned with black and white markings. She carries a powder case and continually dabs her face.*

After several couplets about her beauty, *'She blows powder in* PUG's *face. He coughs.'* Reconsidering, he suggests Covetousness. Vanity disappears. A grating sound of iron on iron comes from the darkness. The seven-foot Covetousness *'is clad in pieces of armour, with iron bands round his arms and forehead. His fingernails are a foot long, and his face is painted with a golden pattern. Hanging from his waist are small iron locks and keys and he carries bags of gold.'* Commenting that 'Judas' only fault was he sold too cheap' and advising, 'Make it, hold it, nothing must you loan./What's theirs is mine, what's mine's my own,' Covetousness hits Pug with a bag of gold. Reconsidering again, Pug suggests Jonson's Vice, Iniquity. Covetousness is replaced by a seven-foot Iniquity, *'a gnarled old man covered in sores and rags, cobwebs and dead spiders. He carries a wooden dagger.'* He speaks Jonson's verse, though abridged, but unlike the other vices, he is dispatched by Satan before he can use his prop, the dagger, on Pug. At a gesture, Satan shows Pug the spinning planet Earth, surrounded by darkness, and sends him there.

Barnes, the adapter, embroiders Jonson's dialogue, sometimes to enhance the comedy, as when Meercraft, outlining his plan to make wine from raisins, indicates that if the price of raisins rises:

MEERCRAFT: Why, then I'll make it out of blackberries.
ENGINE: Blackberries?
FITZDOTTEREL: Blackberries?

MEERCRAFT: *Blackberries!* [[And it shall do the same.]] 'Tis but
  more art
And the charge less.   [II]

Barnes expands Meercraft's fantastic notion of a Master of
Dependences into a Master of the Quarrel Court and Dependencies:

MEERCRAFT: For such there will be [[differences]] *duels* daily
'Twixt gentlemen, and that the [[roaring]] *uncontrolled* manner
Is grown offensive, *and* that those few we call
The civil men of the sword abhor [[the vapours]] *such offensiveness,*
They shall [[refer now]] *now refer* [[hither, for the process]] *their
  quarrels to*
'*The Master of the Quarrel Court and Dependencies.*'
FITZDOTTEREL: I like the sound of it, sir.
Instead of gentlemen settling their quarrels on a field of honour
And being pricked bloody through and through
And ending stiff and cold though they be innocent,
We now settle with words in a Quarrel Court.
MEERCRAFT: And such as trespass 'gainst the *Master's* rule of
court
Are to be fined.   [III]

At this stage of the play, the lengthier explanation clarifies
Fitzdotterel's action and the swindler's scheme.

Barnes places his single intermission at the end of Jonson's Act
III, Scene i, when all of Meercraft's schemes in relationship to
Fitzdotterel have been set in motion. Jonson ends the scene with
Meercraft explaining that Fitzdotterel must have a legal deed of
trusteeship before he comes to the Court. Coming as it does many
pages after the explanation of this Court, this added information is
clumsy. Barnes transfers it to the scene in which Meercraft first
explains the Court. To provide an effective climax, he ends the act
with a brief recapitulation of all the schemes and an expansion of the
original's self-conscious theatricalism. Meercraft tells Fitzdotterel to
meet the Spanish lady at Lady Tailbush's after dinner.

FITZDOTTEREL: *After dinner!* 'Slight, that will be just play-time
It cannot be, I must not [[lose]] *miss* the play!
MEERCRAFT: Sir, you must [[, if she appoint to sit,
And she is president]].
FITZDOTTEREL: 'Slid, it is the 'Devil *is an Ass.*'
MEERCRAFT: [[An]] *Even if* 'twere his dam too, you must now
apply
Yourself, sir, to this wholly, or lose all.
You have the much to think on:

The Spanish lady, the duel, the Duke of Drown'd Land,
The naming of your trustee.
You've not time for fripperies.
FITZDOTTEREL: If I could but see a piece [[—]] *of the play.*
MEERCRAFT: Sir, never think on't.
FITZDOTTEREL: Come but [[to]] one act, and I [[did]] *will* not
care—
But to be seen to rise and go away,
To vex the players, and to punish their [[poet]] *author;*
Keep him in awe—
MEERCRAFT: [[But say that he]] *I hear the author* be one
Who will not be aw'd, but laugh at you; [[how]] *what* then?
FITZDOTTEREL: Then he shall pay [[for's]] *for his* dinner himself.
MEERCRAFT: Perhaps
He would do that twice, rather than thank you.
FITZDOTTEREL: *But 'tis 'The Devil is an Ass.'*
MEERCRAFT: [[Come]] get the devil out of your head[[, my lord,
(I'll call you so in private still)]] and [[take]] *keep*
Your lordship in your mind.
FITZDOTTEREL: Let me see but one act.
MEERCRAFT: No.
FITZDOTTEREL: The first scene,
'Tis in Hell.
MEERCRAFT: No!
FITZDOTTEREL: The prologue?
Let me see the prologue.
MEERCRAFT: NO! NO! NO!
MEERCRAFT pushes FITZDOTTEREL off Stage Left. Curtain.

Barnes makes two substantive changes which improve the original.
He turns Ambler from a feeble plot device into a comic asset, and he
strengthens the play's ending.

In Jonson, the fifth act return of Ambler—whose clothes Pug
steals—has the air of a dragged-in expedient to get Pug out of the
way. To make Ambler's return seem less obviously contrived and
also a comic resolution of a running joke, Barnes foreshadows the
explanation of his absence and adds or amplifies references to him.
First, he has Satan show Pug the hanged pickpocket: *'Lights half up
on a small man dangling from a gallows Up Stage Centre. To the left in the
shadow of the gallows, a* MAN *with a black eye patch is making love to a half
naked* WOMAN, *whilst a* DRUNK *staggers past. No one takes any notice of the
hanged man'* (I). Spectators are not apt to overlook a one-eyed man,
particularly if he is making love to a half naked woman. The man is

Ambler, who does what he later describes. To avoid overemphasis, Barnes brings on the Drunk. When Pug appears on earth, he is not *'handsomely shaped and apparelled'* as Jonson has him (I), but wears *'stolen clothes one size too big for him'*—clothes which include orange shoes, a colour that cannot help but impress spectators, particularly as they do not fit Pug, who *'staggers unsteadily.'* Serving the dual function of introducing Ambler early in the play and of motivating Manly's departure so that Wittipol can talk to Mrs Fitzdotterel alone, Barnes adds dialogue:

> MANLY: I leave you, sir,
> The master of my chamber: I have business *with my Lady Tailbush.*
> *I hear she hath lost Ambler.*
> *WITTIPOL: Who?*
> *MANLY: Her steward Ambler. Lost*
> *She'll be distressed: I must go comfort her.* [II]

Making the lost Ambler—who appears to have been mislaid—a running joke, Barnes adds more dialogue. Everill tells Meercraft that Lady Tailbush

> *Has sent for me in some distress:*
> *Ambler is lost.*
> *MEERCRAFT: Ambler? Who's Ambler?*
> *EVERILL: Her steward, Ambler: lost.* [III]

The next reference to Ambler is the first in Jonson's original. Meercraft tells Wittipol to disguise himself as the Spanish lady and to meet him at Lady Tailbush's.

> WITTIPOL:I know her, sir.
> And her gentleman [[usher]] *steward, Ambler.*
> MEERCRAFT: [[Master Ambler?]] *Lost.*
> WITTIPOL: [[Yes, sir.]] *Who?*
> *MEERCRAFT: Ambler: all lost.* [III]

Picking up the running joke later, Barnes again expands the subject of the apparently mislaid Ambler:

> LADY TAILBUSH: I must send them thanks
> And some remembrances.
> *You've heard of the business*
> *With Ambler?*
> MEERCRAFT: [[That you must, and visit them.
> Where's]] Ambler, *Madam?*
> LADY TAILBUSH: *My steward.* Lost[[, today, we cannot hear of him]].

MEERCRAFT: [[Not, Madam!]] *Ambler lost?*
LADY TAILBUSH: [[No, in good faith: they say]] *We cannot find*
him, he lay not
At home [[to-]] *last* night.   [IV]

At the beginning of Jonson's Act V, when Ambler appears, Jonson
fails to identify him until line 9. Barnes does so immediately:

> *The front of* TAILBUSH*'s house.* PITFALL *enters Stage Right with a basket*
> *of goods, and sees the extraordinary figure of* AMBLER, *creeping in Stage*
> *Left, trying not to be seen. He is barefooted and wrapped in a torn blanket.*
> *We see he is the one-eyed man* PUG *stole the clothes from at the foot of the*
> *gallows.*

He has Pitfall exclaim, 'Master Ambler!' Only then does Jonson's
dialogue begin. In order to remind the audience of the scene they
saw at the start of the play, Barnes changes Ambler's account of how
he persuaded a lady to go with him 'And carry her bedding to a
conduit-head,/[[Hard by the place toward]] *At the foot of the gallows*
near Tyburn, which they call/My Lord Mayor's banqueting-house.
Now, sir, this morning *there*/Was execution *of a little cutpurse,*' and so
forth. Further, Barnes alters Ambler's description of the stolen shoes
to make them vividly '*orange* shoes, *truly a most delicate shade of orange.*'
When he sees Pug, Ambler questions him about them. The result of
these additions and changes is that a clumsy plot device in the
original becomes a major comic asset in the adaptation.

Jonson's conclusion runs down unclimactically. Manly simply
explains to Fitzdotterel that his wife is chaste and that he and
Wittipol never intended to steal his land, which he still owns, but
rather to help her. He then comes forward to deliver a conventional
Epilogue that declares the swindler to be overthrown and hopes the
audience is pleased. In Barnes' adaptation, however, the other
characters react with jeers to Manly's statement that Mrs Fitzdotterel
is chaste. When she reiterates that she has not lost her virtue, they
jeer again:

> FITZDOTTEREL: *Your putcher's cracked, go to a vaulting school!*
> *You lewd wagtail, whore's beef!*
> LADY TAILBUSH: *Whore!*
> *He called her whore.*
> LADY EITHERSIDE: *Whore! whore!*
> MEERCRAFT: *Ahhhh, all those other projects lost I had for you*
> *For raising Dutch windmills on Hampstead Heath;*
> *For the catching, preserving and transportation*
> *Of butterflies—that's a subtle one!*

For the making of periwigs male and female;
The keeping of tame owls in cities
To kill off rats and mice—
    FITZDOTTEREL: *Villains, we've lost it all!*
    MANLY: *Sapskull!* The land is still yours, never by my friend
Or by myself meant to use it.
    But to assist your wife—
    EVERILL: *Gorgons! Hydras!*
    MEERCRAFT: *We've been cozened!*

Amid loud curses and abusive shouts, the men assault Wittipol and
Manly, the women Mrs Fitzdotterel.

But Barnes does not end the play here. Instead, he blends their
cries into those of the damned in Hell, as a final scene begins,
symmetrically balancing the opening scene. In this new scene, Satan
rises from the rear of the stage and towers over it. Beside him is Pug,
with a yoke around his neck and his arms stretched on a wood
frame. At a gesture from Satan, the characters freeze in position and
their curses and shouts diminish in volume. Followed by Pug, Satan
walks among them and concludes that humans cannot fear Hell,
which is 'their familiar daily, though they do not heed the fires.'
Pointing to the pride and hate etched on their faces, he observes:
'They rend their victims with more delight/Than my own legions.'
Lights fade down on humans and up on him, Pug, and the spinning
globe Earth. Satan declares Earth 'out of bounds for all my demons,'
who he fears might be infected 'And lose all sense of good and evil.'
They will go to other planets, but: 'Earth we leave to the damned/
And the pain of living.' As Satan walks upstage into darkness, a
spotlight remains on Pug, who looks at the globe Earth and
shudders. Suddenly, inspiration seizes him: 'Jupiter's the place for
me!/Chief? Where are you, chief?/Send me to Jupiter, Chief,/Chief?!
Chief?!' The lights fade out, the play ends—a striking, startling
conclusion of a work whose comedy and theatricality the adapter
has enhanced.

Eastward Ho!

The title is the cry of the Thames boatmen who announce where
they will take passengers. It also suggests attempts to obtain favours
at James I's court, which lay eastward. There, the new king
distributed honours to such upwardly aspiring citizens as Petronel
Flash, who purchased a knighthood, which the businessman

Touchstone might also have done. Instead, this embodiment of middle-class virtue remained content with his lot and held his aspirations down: 'I hired me a little shop, sought low, took small gain, kept no debt-book' (I). To overstep the boundaries of one's class by travelling eastward, according to him, will result in a journey westward—to Tyburn gallows at the other end of the Thames. Touchstone has two daughters and two apprentices, one of each content to remain in his social class, the other anxious to rise above it. The first two, Mildred and Golding, marry. Of the others, Gertrude—against her father's wishes—weds Petronel, whom Quicksilver, released from his apprenticeship, joins in a scheme to seek gold in Virginia. But Petronel wants Gertrude's money, not Gertrude. He loves Winifred, the wife of the usurer Security, and he persuades her to join him on his trip to the American colony. Tossed ashore by a storm, the travellers—including Security, who pursues his wife—arrive, appropriately, at Cuckold's Haven, where they are humiliated and the men jailed. Now an alderman, Golding persuades Touchstone that the prodigal apprentice is truly converted, as repentant as Petronel, whose wife forgives him, while her father forgives her.

According to Martin Esslin, who commissioned this adaptation for the BBC, Barnes believed himself to be so truly a collaborator that he could almost hear and talk to Jonson, Chapman, and Marston. His collaboration includes the drastic revision of their final act, which he considers a mess.[9]

Before examining this act—Barnes' major alteration—let us analyse other aspects of his adaptation.

A play that is conscious of itself as a play, *Eastward Ho!* contains a character, Quicksilver, who habitually quotes passages from other plays. Although the original audiences of *Eastward Ho!* might have recognized the quotations, it is unlikely that most of today's audiences would do so. Bringing the footnotes into the text, Barnes therefore adds the name of the play, sometimes with its act and scene, for example: '"Ta ly-re, ly-re ro! Who calls Jeronimo? Speak, here I am!"'—*that's from the "Spanish Tragedy," Act II, Scene v; I'm well versed i' the play-books'* (I). He even adds two quotations, one of which—spoken in jail—caps the running joke:

QUICKSILVER: 'Heart, wilt not break? and thou abhorred life,/ Wilt thou still breathe in my enraged blood?'
BLURT: Prettily said.
QUICKSILVER: 'Antonio and Mellida,' Act I, Scene i.
PETRONEL: This is no time for the playbills, sir.   [IV]

In contrast to Quicksilver, who deliberately quotes plays, *Eastward Ho!* has characters who inadvertently paraphrase them. Twice, they parody Hamlet's 'the funeral bak'd meats/Did coldly furnish forth the marriage tables': leftovers of the hot food served at the wedding of Gertrude and Petronel become a cold meal served at the wedding of the thrifty Mildred and Golding. A footman named Hamlet[10] serves a mistress with the name of the Shakespearean Hamlet's mother, Gertrude. Barnes adds another paraphrase (of *Richard III*): in the storm, Security cries, 'a boat! a boat! My kingdom—' (IV).

Some of Barnes' alterations are for the medium into which he adapted the stage play: radio. New characters reveal their names at the start of their speeches or others reveal them before they speak. When a character (Winifred) is silent on stage, Barnes inserts phrases for her to remind the audience of her presence, such as 'Oh, sir' and 'Ay' (III). In a new opening, he sets the scene, explains the title, and provides atmosphere:

> *The River Thames. The muffled sound of oars. Then the cry of the boatman calling across the water: 'Eastward Ho!—Eastward Ho!'*
>
> NARRATOR: It's the cry of the Thames boatman hailing passengers downstream to the Court of James I at Greenwich or onto Blackwall Harbour and the open sea beyond. They go eastward to seek gold and glory. For the east has always been the home of good fortune.
>
> BOATMAN: Eastward Ho! Eastward Ho!
>
> *Music plays: 'Come Bring Us Wine.'*
>
> NARRATOR: Early morning. Goldsmith's Row. The City of London. June 10th, 1605.
>
> *The music fades out.* FRANCIS QUICKSILVER *approaches, slightly drunk, singing:*
>
> QUICKSILVER: 'Come bring us wine in plenty/We've money enough to spend;/I hate to see pots empty,/And a man cannot drink to's friends.'

Like the other songs in the play, this one was not written by Barnes but was taken from a song of the period.

To stress the contrast between the daughters and their husbands, Barnes changes and adds lines, and he rearranges and adds scenes, such as the weddings—with songs, sounds of drinking and dancing, and a drunken preacher. To provide transitions between scenes, he adds new dialogue and sound effects, for example:

> QUICKSILVER: I'll meet thee there, wi'in the hour, and bring your Winnie wi' me.

PETRONEL: The seconds are too, too sluggish. 'The Blue Anchor' wi'in the hour!

'The Blue Anchor' is full. Loud tavern noises: tankards being filled and emptied, yells, curses and coarse laughter. Every time the tavern door is opened, we hear the night wind howling outside.

Then, Captain Seagull demands a full cask from the Drawer (III). Barnes adds comic touches. When Gertrude tries to spruce herself up for Petronel, she asks her sister, 'do my cheeks look well? Give me a little box o' the ears that I may seem to blush.' Barnes adds: '(MILDRED *gives her a tremendous clout; she yelps:*) A LITTLE box o' the ears, sister, a LITTLE' (I). To Mistress Touchstone's question as to whether Hamlet must run beside the coach while it drives, the original has Gertrude reply, 'Ay, by my faith, I warrant him! He gives no other milk, as I have another servant does' (III). Barnes provides a funnier response: 'Ay, he's a footman, is he not?'

Partly for comedy, but also to interrupt long passages whose listeners the audience cannot see, Barnes interpolates dialogue and sounds:

PETRONEL: There spake an angel! To bring her to which conformity, I must feign myself extremely amorous.

QUICKSILVER: Amorous, Sir Petronel!

PETRONEL: EXTREMELY amorous, master Frank, and [[alleging]] *making* urgent excuses for my stay*ing* behind, part with her as passionately as she would from [[her foisting]] *a farthing* hound.

They chuckle with glee.

QUICKSILVER: You have the sow by the right ear[[, sir]]. I warrant there was never child longed more to ride a cock-horse or wear his new coat, than she longs to ride in her new coach. She would run mad for 'em. I lay my life, she will have every year four children.

PETRONEL (stops chuckling): What?!

After Quicksilver mentions what Petronel must endure while Gertrude is pregnant, Barnes has him audibly groan. As Quicksilver continues to talk, he has Petronel continue to groan *'with increasing agony'* (II).

In the original, Bramble—in the tavern—tells Security that Petronel's disguised lady reminds him of Security's wife. The next scene has Security return home to discover that his wife has gone. Augmenting the comedy and utilizing the different medium, Barnes inserts a new scene between the two:

OTHER CUSTOMERS *shout for wine as we fade into the stormy night outside* SECURITY*'s house. High wind, distant thunder.* SECURITY *and* BRAMBLE *approach along the street.*

BRAMBLE: But art certain 'twas not thy wife?

SECURITY: 'Twas not. No, no, *ha, ha, ha.*

BRAMBLE: But 'twas her gown.

SECURITY: No, no.

BRAMBLE: But 'twas her scent.

SECURITY: No, no—her scent, you say?

BRAMBLE: Crushed lavender and myrtle.

SECURITY: No, no. *(They reach* SECURITY*'s front door.)* Now let's i' our homes and out o' the tempest. Goodnight, Master Bramble.

BRAMBLE: Goodnight, Master Security. I couldst've sworn 'twas—

He walks away as SECURITY *opens his front door and goes into his house. A cat miaows.*

SECURITY *(calling)*: Winnie, thy Cu hath returned—Winnie, thy Cu—Winnie—? *(He searches through the house.)* Winnie—Wife, I say—Out o' doors this night? Where couldst—? Winnie—*the scent! the scent! 'Twas* her scent!

He then continues, as in the play, 'Billingsgate, Billingsgate, Billingsgate! She's gone with the knight!' and so forth (III).

Equally funny is Barnes' new radio sequence in which Winifred almost drowns:

A great wave finally swamps their boat. Screams, shouts and curses as they are flung into the water. The storm rages as they desperately start swimming. It rages too on the bank where TWO MEN *have seen the disaster dimly through the wind and rain.*

1st MAN *(slowly)*: Didst see that boat o'erturn?

2nd MAN *(slowly)*: Bad weather t' be abroad on water.

1st MAN: There's a woman.

2nd MAN: See how the rude water takes up her clothes.

1st MAN: Women love to have their clothes taken up.

2nd MAN: The next wave will drown her.

1st MAN: Ay. Some vigilant body shouldst jump in and save her.

A pause.

2nd MAN: She 'scaped it.

1st MAN: She swims like a mermaid.

2nd MAN: Ay. She's up on the shore.

1st MAN: A handsome woman.

2nd MAN: Most handsome.

An exhausted WINIFRED *is heard splashing up the parapet steps.*

Then, as in the original, the First Man asks, 'How fares my lady?' (IV). The contrast between the dispassionate commentary (sometimes sexual) and Winifred's danger, set at a distance because the audience does not see her, is hilarious.

Barnes' most drastic change is the play's ending, which reconciles repentant sinners and exemplars of middle-class morality. Although critics often regard this conclusion as parody, the play's genial spirit—which they also note—tends to soften any mockery. Are Golding and Mildred uninteresting models of virtue? Of course, but they are still models of virtue. Is Touchstone naïve and Quicksilver's repentance a sham? Very likely, but the only ethic of Touchstone's that the play clearly derides is revenge; his middle-class values remain unchallenged.

Barnes' adaptation unmistakably and uncompromisingly denounces Touchstone, Golding, and Mildred. Going further than parody, he satirizes the middle-class values of all three. It is not their hearts that are touched but their purses. For reasons of profit and reputation, two businessmen and a woman who is daughter of one and wife of the other forgive apparently repentant sinners—whose repentance, in this version, is much more clearly apparent than real.

To prepare this conclusion, Barnes renders the trio less sympathetically than his collaborators do. He adds passages which demonstrate that in addition to possessing middle-class virtues, the businessman Touchstone has middle-class vices. When Quicksilver asks whether he should not trust *gallants*, Barnes gives Touchstone a reply that encompasses more than gallants: 'No, never trust, if thou wants t' thrive i' the City. Trust and you'll end in Moorfields, beggar-naked and shivering wi' the cold' (I). He has Touchstone tell Gertrude, 'Marry then, marry, you're so set upon the matter. I'll make today a holiday and close my shop—though I swear 'twill be easier losing a daughter than a day's hard profit' (I). To make Golding and Mildred less attractive, he adds dialogue to their decision to marry. Golding observes that 'when sense first rules, love creeps slowly in.' 'But not in tatters,' Mildred corrects him, and she points out that their 'blood's cool, eyes clear, not hung up on passion's torture-wheel. And thus we gain advantage.' Not blinded by love, they will not be disillusioned after the honeymoon. 'We expect small profit from this our venture at the first. Our partnership's no gambler's throw. But with much honest effort, tender care, 'tis certain, love will grow' (I). By stressing the initial joylessness of the loveless match, and by employing terms relative to their class ('not in tatters') and commerce ('profit' and 'partnership'), Barnes ensures against the audience's admiring this couple. Mildred is indeed her father's daughter, Golding the apprentice who follows his master's steps.

In the new concluding scenes, the repentance of Petronel and Quicksilver is obviously a sham. As the prisoners mumble their prayers, Petronel confesses to Quicksilver, 'I do not feel penitent, only penniless.' Quicksilver's theatregoing now profits him: ''Tis not a matter of feeling penitent, but seeming penitent. The show, the show! The citizens live by show. Wi'out it all would collapse. Bend knees and neck, they'll not ask to see thy heart. . . . Jus' take thy cue from the playbooks.' So he does. When the Goldings arrive, Petronel declaims, 'Accursed that ever I was born, dear friends, you find me in this last sad resting place. Amid insufferable shame and misery,' then inquires about bail. Quicksilver commits himself to God and acknowledges that his former wantonness and prodigality justify his present condition. Slyly, they try to bribe the Goldings. In supposed confidence, Petronel confesses, 'I had marked one quarter of my calculated profit from the venture for you, Master Deputy, being of my wife's family.' Although Golding gives no sign of offering thanks, Petronel continues, ''Twas a trifle. If the voyage had proved success-ful, we wouldst ha' gained millions; a quarter wouldst not've been missed. If we failed, you'd not lost a groat.' On cue, Quicksilver insists they would not have failed. Pilfering one of Seagull's earlier speeches that he had cut, Barnes aptly has Quicksilver explain, 'I heard from the Captain's own lips—Captain Seagull, who'd just returned from those far lands—that gold is more plentiful there than copper is with us. Why, all their dripping-pans and chamber-pots are pure gold.' He muses philosophically, 'Now we've lost it all. *(A collective sigh from the listeners.)* And justly for our wicked ways. All I ask of thee is that my old master, Touchstone, come see us and hear our pleas for forgiveness.' The point is not lost on Golding, who agrees to speak to Touchstone and promises, in a strikingly satiric sentence, 'As a true Christian, he'll quickly see where his duty and perhaps his profit lie.' With equal satiric force, Barnes has Mildred implore her father, 'They truly repent—recall the gold dripping-pans and chamber-pots.' Golding arranges a private meeting between the master and his former apprentice. Quicksilver remarks that Touchstone's vengeance is unprofitable. 'You ha' taken up all Sir Petronel's debts and his ship as bond for 'em. But his debt canst not be paid whilst he languishes in prison and the ship, whilst she languishes in the harbour, loses you money hourly. . . . A ship not trading is wasting.' In his own case, Touchstone's reputation is at stake: 'If an apprentice is proved guilty o' stealing, his master is proved guilty o' gullibility.' Quicksilver proposes a solution: 'Let I,

Sir Petronel and his Lady take up the ship and sail her boldly to Virginia in return for half the profits. Then instead of certain mounting debt you'll look to ha' fair prospect of profits.' Sealing the bargain, he links profit, reputation, and Christianity: 'Consider then, by this one act of forgiveness, all sighs and curses'll turn to smiles and warm looks. You'll be following in Christ's way and in the way of profit, too.' Touchstone approves the lad's 'welcome concern for repentance and profit.' The freed sinners leave for America, which as Touchstone says is 'the place for the "quick" and the "flash".'

In this changed conclusion, Barnes more effectively parodies the conception of repentant sin and triumphant virtue than his collaborators do; the satiric thrust—comedy derived from greed and gulling—is maintained; and the characters are more consistent than before: Quicksilver remains clever and the business people are interested in the acquisition of money plus the reputation of soundness, shrewdness, and devoutness. Although *Eastward Ho!* by the three Jacobean collaborators is a very good play, it is a better play when the fourth collaborator, with a twentieth-century view of the seventeenth century, joins their company.

Adaptations from Foreign Languages

As indicated in Chapter 2, Barnes has edited and adapted for performance works originally written in languages other than English. This section will first examine his version of Synesius of Cyrene's *Eulogy of Baldness* in tandem with poems and songs by Bertolt Brecht and Frank Wedekind—none of which he greatly altered. Next, it will explore his adaptations of German plays: his bringing together Wedekind's two Lulu plays, *Earth Spirit* and *Pandora's Box*, into a single work, *Lulu*; his version of Wedekind's short play *The Singer*; and his rendering of Christian Dietrich Grabbe's *Don Juan and Faust*. Although he adapted these to a greater degree then the works in the first group, his changes—to roughly the same extent (hence, their chronological treatment)—alter the originals far less than the changes in his adaptation of Georges Feydeau's *The Purging*, the final work studied. In it, he gives an emphasis and ending quite different from those of the original.

A Eulogy of Baldness, The Two Hangmen: Brecht and Wedekind

In these works adapted for radio—the first, an essay; the second, poems and songs—Barnes' alterations are minimal. He deletes what would either sound clumsy or be incomprehensible to an English audience and he attempts to provide good spoken English that gives the impression the work was originally written in English.

As his narrator states in the introduction to *A Eulogy of Baldness*, Synesius of Cyrene (in Lybia)—born 370 AD and died forty-four years later—found no difficulty in reconciling Christianity with neoplatonism. Although he had not yet been converted to Christianity, the Cyrenese people urged this aristocratic landowner to become their Bishop, which he did. Synesius' many writings include verse and essays on rhetoric, science, and philosophy.

In *A Eulogy of Baldness*, he attempts to refute Dio Chrysostem's eulogy of hair. Admitting he was distressed when he began to lose his hair, Synesius became—or claims he became—accustomed to his baldness. Arguing against Chrysostem's praise of hair, he declares that if a man's mind is garbed with intellectual vestments, it matters nothing if his head has no hairy attire. Reasoning by analogy, first with the animal kingdom, he points out that the dumbest animal is the hairiest, the sheep, and that all hairy beasts are unintelligent compared to man, who has less hair than they. Thus, the man with no hair is to the normal man what the normal man is to beasts. Among humans, those who are regarded as wisest are Diogenes and Socrates, both bald. Admittedly, Apollonius is a hairy philosopher, but he practised demonology. Soon, Synesius' analogy extends to the heavens, whose bodies stand nearest the Creator. The sun, moon, and planets are spheres, which resemble a bald head. Confronted with pictures of Zeus, whose locks are thick, he asserts that such images are not the true Zeus, who is really bald, but Zeus designed to appeal to the masses. He mentions a theatrical performer whose barber shaves his head to increase his strength: he butts his bald head against a trained ram and breaks vases on it. Delighted, Synesius concludes not only that baldness endows one with strength, but that if fortune were unkind to the philosopher, he could earn a living in the theatre. He goes on to cite the long-haired Lacedae-monians, who lost the battle of Thermophylae—because of their long hair, according to him—and the victorious soldiers of Alexander the Great, who shaved their hair before they went into battle—the reason they won, he asserts. Long hair signals immorality, for both effeminate and (he sees no contradiction) adulterous men wear it.

Barnes took a literal translation of *A Eulogy of Baldness*, not intended to be spoken aloud, and turned it into a work that could be so spoken. His adaptation consists of deleting passages difficult for present-day audiences to understand—including discussions of neoplatonism, Grecian rites, and Egyptian deities—and altering passages so that they sound like good spoken English, for example, a reference to the bald Odysseus whom Penelope's long-haired suitors mock: '[[Him they counsel, when he is torch-bearing and kindling a light produced by man's hand, to desist from his work]] *When they found him carrying a torch, they told him to put it out,* for his head [[suffices to]] *alone would* light the whole house.'[11]

'What is so marvellous about the piece,' says Barnes, 'is that as he progresses he loses all sense of proportion. It reveals the writer more than he ever bargained for. His obsession with baldness reaches absolutely fantastic heights. What is so endearing is you can really sympathize with his disappointment that his hair has gone.' As Barnes states, 'I didn't do much to it. I just turned it into a monologue. I've kept the adaptation down because it's too good.'

With the Brecht and Wedekind verse as well, he kept his adaptation down, also because they are good. Yet, as with *Eulogy of Baldness*, he did adapt them. While faithful to their spirit, he is not always faithful to their letter. As he sees it, his role is the same as that with Jacobean plays: to make the work (play, essay, poem) comprehensible and immediate to English audiences of his own day. Rather than take the Brecht and Wedekind poems generally or *seriatim,* which would involve much repetition and would duplicate the discussion of Barnes' Jacobean renderings, let us examine a typical poem, Brecht's *In Dark Times (In Finsteren Zeiten),*[12] written 1936–38. Here is Barnes' version, written forty years later:

Looking back
They won't say: the nut tree shook in the wind.
But: the oppressors crushed the workers.
They won't say: a child made the flat pebble skim across the
    water.
But: wars were started.
They won't say: a woman entered the room.
But: the great powers conspired.
They won't say: these were dark times.
But: why did the poets keep quiet?

The language is simple, the verse vivid: the beauties of ordinary life contrasted with workers crushed by oppressors and the conspiracy of great powers, the silence of poets who failed to expose oppressors and powerful regimes. The symmetry stresses these contrasts: lines that begin 'They won't say,' followed by lines that begin 'But'; and the horrors of the latter lines shockingly implicate the poets, who by remaining silent join the oppressors and great powers, and therefore become culpable.

But Barnes' poem is not simply anglicized German. In a few important respects, it differs from Brecht's. Instead of employing the recurrent *when*, as Brecht does after the first three times he uses *But*, Barnes adds a first line: *Looking back*. The effect of this new phrase is to retain the idea of the past but to diminish the continuing emphasis on it. He thereby strengthens the poem's contemporary relevance. Also diminishing the emphasis on the past, and stressing contemporaneity, he does not say *house-painter* (the literal translation of Brecht's *Nussbaum*) or *Hitler* (to whom the word refers); instead, he has *oppressors*, which generalizes the reference. Unlike Brecht, he does not repeat the phrase *the workers*, against whom the great powers conspired. The conspiracy is therefore not against only one social class; this change harmonizes with Brecht's *woman* who entered the room (Brecht does not call her a working-class woman). Barnes' change from wars being prepared for to wars being started may be unfortunate, in that poets could be politically effective during preparations for a war but not after its outbreak. If so, this seems the only weakness in an otherwise skilful and vivid adaptation.

Lulu

Lulu, the heroine of Frank Wedekind's *Earth Spirit* and *Pandora's Box*, embodies the sexuality that is the spirit of the earth and she unleashes a multitude of unforeseen disasters. Men and woman alike are drawn to her. When her wealthy husband Goll discovers her behind a locked door with the artist Schwarz, he breaks it open and dies of a heart attack. When the naïve Schwarz, her new husband, learns of her promiscuous past, he kills himself. She shoots her next husband, the newspaper editor Schön, then takes up with his choreographer son Alwa, with whom she makes love on the couch on which his father bled to death. An acrobat-strongman, an aristocratic lesbian, and a young student whose father is chief of police move into her orbit, to their ruin. The acrobat becomes flabby through lack of exercise; the lesbian Countess contracts cholera so that she can exchange places with Lulu in prison (where she is sent after Schön's murder) and thus permit Lulu to escape; believing Lulu to be dead, the student kills himself. Two people are immune to her charms. Unsuccessfully, the white slaver Casti-Piani—who falls under no woman's spell—attempts to blackmail her into letting him sell her to an Egyptian brothel. Successfully, Jack the Ripper—in England, where she, her male and female lovers, and the man who people think is her father have fled—kills her.

In adapting these two plays into one, Barnes makes numerous cuts and condensations. Gone is the Prologue to *Pandora's Box*. When Schön explains Lulu's background to Schwarz, Barnes eliminates all details concerning her other names. Retaining only the simple explanation of the two women changing clothes, he deletes all other particulars about how Countess Geschwitz contrived Lulu's escape.

But the adapter does more than cut dialogue. As Barnes states, 'There are lots of changes, in the sense that by choosing what I think the author was saying and emphasizing certain aspects—making directorial choices, really, in the text—one is moving the play in a certain direction. You can't say that's a straightforward editing job. I take that to be an adaptation.' In the Prologue to the first play,[13] he slashes references to the audience's sensuality, the soulless characters of the drama, people's animal-like behaviour, and the popularity of farces and Ibsenite drama with well-mannered animals. What remains acquires greater emphasis: Lulu's seductiveness. Barnes further stresses this by having Lulu appear not in the Pierrot costume specified by Wedekind but '*in a glittering, skin-tight, one-piece suit.*' Instead of the Animal Trainer tickling her under the chin, Barnes' Lulu '*coils herself sinuously around his body.*' Wedekind's Animal Trainer fondles her hips; Barnes' Ringmaster '*strokes her legs*' (p. 1). This aspect is in the original, perhaps minimized by Wedekind because of stringent censorship regulations (which he flaunted to some extent, though less daringly than what one is accustomed to nowadays). In Barnes' adaptation, sensuality is far more prominent.

Other changes also emphasize certain aspects, as he puts it. When Wedekind's Lulu examines the painting of Schön's fiancée, she exclaims, 'Look! Enchanting! Charming!' (ES, p. 388). Barnes' simply states, 'She's lovely' (p. 4), which makes the statement perfunctory, a conventional compliment. By cutting digressive dialogue, Barnes stresses more emphatically than Wedekind Goll's perverse lust for young girls. In the original, Alwa invites Goll to see a dress rehearsal of his ballet. He mentions a dancer as the young Buddha, Schön refers to the dancer's mother, Alwa talks of dining afterwards, he refers to young girls in the performance, Lulu suggests seeing a regular performance, Goll worries about not supervising Schwarz's painting, Alwa talks of young girls in their tights, Goll refers to the painting again, Schön speaks of the need to hurry, and finally Goll agrees to go. Except for retaining Goll's concern about supervising the painting, Barnes cuts virtually everything else to focus on the young girls in their tights. As soon as Goll hears about them, away he goes.

Some of Barnes' changes strengthen themes of business and class relationships. Wedekind's Schön suggests that if Goll were to finance the impoverished artist Schwarz, it would be 'a matter of arithmetic' (ES, p. 390). Barnes more clearly links the subject to business: 'It'd just be a minor problem in accountancy for you' (p. 5). After Wedekind's artist spits at Goll and Schön, who have just left, he complains that wealthy patrons like them give poor artists both a breadbasket and a muzzle. Barnes' also spits, but his reply is more pointed: 'A man must eat but he has to be broken first' (p. 7). One or a few changes in emphasis would be of relatively little importance, but their accumulation amounts to a great deal.

The English adapter adds as well as changes. To clarify why young Hugenburg fears he will be expelled from school if anyone learns he is at Lulu's, and to enhance the aura of perversity, the acrobat Rodrigo has new speeches: 'Alfred, you've been selected to attend one of Lulu's intimate afternoon soirées. *(He laughs.)* Only close friends like the old man and me and young boys like yourself are invited. But there's one thing I can promise, it'll be an afternoon you'll remember!' and he warns the old man not to give the boy too much liquor 'or he won't be able to do himself justice and Lulu'll make us suffer for it' (pp. 35–36). When Schön states that in two weeks he will announce his engagement to an innocent young lady, Barnes has him add, 'She's going to make a new man of me' (p. 4)—a telling commentary on the pompous, degenerate, wealthy man's view, which is entirely unrealistic, of the ennobling effect of the innocent on the corrupt. With the suicide of the artist comes news of a revolution in Paris. This, considers Schön, will help him weather the scandal. Barnes has him add, 'a revolution's bigger than a suicide. Artists are killing themselves every day' (p. 22).

Making fine use of the technical resources of today's theatre, Barnes takes the circus milieu of Wedekind's Prologue to the first play as a *leitmotif*. Frequently, he employs its music between scenes, and his directorial imagination embroiders the transitions, as in the bridge between the first and second scenes of Act II. Following the former, '*discordant circus music*' plays. Then: '*Spots up on the distorting mirrors. Only the centre panel is dark. Men and women in death masks waltz in front of them.'* As they do so, *'Their grotesquely distorted images form a moving Dance of Death fresco'* (p. 54). At the end of Act I, Scene iii, after Lulu entices Schön to break his engagement, Barnes adds: *'Wedding bells peal out above the crowd's roar, which fades down immediately. Spot up on* LULU *in front of the mirrors, dazzling in black underwear and a white bridal veil.* SCHÖN*'s Spot slowly out as he turns and sees her walk slowly Down Stage Right in front of the curving wall of mirrors as the Wedding March plays over.'* This music continues as Lulu stops *'in front of the first mirror. Circus music up.* FERDINAND, *a bearded gamekeeper, enters with a white negligee. As* LULU *takes off the veil and* FERDINAND *helps her on with the negligee, Spot up Down Stage Left on* SCHÖN *watching them.'* When they kiss, Schön *'reacts violently.* FERDINAND *exits.* LULU *adjusts the negligee and finally turns away, smiling.'* Then, lights go up on a room decorated in German Renaissance style, as in the original (pp. 32–33). Since Barnes concludes the first act with Lulu's murder of Schön, he begins the second act:

> *An unseen Judge raps three times for silence. A bell tolls mournfully. Distorted circus music is played at a very slow speed.*
>
> *Spot up Up Stage Centre on a monstrous swaying image of* LULU *in a fairground distorting mirror dressed in a prison smock and behind bars.*
>
> *Music fades down and* LULU*'s spot is snapped off.*

Then, lights go up on the German Renaissance room (p. 45).

Unrestrained by censorship, Barnes makes more explicit, through additional stage business, the perversity of the original. He has Lulu and the lesbian Countess Geschwitz kiss onstage before the latter *'ecstatically'* agrees to take Lulu's place in a brothel (p. 68). Alone, Geschwitz *'sees* LULU*'s handkerchief in the chair. She picks it up and smells it. Hiding it in her muff she bends down on the sofa and smells where* LULU *has been sitting'* (p. 35). When Prince Escerny wants Lulu to confirm his hope that she would rather tyrannize a single special person than receive the applause of the multitude, Barnes' added stage directions grotesquely and comically highlight the perversity of royalty. After she steps behind a screen to change, he *'reacts with pleasure as she puts her underclothes on top of the screen. She throws her stocking over.* ESCERNY *furtively picks it up and starts playing with it.'* Then, he twists it around his neck. As he continues to talk, *'He nearly strangles himself with the stocking.'* Soon, he pockets it *'as* LULU *steps out from behind the screen in a short pleated petticoat, white satin corset, white stockings and carrying white boots with spurs on the heels.* ESCERNY*'s walking stick jumps upright in his hand at the sight. His eyes continually go back to* LULU*'s glittering spurs. She crosses to the centre table and sits on it to put on her boots.'* In a moment, he is by her, bending down and spinning the spurs more and more quickly and furiously. When she tells him he has never been loved honourably, she 'kicks *the delighted* ESCERNY *on to the floor. She slides off the table and crouches beside him.*' Soon, he crawls between her thighs and she rests a foot on his back. '*He jerks sideways and she finds herself astride him.*' When she leaves, '*she kicks him on the backside. He gasps with joy*' (pp. 26–28).

As this scene indicates, Barnes adds farcical touches to the play's grotesque sexuality. After Lulu leaves the perverted prince, Alwa enters and the two men talk. The prince '*takes out a handkerchief to wipe his brow, instead it is Lulu's stocking.* ALWA *reacts*' (p. 29). When Lulu leans over young Hugenburg and invites him to smell the orchid between her breasts, Barnes adds a stage direction: 'HUGENBURG *nearly slides off the chair*'; and when the youth asks her father's name, Barnes has him direct the question not to the old man but '*to* LULU *who is on top of him*' (p. 37). Upon Alwa's entrance, the youth, the old man, and the acrobat hide. Barnes' new stage directions counterpoint farce to Alwa's sincere declarations of love: '*She opens the champagne, the cork shoots into the air.* ALWA *grows more agitated. He lifts the table cloth.* HUGENBURG *pulls it down. When* ALWA *bends to look* LULU *pretends she has done it.*' Soon, the table moves. '*As he bends down to investigate* LULU *interposes herself.*' He begins to tell her how much she means to him. '*As he goes to embrace her* HUGENBURG*'s hand creeps out and covers* LULU*'s breast.* ALWA*'s hand covers* HUGENBURG*'s thinking it is* LULU*'s*' (pp. 39–40).

To the horror and violence of the conclusion of Wedekind's second play, the murder of Lulu by Jack the Ripper, Barnes adds the ludicrous, even the comic. Jack carries Lulu into her cubby-hole. As Wedekind has it, the audience hears Lulu cry, 'No!—No!—No!— O!—O.' Soon, Jack emerges and puts a wash-bowl on a stand. 'That was a piece of work!' he exclaims as he washes his hands. 'What a damned lucky fellow I am!' Looking about, he complains, 'These people here don't even have a hand-towel! What a horrible, poverty-ridden hole!' Drying his hands on Geschwitz's petticoat, he remarks, 'This monster is perfectly safe from me,' then tells her, 'It'll soon be all over for you too' and leaves. Alone, Geschwitz cries for Lulu, begs to see her again, and finally collapses, exclaiming, 'Oh, damn!' (PB, pp. 538–539). For his English audiences, the adapter's ludicrous and comic additions stress their native country (all ellipses in the following quotations are in the original):

> *A crescendo of screams. An unnaturally loud tearing sound. Silence . . .*
> *Then* JACK*'s orgastic cries are heard. He staggers out.*

JACK: I'm so lucky . . . I'm so lucky . . . *(As in a dream he slowly raises the bloodstained knife high like a chalice and licks it. A pause then his manner changes abruptly. He crosses briskly to the wash basin whistling 'Land of Hope and Glory.' He washes his face, hands and knife and looks around.)* Miserable hole. They haven't even got a towel. *(He crosses menacingly to* GESCHWITZ, *bends down and wipes the knife on her dress; to her)* Monster . . . You haven't got long either. *(He puts the knife away, goes to door and pauses.)* A good night's work.

He exits. Lights dim to a Spot on GESCHWITZ, *lying clutching her stomach.*

Calling for Lulu, she dies, without a curse but with circus music (p. 82).

Lulu is an adaptation in the best sense of the word. As Martin Esslin asserts in his Introduction to the published edition, *Lulu* succeeds 'in fully preserving Wedekind's original intention, while compressing the action into the span of a single evening's performance (p. vi). Furthermore, one may add, while it preserves this intention, it strengthens what is implicit in Wedekind's work with a theatricality and comic ludicrousness appropriate for audiences of the late twentieth century.

The Singer

The shorter of two one-act plays that comprise *Frontiers of Farce, The Singer* is an adaptation of a Wedekind work whose untranslatable German title *(Der Kammersänger)* is an honorific bestowed by royalty on an outstanding singer employed in the court's opera houses.

Bothered with flowers and letters sent by numerous admirers, Gerardo—the title character—instructs his Valet to inform all callers that he is out. He plans to employ his remaining time to rehearse songs from *Tristan and Isolde*, which he is to sing the following evening in another city. He receives no opportunity to rehearse. Hidden in his room, sixteen-year-old Isabel Coeurne, who says she is twenty-two, offers him roses and herself. After Gerardo gets rid of her, the composer Duhring—who for fifty years has written operas although no one has demonstrated the slightest desire to produce them—sneaks in, harangues Gerardo about artistic integrity, and implores him to hear his opera. Forget silly notions about art, Gerardo advises the older man. A professional artist, Gerardo explains, is one who performs or has his work performed for payment. He recognizes that he himself is a luxury of the bourgeoisie, a showpiece for people to gawk at and make money from, and he has no use for romantics who fail to recognize the nature of the world in which they live and the relationship between art and the marketplace. After Duhring leaves, Gerardo's lover Helen interrupts to announce that she has left her husband and children, and that unless he takes her with him she will kill herself. He cannot do this, he explains, since his contract forbids him from travelling with a woman—not because sexual activities will interfere with his voice but because people think they will and business will suffer. True to her word, Helen shoots herself. The Hotel Manager arrives, surveys the scene—which to him is commonplace—and expeditiously arranges matters. Gerardo leaves to catch his train and fulfil his contract by singing the romantic *Tristan* music the next night.

Many of Barnes' additions are directorial pieces of farcical business that make visual or audible one character's attitude toward another. When Duhring pleads with Gerardo to listen to his opera, Barnes has him fall on his knees and clutch Gerardo's legs. Then: 'GERARDO *tries to move away.* DUHRING *clings to his leg and is pulled across the room*' (p. 47). While Helen is trying to persuade Gerardo to break his contract, he practices vocal exercises. When she tells him she cannot live without him, '*she grabs his lapels and jerks him close and they fall on the floor*'; upon her claim that to lose him would mean to lose life itself, '*He tries to get up but she pushes him over*' (p. 58).

Employing theatricality and comedy that stress Wedekind's grotesquery, Barnes alters the ending. After Helen agrees to return to her husband and children, Wedkind simply has her press Gerardo's hand, pick up her muff, remove a revolver from it, shoot herself in the head, and fall; and he has Gerardo cry her name, then collapse into an armchair. Barnes goes further: As Gerardo moves away from her to get her cloak, '*he does not see her take a gun from her muff and point it at him. She changes her mind, puts the gun to her mouth and shoots herself. The mirror behind her shatters. Blood pours out of her mouth as she falls slowly to the floor.*' He '*stares at her in horror,*' then addresses her corpse: 'Helen. How could you? After you *promised?*' Unlike Wedekind's Page Boy, who is shocked at seeing the dead body, Barnes' is self-possessed: 'Leave it to me, sir, I know exactly what to do.' After he leaves, Barnes has Gerardo address the corpse again: 'No consideration for anyone but yourself, Helen. Self-indulgent to the end. You do exactly what you want and leave others to take the consequences. *(He looks mechanically at his watch.)* What about me, the man you said you loved?' He complains of her excessive romanticism, which he calls 'a disease more deadly than typhus. The Germans get it worst.

Always having to kill themselves or somebody else. You never had any sense of proportion, Helen' (p. 62). As in the original, Gerardo laments that if he leaves he will be considered a beast and if he stays he will be financially ruined for having broken his contract. He asks the Hotel Manager to send for the police. Also as in the original, the Page Boy's inability to find a policeman promptly provides Gerardo with an excuse to fulfil the terms of his contract. In Wedekind, he springs up; lets Helen's body fall; exclaims, 'I must sing *Tristan* tomorrow night in Brussels!' and leaves, bumping into furniture as he does so (p. 580). In Barnes, Gerardo's professionalism is more pointed:

> PAGE BOY: I can't find the police, sir.
> GERARDO: No. I can't wait. I must sing *Tristan* tomorrow.
> *He dumps* HELEN *on the floor again with a thud, gets up, clicks his fingers for the* VALET *to follow him and exits determinedly. The lights dim down slowly as* MÜLLER *and the* PAGE BOY *gather round the body on the floor and* GERARDO *is heard singing exquisitely, with full orchestra, an aria from* Tristan and Isolde *in the gathering darkness.*   [p. 64]

Many of the adapter's changes from the original emphasize Wedekind's themes. As Barnes says in his Introduction, 'Wedekind pointed out the reality behind the pretensions of high culture: that even here everything is still "addition and subtraction, the rest is conversation."' The glamorous title character, 'battered by rapacious art-lovers and would-be artists, tries with increasing desperation to make them see he is as much a wage slave as any factory worker.' Even in the dignified world of opera, 'the capital ethos still prevails, seeking to substitute monetary values for human and artistic ones' (pp. vii–viii). To this statement, one should add that the capitalist ethos succeeds. In the play itself, Barnes' changes demonstrate this to be the case. More frequently, and therefore more clearly, his Gerardo is a professional, to whom payment for his work is of paramount importance. At the play's start, after Gerardo demonstrates how properly to fold his trousers, Wedekind has this exchange:

> VALET: Your Excellency perhaps was once a tailor.
> GERARDO: What?!—Not quite that—Idiot! *(Giving him the trousers)* There, pack them, but be quick about it.   [p. 548]

Barnes changes it: 'You're very professional, sir.' 'I always try to be.' 'Have you ever been a valet, sir?' 'I've been everything. Except an idler and a parasite. See if I've left anything in the bedroom' (p. 42). After Gerardo explains to Helen that his contract forbids him from travelling with a woman, Wedekind has her declare, 'That's incomprehensible to me. I don't understand how a decent person could sign such a contract.' Gerardo responds, 'I am first an artist and second a human being!' (p. 570). Barnes alters the emphasis to include money: 'How can an intelligent man sign such a contract?' 'My rights as an intelligent man don't come into it. I'm just an artist, who wants to be paid' (p. 57). When he pleads with her to listen to him, Helen—who by this time understands that to Gerardo time means money—says sarcastically that he has only ten minutes before he must go. Barnes has him add: '*(looking at watch)* Eight and a half actually' (p. 58).

A major change occurs early in the play: the scene between Gerardo and the sixteen-year-old Isabel Coeurne. When she offers herself to him, he tells her she is too young, but Barnes adds stage directions which indicate that despite (or because of) her youth she sexually attracts him: at one point he examines her low-cut dress, at another leans over her. Not only does Barnes change Gerardo's age—from the middle-young thirty-six to the almost middle-age thirty-eight—he gives the singer a touch of vanity, regret, and a feeling that he is perhaps not *that* much older than she. Ostensibly explaining he is too old for her, Barnes' Gerardo says, 'But I'm thirty-eight—thirty-six years old' (p. 44). When Gerardo tries to get rid of her, Wedekind has him stress for her benefit the idea that she is dazzled by the romantic nobility of his appearance on stage. Barnes has him stress his awareness of his sexual attractiveness on stage: 'It's not my fault you've fallen in love with me, is it? It's my manager! I told him about my costume. But he insisted. The breeches're too tight and the shirt's too open at the neck. You can see the hairs on my chest when I sing. It's sheer provocation. I told him. He wouldn't listen' (p. 45). Finally, when Wedekind has him get rid of her, he talks to her about the dignity of art and of opera, and he fobs her off with an autographed picture. As elsewhere, Barnes goes further:

GERARDO: You're so young, so beautiful. And there's just time.
He looks quickly at his watch, grabs her hand and disappears with her into the bedroom Down Stage Right. There is a scream and ISABEL *rushes back out sobbing with fright.* GERARDO *appears in the doorway frustrated.*
[p. 46]

He *then* talks about opera and gets rid of her by giving her an autographed picture.

Barnes' changes in this scene stress a major theme. All of the people who pester Gerardo live in worlds of romantic unreality. Gerardo, however, is a realist who shatters their illusions. More clearly and more comically than in the original, he shatters Isabel Coeurne's illusions too. Although she throws herself at him, she is unaware of consequences, for she has no understanding of the nature of sexual love. Fully aware of it, and of the fact that he has *just* enough time to indulge himself, Barnes' Gerardo brings reality into his relationship with her as he later does with the other romantic intruders.

Don Juan and Faust

At the start of Christian Dietrich Grabbe's *Don Juan and Faust*, Juan contrives to make the Governor, Anna's father, and Don Octavio, her betrothed, leave her alone at home, but they thwart Juan by locking the door behind them. In his study, Faust summons the Devil, with whom he makes the traditional pact. Trying to persuade Faust to diminish his aspirations, the Devil shows him Anna, with whom he falls in love. Faust agrees to let Juan kill Anna's fiancé, then abduct Anna himself. Although Anna falls in love with Juan, she refuses to compromise her honour or Christian faith. Juan—who, like Tirso de Molina's original character, mocks the laws of God and man—kills Octavio, then—after Faust abducts Anna—kills her father. Immediately after Faust's departure, the Devil informs Juan that they have gone to an ice palace he built for Faust atop Mount Blanc, a name whose connotations of purity comment ironically on the diabolical activities there. Because Anna will not become involved with a married man, Faust has his wife killed—to no avail, for she still refuses to gratify his desires. Upon learning that Juan killed her father as well as her husband, she asks Faust to avenge her. When she tells the German she hates him, his temper overcomes his judgment and he commands her to die, which she does. Forlorn, Faust decides to go to Hell before his contract expires, but not until he sees Juan's torment when he tells him of Anna's death. Instead of despairing, Juan laughs defiantly, since other women exist. The Devil strangles Faust. At Juan's invitation, the Statue of the Governor arrives for dinner, shakes Juan's hand, and drags him into the pit. The Devil promises to chain him to Faust, both of whom, he says, arrived at the same destination by different coaches.

As with Wedekind's plays, Barnes' changes in *Don Juan and Faust* are primarily for emphasis and production. He makes internal cuts—within scenes and within speeches—to streamline and, in this instance, to reduce the lyricism of Grabbe's play, which unlike Barnes' adaptation is in verse. Partly for this reason, Barnes cuts the entire scene with two Gnomes (II,iv): it is lyric, not dramatic. His other relatively major alterations are to change the time and set of the duel between Don Juan and Anna's father from a different scene after Juan kills Octavio to the same scene, just after Faust abducts Anna—an alteration that gives the events greater dramatic intensity because they occur rapidly upon each other—and to costume the Devil not as a Knight, as Grabbe does, but as a Devil—which is more impressive for modern audiences.

In providing prose paraphrases of Grabbe's verse, Barnes retains the antitheses and the vivid imagery of the original. 'If you were a man of honour,' Anna tells Faust, 'you'd let me go.' 'I am a man of power,' he replies. 'And power creates its own honour' (IV,iv). Barnes' paraphrase employs Grabbe's imagery, as when the Devil states, 'Happiness is a worm which crawls no further than its power permits' (I,ii).

Many seemingly modern inventions of the adapter are in the 150-year-old play. It is Grabbe who has the Devil say (in Barnes' rendering) that God 'wanted to rule and I, His equal, wanted to rule as well. But I made the mistake of being frank and open about it. He lied, called the chains "Love" and hey presto, the angels heard the sound of the word and not the rattle of the chains' (I,ii). It is Grabbe who has this exchange between the dying Governor and Juan (again, in Barnes' accurate version) after Juan refuses to give up Anna: 'There is a God.' 'It doesn't interest me. This earth is so full of delights, I haven't the time or patience to brood about the Being who created it. If it is God, so much the greater is His glory. The best compliment you can pay a cook is to enjoy his cooking' (I,iv). Also accurately rendered is the exchange between Juan and his servant Leporello about Anna's servant: 'How goes it with Lisette?' 'Just the same way it would with you and Donna Anna after you've enjoyed her. Let's leave Rome. In nine months she'll be suing me for marriage!' (I,iii).

Barnes' alterations stress, more strikingly for today's audiences, the qualities of the original. To demonstrate Faust's superiority to the Devil, for instance, Grabbe's Faust reprimands him for the ice palace he has created: 'Miserable, the art that you show here!/ Unworthy of her gaze is this your castle!/This hall as well! It makes me feel ashamed!/You want to be a Devil, yet you can't/With splendour dazzle, even though it's false.'[14] Barnes' Faust is more supercilious: 'Rubbish! It's all rubbish! You call this a palace? It's a shack. Just thrown together. The place isn't worthy of Donna Anna. It's humiliating for me to have to bring her here. You and your so-called magic arts! I expected to be dazzled. Instead I'm depressed. It's so *vulgar!*' (II,i). Barnes also increases the comedy.

When Juan has Leporello provoke Octavio in order to give him an excuse to replace his servant in the duel, Grabbe has this exchange:

> DON OCTAVIO (*to* DON JUAN):   Who without cause
> Calls me a scoundrel, he is one himself.
> LEPORELLO (*to* DON JUAN): This man, he treats me like a common drunkard.
> You know me, sir; I beg you, tell the truth:
> That I get drunk, how could it ever be?
> The grapes to make me drunk have not yet grown.
> DON JUAN: Offend my servant, you offend me too.
> So draw your sword.   [p. 466]

Barnes' funnier version has them argue:

> OCTAVIO: Who's the scoundrel who calls me a scoundrel?
> DON JUAN: Are you calling me a scoundrel?
> LEPORELLO (*raising his glass*): He called *me* a drunkard.
> DON JUAN: I've been insulted!
> OCTAVIO: I've been insulted!
> LEPORELLO: I've been insulted!
> OCTAVIO: He stepped on my foot!
> DON JUAN: He called me a scoundrel!
> LEPORELLO: He called me a drunkard!
> DON JUAN: Draw your sword.   [I,iv]

Very sardonic is the more urbane comedy which Barnes inserts into the scene wherein Faust agrees to go to Hell earlier than his contract demands. As Grabbe has it: 'Devil, in one hour I am yours!' 'Doctor, in one hour?' 'Certainly.'/'Sir, that is a great, great deal, it is/Self-conquest. This I will reward you for/With magnanimity.' 'Hypocrite!' (p. 499). As Barnes renders the exchange: 'Devil, in one hour, I am yours!' 'What?' 'In one hour I give myself to you. You can claim the contract.' 'In one hour.' 'Yes.' 'But you have years yet.' 'One hour.' 'This sudden flush of nobility won't get you any reprieve. You're too far gone.' 'I know.' 'So be it. I must say, this is most generous. I hardly expected such—such self-sacrifice. You're a man of honour, sir, a gentleman.' 'Hypocrite!' 'Not at all. I am truly touched by your gesture' (II,iv). Barnes strengthens the cynical tone of the original. When Juan waxes rhapsodically about the wonderful Roman air, once breathed by Caesar and now by his beloved, Grabbe's Leporello says it comes from the local tavern. Barnes' says it comes from the local cesspool and open sewer.

Some of Barnes' alterations further emphasize the class consciousness of the original. When Juan is indignant that Leporello palms himself off as a count in order to court servant girls, Leporello says he always does so. Barnes has him add, 'It's easier for the rich to make love and not pay for it' (I,i). As in Grabbe, Juan tells Anna that Octavio turns his stomach, but Barnes has Juan call Octavio's speeches 'the bourgeois approach, the pretty commonplaces' (I,iii). Increased class consciousness informs the reassignment of speeches. Grabbe has Juan say that he embraces the girl he loves, marries the one he hates or who has money. Barnes has him say, 'I embrace the woman I love, marry the one I hate.' It is his servant who tauntingly adds, 'Or who has money' (II,ii).

Barnes also adds. To make Rubio, the Police Commissioner, more distinctive, he gives him the humorous habit of repeating phrases, as when Rubio drunkenly says (italics indicate additions), 'I can't stand on one leg anymore. *I said anymore.*' When Rubio passes out, Barnes adds a comment by his companion Negro: 'And he's the Commissioner of Police. If only I were Commissioner. They'd see things. I said things. He's got me doing it now' (I,iv). When Juan agrees to attend Anna's wedding, Grabbe has Octavio say that he and the Governor will be honoured, and Juan respond that the honour is his. To Juan's response, Barnes adds:

GOVERNOR: No, the honour is mine.
DON JUAN: No, the honour is mine.
GOVERNOR: Mine, sir.
DON JUAN: Mine, sir.
GOVERNOR: SIR!
DON JUAN: I accept, sir, and the honour is yours. [I,i]

When Faust commands the Devil to be taken away and tortured, Grabbe simply has the Devil cry out as he is torn away. Between command and outcry, Barnes adds grotesque comedy:

FAUST: Devil, take yourself away and be tortured as commanded.
DEVIL: You can't do this to me. I'm—
FAUST: Read the contract—Paragraph Four.
DEVIL *(whips out the contract)*: Paragraph Four. 'I will obey.'
FAUST: Obey!
Fierce fires burn in the doorway Up Stage Centre.
DEVIL: Everyone's a damn lawyer now! *(A great wind blows and he is dragged irresistibly Up Stage Centre.)* Not me. I'm too important, I'm below all this—. I'll be r-e-v-e-n-g-e-d. *Aaaahhhhhh.*
He is dragged into the fiery doorway Up Stage Centre and disappears. The fires go out immediately. [II,i]

Furthermore, Barnes' additions fortify Grabbe's themes, one of which is the greatness that inheres in being true to oneself despite external constraints, as when the Devil tells Juan where Faust has taken Anna: 'I serve him faithfully and can still betray him. *That's the way I am. Remember this, one must always be true to one's nature*' (I,iv). Emphasizing this theme, Barnes has Juan cry, as he sinks into Hell, '*Damn you, Satan! This is my last cry on earth: King, Glory, and Love! Damn you all!*' (II,v). Even more than in the original, Juan is unregenerate to the end.

In harmony with the satiric mockery of the original, Barnes provides an impressive finale for the end of the first of his two acts (Grabbe's Act III, Scene i). As Grabbe ends the scene, wherein Juan kills the Governor, the Governor's servant Gasparo enters with a priest. Gasparo finds his master (as Barnes renders it):

GASPARO: Dead.

PRIEST: We're too late then. Almighty God, forgive his sins!

GASPARO: The plea is superfluous. I served him for years and know he committed no sins.

PRIEST: What?! But he just fell in a duel.

GASPARO: He fell in a battle over Octavio's blood and Donna Anna's honour.

PRIEST: Only God—not man—can mete out punishment, my son.

GASPARO: God punishes the wicked so seldom, the Governor probably thought it might help if he lent Him a hand.

In the original, the two then remove the body and the scene ends. In the adaptation is an additional passage:

PRIEST *(pointing to* OCTAVIO*'s corpse)*: Who's this?

GASPARO: Octavio.

PRIEST *(removing the napkin from the corpse's face)*: Oh, yes, I just married him, didn't I.

GASPARO: I'll get servants.

PRIEST: I can perform the last rites on both of them at once. It'll save time. I suppose this is what you Spaniards call a blood wedding. 'Adjuro—'

GASPARO *exits Stage Left whilst the* PRIEST *opens his Bible and intones the last rites over the two dead men as the lights fade out.*

Using his directorial imagination, Barnes embellishes the duel between Juan and Octavio. In Grabbe, a stage direction indicates that they duel. After Octavio falls, people in an offstage room toast (in Barnes' words): 'May Donna Anna and Octavio live a thousand years.' As Barnes describes the duel, music from the ballroom and shouts from the guests accompany it. *'Despite themselves,* DON JUAN *and* OCTAVIO *find they are fighting in time to the music, which grows livelier and faster. At the climax,* OCTAVIO *lunges,* DON JUAN *parries and hits* OCTAVIO.*'* After he dies, Juan *'bends over him, and wipes his sword on* OCTAVIO*'s shirt as a fanfare is heard in the ballroom and* GUESTS *shout "A toast, a toast!"'*—followed by the one quoted above (I,iv).

Like *Lulu* and *The Singer, Don Juan and Faust* is part of a German dramatic tradition that includes the work of a recent playwright whom Barnes admires, Bertolt Brecht. Like the others, this adaptation is faithful to the spirit of the original, which it translates with skill and theatrical imagination for audiences of the late twentieth century.

The Purging

As Barnes states in his Introduction to *Frontiers of Farce*, the double bill of which Georges Feydeau's *The Purging* is the longer one-act play, Feydeau's later works, including this, 'strip away the false romanticism of "Oo la-la and Gay Paree" . . . and show us instead that a Frenchman's main concern is not sex but money and the state of his bowels' (p. vii). To a greater extent than his other adaptations of plays written in foreign languages, *The Purging* changes the original and thereby becomes a collaboration. Like his adaptations of *The Devil is an Ass* and *Eastward Ho!* it improves upon the original.

In the opening scene, Feydeau has Follavoine, his central character, look up 'Iles Hébrides' in his dictionary under the letter Z,[15] since he does not know how to spell it and it is pronounced *eel Zay-bred*. Mocking Follavoine's ignorance, his wife Julie tries to find it under *E* (p. 163). Taunting her, he sarcastically asks, 'Why not also look it up under *H?*' (p. 164)—where, of course, she finds it. When Follavoine sees that she is in her dressing gown, wearing hair curlers, and with her stockings around her ankles, at eleven a.m. he implores her to dress, since they expect luncheon guests: Mr and Mrs Chouilloux and his wife's cousin, Truchet. Julie is more concerned with their child, Toto, who has not had a bowel movement that morning and refuses to take a laxative. A manufacturer of chamber-pots, Follavoine is anxious to make a favourable impression on Chouilloux, since the French government contemplates issuing chamber-pots to every member of the armed forces and Chouilloux is chairman of the committee that will make a recommendation.

Follavoine markets what he boasts is an unbreakable porcelain model, on which he holds a patent. When he demonstrates two samples for Chouilloux, they break. Enter Julie—still in dressing gown and hair curlers. Ignoring her husband's distress and the importance of their guest, she insists Follavoine give Toto a laxative. Bringing the seven-year-old onstage, she enlists Chouilloux's aid. The boy behaves like a brat and refuses. Unsuccessfully, Julie tries to bribe him. After she insults Chouilloux, she attempts to persuade her husband to take a spoonful of the laxative to show their son how easy it is. 'Baby,' as he is frequently called, says he wants Chouilloux, not his father, to take it for him. Although Chouilloux protests when Julie tries to make him swallow a spoonful, he accidentally does so. When he refuses to take a second, she argues, and tells him his wife is cuckolding him with her cousin. At this point, the laxative starts to work and Chouilloux runs to the lavatory. By the time he returns, his wife and Truchet have arrived. He accuses them of cuckolding him; they deny it; he points to the Follavoines as the source of his information, challenges Truchet to a duel, and leaves. Truchet then challenges Follavoine to a duel and leaves. So befuddled is Follavoine, he takes the laxative and downs it in one gulp. Too late, he realizes what he has done and dashes out of the room. When Julie, who had left, returns, Baby holds up the bottle to receive credit for having taken the medicine. As Feydeau ends the play, Follavoine returns, goes berserk, and leaves. As we shall see, Barnes' conclusion is different.

Streamlining the comedy, Barnes makes extensive cuts. More significantly, he makes changes as well. In regard to the dictionary sequences, some of his changes derive from the different language. In English he has Follavoine look up the Azores under *O*. But he also uses English to add a joke not in the French. Feydeau's Julie tells Follavoine that he will find Hebrides under *E*, not *Z*; Barnes', that he will find the Azores under *I*, not *O*, then looks it up (here, as in later quotations, ellipses are in the original): 'O for Azores . . . An illiterate. A fully functioning illiterate. Thank God Baby's'—and she begins to look up the word under *I*—'Illegitimate' (p. 6).

The passage just cited illustrates another characteristic of Barnes' adaptation: he changes remarks that are not particularly funny to those that are. Julie's comment that her husband is a fully functioning illiterate is Barnes'; Feydeau's Julie calls him a porcelain manufacturer. Feydeau has Julie provoke Follavoine (in Barnes' rendering): 'That's how you'd like me to be, isn't it?!' Feydeau's husband responds: 'What do you mean, "like you to be"? Like you to be what?' (p. 167). Barnes makes him comically insulting: 'How

I'd like you to be is invisible' (p. 9). When she complains it was not easy for her to carry Baby for nine months in the depths of her womb, Feydeau's Follavoine asks where she got such a far-fetched expression. Barnes' exasperatedly asks, 'O why didn't he stay there?' (p. 32). After Chouilloux runs out of the room in search of the lavatory, his wife and Truchet are heard in the hallway. Follavoine tells Julie to deal with them while he sees how Chouilloux is. When she protests she does not even know them, Feydeau's husband exclaims, 'I don't care, do what you like!' (p. 198). Barnes' says, 'Don't worry, just be your usual charming self and I'm sure they won't stay long' (p. 35).

Also for comedy, Barnes adds entirely new passages. As in the original, the maid Rose tells Follavoine, who asks if she knows where the Azores (or Hebrides) are, that his wife, not she, puts things away and he explains they are islands, that is, earth surrounded by water. Next: 'You know what earth surrounded by water is?' 'Mud?' 'MUD?! *So much for the French educational system*' (p. 3). When Julie interrupts Follavoine after he has smashed the chamber-pots, Barnes creates new dialogue between her and Chouilloux: 'What's that mess on the floor?' 'Unbreakable porcelain' (p. 24).

In addition to new verbal humour, Barnes improves the farcical business. In the original, Follavoine takes Chouilloux's hat, Chouilloux sees the water-bucket Julie left in the room, Follavoine puts the hat on a cabinet, and, attempting to hide the bucket, he dashes between it and Chouilloux. Barnes rewrites the scene: 'FOLLAVOINE *takes* CHOUILLOUX*'s hat and gives him the bucket in exchange. Seeing what he has done he quickly snatches it back, then in his confusion puts* CHOUILLOUX*'s hat in the bucket and hangs the bucket on the hat stand*' (p. 19). Feydeau has Follavoine break two of his supposedly unbreakable chamber-pots. Barnes has him smash an additional six, then go to another cabinet, from which he removes a chamber-pot from a different batch. Instead of smashing, however, the bowl flies off as Follavoine swings the chamber-pot over his head, leaving him with the handle in his hand.

The substantive changes in *The Purging* concern focus and ending. Whereas Feydeau focuses on the child and the concern over his laxative, Barnes focuses on the father and the concern over his business. Throughout the play, the adapter adds dialogue for this purpose. Unlike Feydeau, Barnes raises the subject of Chouilloux early in the play—the fifth speech, wherein Follavoine tells Rose not to forget to announce Chouilloux the moment he arrives. A few pages later, Barnes has him remind his wife that Chouilloux is due at any minute. When Julie complains that she does not care about him, Barnes adds this exchange: 'Chouilloux could be worth two million francs to us.' 'You can have my interest in him for two centimes' (p. 11). Unlike Feydeau, Barnes does not permit the audience to forget the importance of business and money to the bourgeoisie. When his Follavoine considers what the government contract might mean to him, he daydreams of a business empire: 'I'll be the exclusive supplier of chamber-pots to the Armies of France. *And that's only the start. We could spread across the face of the globe: Europe, Africa, Asia and beyond. From Pole to Pole they'll all be using Follavoine chamber-pots. Today France, tomorrow the world!*' (pp. 16–17)— the anachronistic reference to Hitler's mad fantasy making Follavoine's more ludicrously comic. Barnes expands the references to money, as when Follavoine tries to calculate his earnings: 'Let's say the peace time strength of the army is what—three hundred thousand men? *Yes, three hundred thousand. But there'll be new recruits coming in yearly. Ah, but when the old ones retire, they'll take their chamber-pots with them as mementoes of their army days. It's a gold mine!* If each pot costs . . .' After Truchet challenges Follavoine to a duel, Julie tells her husband that everything has been his fault. Barnes gives a new emphasis to Follavoine's response: '*I'm ruined . . . Contract down the pan* . . . I have to fight a duel at dawn' (p. 36).

These significant shifts of emphasis foreshadow the ending, which Barnes changes and thereby conclusively focuses the play on the father's concern with money and business. As Feydeau ends the comedy:

> FOLLAVOINE *(bursting in, wearing his coat and hat)*: No! No! I'd rather go away! I'd rather leave home!
> *He goes to his desk, from which he takes papers which he nervously arranges in a folder before he leaves.*
> JULIE *(without even noticing her husband's state)*: Bastien! Baby took his laxative.
> FOLLAVOINE: I don't give a damn!
> *He leaves angrily.*
> JULIE *(indignantly)*: He doesn't give a damn! He doesn't give a damn! *(To Toto)* Well, there's your father for you! He doesn't give a damn! Oh! Luckily you have your mother! Love her with all your heart, my darling, love her with all your heart!
> *She covers Toto with kisses.*   [p. 201]

Barnes' ending is entirely different:

> FOLLAVOINE, *who has been stuck in the doorway clutching his stomach, staggers back to the hatstand and puts on his hat.*

FOLLAVOINE: That's it, I've had enough. That's mine I think!
He crosses to his desk and snatches up the chamber-pot.
JULIE: Baby's such a good boy. He's taken all his medicine.
FOLLAVOINE: Goodbye. I'm going.
JULIE: Where to? The Azores?
FOLLAVOINE: Shit!
FOLLAVOINE *lashes out at her with the chamber-pot, misses and hits the edge of the desk instead. The chamber-pot does not break. He stares at it, bangs it against the desk again and again; then staggers out waving the unbroken chamber-pot and sobbing.*
FOLLAVOINE: Monsieur Chouilloux! Monsieur Chouilloux! Monsieur Chouilloux!
Sound of toilet being flushed. [p. 37]

At the renewed prospect of a lucrative government contract, intestinal pains vanish and marital problems become unimportant. Only one thing matters: money. Not only is Barnes' changed ending funnier than Feydeau's, which—atypically for Feydeau—simply trails off unsatisfactorily, it underscores the theme and it provides a classically symmetrical balance to the play's beginning: both refer to the Azores; and at the start, Follavoine waits for Chouilloux, while at the end, he runs after him.

In harmony with the changed conclusion is the changed title. *On purge Bébé* means *Giving Baby a Laxative.* The title is ironic (the characters try but fail to give him a laxative) and emphasizes the domestic situation. Barnes' *The Purging*, which is not ironic (the bowels of two businessmen are purged), emphasizes the father's business situation.

Common Features with his Original Plays

What have the Jacobeans, Wedekind, Grabbe, and Feydeau in common? Barnes' response describes his own plays as well: 'Extreme theatricality. They have huge size, passions, and extremes of emotion.' Like some of his critics, he calls himself Jacobean. Opposed to naturalism, he regards Jacobean drama as 'a strong tradition in English literature. But we lost the golden pathway, which is theatrical, poetic—theatrically poetic—and richly textured. When we see it, we recognize it in an enlarged, inflamed, and glorious way, touching us, but not actually a photographic reproduction of the life we lead.' The statement also holds for Brecht—including the phrase about passion and extremity of

emotion, for Brecht's coolness and apparently dispassionate manner
are means by which he depicts the passions and emotions of his
characters. Barnes' introductory comment on *The Singer* and *The
Purging* applies to other works he has adapted, and to his own, too:
'They are . . . on the outer limits of farce where everything is pushed
to extremes of pain and cruelty, which is the very source of both the
comic and the tragic' (p. viii).

The very terms he uses to praise other writers apply to himself.
Take, for example, his tribute to Ben Jonson:

> I find Jonson close and sympathetic for his voracious appetite for
> words, his ability to create monsters, his moral conscience and the
> distinct discipline of his intelligence. He pays the audience the
> compliment of expecting them to use their brains; he has some-
> thing to say and they must pay attention. I admire his lack of
> sentiment, the polished surface. I adore the brilliant colours, the
> handling of large bold designs, the baroque excesses, the piling of
> concrete images and incidents all allied to a strict sense of form. I
> love the brutality. He was never crippled by ghastly good taste.
> The one-word motto over our writing desks is 'MORE.' Jonson
> makes me laugh, which helps.[16]

Substitute Barnes for Jonson and the tribute fits. The appetite for
language, the creation of monsters (that is, figures larger than life),
the moral conscience, the intelligence, the demand that the audience
use their intelligence, the unsentimentality, the large and bold
designs, the accumulation of concrete images and incidents, the
sense of form, the brutality, the mockery of conventional ideas of
good taste, the excess, the comedy—these also describe Grabbe,
Wedekind, and Brecht. Some of these terms—such as the creation of
monsters, the large and bold designs, the sense of form, the comedy,
and the excess—describe the Feydeau and Marston plays he has
adapted, and several characterize the passionate eulogy by Synesius.

Such qualities are theatrical, and the term theatricality includes a
play's visual characteristics. Jonson's theatricality, says Barnes—and
once again the statement applies to his own and that of Marston,
Grabbe, Wedekind, Brecht, and Feydeau—represents 'the fusion of
the verbal and visual before a live audience.'[17] Many of the works he
has adapted have a self-conscious theatricality, as his original plays
do. In *Antonio's Revenge*, one character suggests to another that they
'talk as chorus to this tragedy' (I). After Justice Overdo delivers a
soliloquy in *Bartholomew Fair*, Winwife asks Quarlous why that man
is talking to himself. *Eastward Ho!* has Quicksilver quote lines from
other plays. In *The Alchemist*, a character wears the costume of

Hieronymo of *The Spanish Tragedy*. *Volpone* has Peregrine tell the audience that Sir Politic Would-be is a fit subject for a play. In *The Silent Woman*, a character refers to Ben Jonson. *The Devil is an Ass* refers to the play *The Devil is an Ass*, which Fitzdotterel plans to see at the Blackfriars Playhouse (where it was originally performed)—or, more accurately, he plans to see part of it, for he wants to embarrass the author by leaving early. In *Pandora's Box*, the sequel to *Earth Spirit*, Alwa has written a play called *Earth Spirit*, which eunuchs and concubines are performing for the Sultan of Turkey. Barnes' use of popular culture resembles that of Jonson, who in *Volpone* has a snake-oil salesman and in *Bartholomew Fair* a ballad-hawker and a puppet show.

Also characteristic of his own plays is the vulgarity he admires in Jonsonian comedy. 'It's not sexual, it's a more farty vulgarity. Here we have a classic who can be very coarse; and this is something that makes some people's nostrils twitch. . . . On the one side you get the intellect, and on the other the farts and the lavatories.'[18]

In the works he has adapted, he finds contemporary significance. 'Just substitute collapsing insurance companies, washing machine companies and spiralling Australian mining shares for Meercraft's money-making schemes for draining the Fens and manufacturing bottled ale.' All of Jonson's confidence tricksters, he declares, have a remarkable modernity.

Jonson will always be contemporary because his perennial theme is greed. His heroes, Meercraft, Face, Subtle, Volpone would relish [then Prime Minister] Ted Heath's England. They have their eyes fixed on the main chance. For them lame ducks are only ripe for plucking. They are too busy making money to worry about the sick, the weak and ignorant. It is a vision of our free market economy, a maelstrom of greed and ruthlessness. One million unemployed and speculators making fortunes on the market. . . . The only difference between then and now is the scale was smaller, and Jonson's characters had a vitality our grey, respectable money élite deliberately lack.

Jonson, he claims, is a major poet of 'money and its power. He thunders like the Israelite prophets against it.'[19] As in earlier quotations, one can substitute the names of Barnes, Wedekind, and Brecht for that of Jonson.

The appropriateness of making such substitutions may be more convincing if one first sees a statement, then the play to which Barnes applies it: 'The moral of that is: con-men survive, and the only way we can survive is by becoming con-men ourselves.' Brecht's

Mahagonny? Wedekind's *Marquis of Keith?* Barnes' *Time of the Barracudas?* No. *The Alchemist.*[20]

The perversity of the upper classes *(Lulu)*, the hypocrisy of the bourgeoisie *(The Singer)*, the fraudulence of religion *(Don Juan and Faust)*, the bourgeoisie's obsession with money *(The Purging)*—these are among the themes of Barnes' mature plays. What his narrator says of Brecht and Wedekind in *The Two Hangmen*, one can without distortion say of Barnes. They 'sang without fear, knowing the world to be bad but believing it can be changed and oppression defeated. They ask us to face life without conventional props and a tenacious hope for the future. For the death of God and authority need not lead to despair but the elimination of fear of punishment; a great jubilation, a great "yes" to life.'

7 | *Turning On A Sixpence*

Except perhaps with minor writers, influences and derivations seldom come in tidy packages. Although Barnes is familiar with Swift and Shaw, in whose tradition of satiric comedy he belongs, he is unconscious of their direct influence on his work. He is conscious, however, of the influence of Ben Jonson and his fellows, with whom he strongly identifies. Deliberately dissociating himself from the naturalistic tradition, he just as deliberately insists that the non-naturalistic tradition, as exemplified by Jacobean drama, is also powerful. With Jacobean extremity, he calls naturalism 'a current fad' whose proper place is television. On the stage, he is uninterested in plays with 'just two people and a table.'[1]

As indicated earlier, the affinities of Barnesonian transformationalism to the work of America's Open Theatre are coincidental— unless one invokes the *Zeitgeist*. Barnesonian transformationalism also has affinities to the theatricalized plurality of realities in the plays of S. I. Witkiewicz, the Polish *avant-garde* dramatist of the between the wars period, whose innovative drama swiftly and daringly shifts from realism to fantasy, and combines farcical comedy, philosophical discourse, and social commentary. Although Barnes admires Witkiewicz's plays, particularly *The Water Hen*, his affinities to the Pole are entirely coincidental: he did not read Witkiewicz's works until after he had written several of his own mature plays. Nor need one point to E. E. Cummings' *Him*, with which his work has coincidental affinities, to account for his employment of popular culture. As a filmgoer and film reviewer, Barnes is certainly familiar with such comedians as Buster Keaton, who combines farce with acrobatics, and the madcap Marx Brothers, who at the drop of a hat suddenly shift gears and perform outrageous actions not logically related to those they have just performed. He is familiar, too, with English music-hall singers and comedians, of whom Max Wall and Sandy Powell are particular favourites.[2] Just as he was 'mad on movies,' so has he been mad on musicals, both on stage and screen, and in these, characters burst into song at the slightest provocation, or without provocation. Also important are the influences of Artaud and Brecht, which he more than acknowledges: he boasts. 'One should only take from the best,' he says.

In his penetrating Introduction to *The Bewitched*, Ronald Bryden observes that this play crystallizes apparently unconnected tendencies that preceded it. In English drama of the 1960s, says he, a new blend of comedy and disillusionment appeared.

> In the black farce of Joe Orton, the metaphysical wit of Tom Stoppard, the Goyescan horror of Edward Bond's *Early Morning* and *Lear*, there is a common note which one could only, at the time, describe loosely as Jacobean—a sense of things falling apart, a bitter delight in their new randomness, an appalled disgust at the superstition and brutality revealed by the collapse of the old order, which brought to mind Ben Jonson, Donne and Webster. . . . Peter Barnes gathers all these threads together in *The Bewitched*.   [pp. viii—ix]

Bryden's conclusion applies not only to *The Bewitched*, but to all Barnes' mature plays, beginning with *The Ruling Class*, which appeared at the end of the 1960s.

One can trace these threads, or developments, to the mid-1950s. From the continent came two major influences: that of Samuel Beckett, whose *Waiting for Godot* opened in London in 1955, and that of Bertolt Brecht, whose theatre company, the Berliner Ensemble, performed in London in 1956. In England, one sees Beckett's influence in the work of Harold Pinter. Most of Pinter's plays—and certainly those of the late 1950s and early 1960s—conform to the naturalistic tradition of production. In fact, the performance style of such works as *The Room* (1957), *The Dumb Waiter* (1957), and *The Caretaker* (1960) prompted some reviewers to link them with the realistic *Look Back in Anger* (1956) and with Arnold Wesker's *Chicken Soup with Barley* (1958) and *Roots* (1959). Whereas the Beckett tendency revealed its most significant English manifestation in the drama of Pinter, whose theatrical style was naturalistic, the Brecht tendency did so in the plays of John Arden and the productions of Joan Littlewood, neither of which were naturalistic. After presenting Elizabethan and Jacobean dramas in the 1950s, and *Mother Courage* in 1955, Littlewood produced at the turn of the decade plays like *The*

Hostage (1959) and *Oh, What a Lovely War* (1963), which are Brechtian and which—like the plays of Barnes—combine social satire with popular songs, music-hall routines, and farcical comedy. One of the major threads gathered by Barnes is that of Brecht-Littlewood, and he carries the innovative techniques of Littlewood, who did not produce the work of a great contemporary English dramatist, to a triumphant conclusion.

Although one may relate Barnes to traditional types of drama and theatre, as I have just done, one should also recognize his uniqueness. As he points out, 'one acknowledges influences, but one is just picking up certain aspects and then using them to one's own ends. In stealing, you sort of forget where it's come from and then make it your own.' This is what he does. His mature plays are *sui generis*. What reviewers have said of *The Ruling Class* and *The Bewitched* apply to all his mature plays. He is 'fully in command of his own world.'[3] His theatre 'is like nothing we have seen on the stage before. It presents us with the most outrageous improbabilities, and they seem as inevitable as tomorrow's breakfast.'[4] He matches his 'vast subject matter' with 'the wealth of his invention and the sheer power of his language.'[5] Affinities and tradition notwithstanding, Barnes is indeed a true original. Barnesonian transformationalism, which makes his theatre continually turn on a sixpence, as it were, is a distinctive package of comedy, shock, erudition, popular culture, diverse types of theatricality, and bitter social commentary that bounce off each other and, paradoxically, embrace each other to form an organically unified whole.

At present, many readers and spectators, including reviewers, are unaccustomed to plays that turn on a sixpence in this manner. They expect the stylistic homogeneity to which most drama has accustomed them. If a play begins in a Chekhovian manner, they expect its style to be Chekhovian throughout; if it suggests discursive philosophical drama, they expect it to be discursively philosophical throughout; if farcical, then farcical throughout. Unlike such plays, Barnes' create stylistic unity from heterogeneous theatrical modes. Shifting from realism to different types of theatricalism, from seriousness to parody, from pathos to farce or to savage derision, they then switch back and forth, and in different sequences, again and again. Such turnings on a sixpence permit audiences to take nothing for granted. In effect, they confront and challenge spectators and readers. Once audiences become accustomed to Barnesonian transformationalism and his distinctive shifts of mode receive widespread recognition as a major, organically unified theatrical style of its own, Harold Hobson's prophecy, in his Introduction to

The Ruling Class—and here we return to the essay from which this book draws its first quotation—may become accurate. Together with Barnes' later work, this play may 'prove a turning point in the drama of the second half of the twentieth century' (p. vii).

Postscript: *Barnes' People*

In September 1980, while this book was in press, Barnes completed seven original monologues for BBC radio. The ironic early title, *A Barnes Half-Dozen*, was finally rejected in favour of the simpler, apt *Barnes' People*, consisting of *Confessions of a Primary Terrestrial Mental Receiver and Communicator: Num III Mark I, The Jumping Mimuses of Byzantium, The Theory and Practice of Belly-Dancing, The End of the World—and After, Yesterday's News, Glory*, and *Rosa*.

Surprisingly, the vociferous anti-naturalist Barnes employs the medium of radio in a realistic manner. Motivating each of the monologues, he provides legitimate reasons for his people to speak aloud. In *Confessions*, Lilly talks to himself on how no one suspects that a person as apparently ordinary as himself, holds enormous cosmic powers and is the greatest earthling since such other communicators as Buddha, Moses, Christ, and Mohammed. In *Mimuses*, set in Byzantium during the days of Justinian and Theodora, an aged holy man prays to God, whom he expects to meet soon, about the chief conundrum of his life. True to his name, Maya (illusion), he wonders which was illusion, which reality: were the male and female clowns of the title apparent sinners who were really chaste or actual sinners who pretended devoutness? In *World*, Reverend William Miller, who predicted the end of the world, speaks to God while he awaits the event and, after the clock's final stroke, when the world remains. *Glory* is an oration to a crowd at the Olympic games of 165 AD by a man about to step into a pyre in order to achieve glory by suicide. In *Yesterday's News*, an amoral 113-year-old former prostitute, white slaver, drug dealer, and murderess speaks into an interviewer's tape-recorder, making a sexual overture to him as she does so. In *Belly-Dancing*, a woman talks to herself to pass the time while she practices before a mirror, proud that she has abandoned the monotonous duties of wife and mother for the artistic creativity of belly-dancing, unaware that her exercises are even more monotonous. The title character of *Rosa* is a social worker who tape-records her cases: indigent old people who she recommends be admitted to Residential Council Homes, though such places are virtually as wretched as the slums they would leave. Lamenting not only the loss of her early idealism, which motivated her to battle, usually in vain, for more funding and better conditions, but also its misdirection, she recognizes that revolution not patchwork will really help the old. Frustrated, she resigns. But even her resignation is futile. Turning back the tape, she erases her words and prepares to redraft her report and continue a little longer, with the help of a drink.

Like the people who populate his stage plays, Barnes' radio people often derive from or allude to authentic historical characters. *Mimuses* and *Glory* are based on real people. William Miller is based neither on the author of 'Wee Willie Winkie' nor on Barry Goldwater's vice-presidential running-mate when he opposed Lyndon Johnson for the American presidency in 1964, but on an adventist who in 1843 prophesied the end of the world, and the mathematical calculations for determining judgment day are his. So famous was this Miller, in fact, that *The Macbeth Travestie*, staged in New York in 1843, had him, together with a Yankee peddler and ragpickers, make prophecies.[6] Of course, all the movements named in *Belly-Dancing* are authentic as are the case histories in *Rosa* whose title alludes to the revolutionary Rosa Luxembourg.

The themes and techniques of *Barnes' People* link to, and in some cases distil, the author's stage plays and adaptations. With the statement that Maya 'lived on five olives and muddy water' *(Mimuses)*, one enters familiar Barnes territory—that of *Noonday Demons*, to be precise, where Eusebius has the same diet. Lilly is bewitched by the fantasies that give meaning to an otherwise meaningless life, and in a godless age like ours, belief in extra-terrestrial beings may, for some, replace belief in the divine Being. *Mimuses* makes prominent a theme of *Noonday Demons*, the impossibility of objectively verifying a subjective, religious experience. The titular mimuses are in show biz, and the 113-year-old woman recounts sex shows she staged in her brothel, with special rates for Rotarians and Freemasons. *Glory* focuses on a minor theme of *Red Noses, Black Death*, an unimportant person's belief that he merits a prominent position in people's eyes. The 113-year-old woman is spiritual kin to Wedekind's Lulu, and the belly-dancer, first cousin to the composer in *The Singer*, rejects the cheap tricks of commercial, cabaret-style belly-dancing. And class stratifications based on wealth and position permeate all seven monologues.

The concluding monologue, *Rosa*, is to the others what *Red Noses, Black Death* is to the earlier stage plays. In both, red signifies more than a colour; and in *Rosa*, the contemporary bleak death of the elderly poor parallels the medieval black death. Although Rosa resembles Charlie Ketchum, in that she too is an individualist who resents institutionalized conformity, she more closely resembles Father Flote. Like Flote, she wants to help humanity. Like him, she gains the insight that slow, lawful, orthodox progress (SLOP, the acronym Flote creates) is ineffective, since 'individual acts of goodness only institutionalize the injustice and therefore make it permanent. . . . Chipping away a few bricks is useless. Only hammer blows will break [the system] down.' Rosa envisions an army of the elderly poor, 'a Geriatric Terrorist Army!' Perhaps deliberately linking *Rosa* and *Red Noses*, Barnes adapts a gag from the stage play. 'Our Homes answer the question, "Is there life before death?" with a resounding "No"', says Rosa, recalling 'Why if we live after death do we have to die?' (II,i).

In these radio monologues, Barnes piles up images with Jacobean excess. The 113-year-old woman recites a prospectus of sexual delights offered in her brothel, for instance, and Rosa lists the horrors of poverty ('Dr Rosa is tired of seeing old men and women wrapped in blankets staring up at the ceiling and turning yellow— tired of that bloody smell of urine, spit, stale cabbage, disinfectant and defeat—tired of men so lousy no one can go near them till they've been scrubbed with a long-handled brush', etc.).

Like the stage plays, the radio monologues have an invented, richly textured language that differs for each character. The language of *Confessions* is filled with computer-like sci-fi jargon ('the Supreme Council of Urokinase on Alpha IV', 'the most important paranormal event ever to be taken', 'according to the solar data boys at Xenon'). The vivid earthly imagery of the holy man of *Mimuses* ('Persecutors of men of God, may your wombs be blasted and your instruments of procreation drop off!') contrasts with the equally vivid apocalyptic imagery of Reverend Miller ('You come with clouds—you rise up in anger and the dark angel's bright sickle cuts the vines—the sun is veiled and man hovers in the middle air—the earth reels—the world crumbles and ends'). Whereas the language of *Glory* is elegantly phrased and ironic, as befits its patrician speaker, that of *Yesterday's News* conveys a sense of rambling, as befits its 113-year-old speaker. The belly-dancer's monologue is cliché-ridden ('Now I'm being fulfilled', 'belly-dancing's more than just an exercise, it's an art'). Embattled in her dealings with the Establishment, Rosa even battles with herself ('That's unfair, Rosa. I want to be unfair'), and her acerbic imagery would be appropriate to none of the other monologists ('They live in a part of the East End of

London which looks as though it has been dismembered and the dead pieces left lying about').
Even the modern gags are appropriate to speaker and situation. 'I must stay silent. The Saturnian we call Jesus Christ said too much, though not the half of it, and had to let himself be murdered by the rabble. Naturally, once bitten . . .' *(Confessions)*. 'All were amazed at my strength and the fact it was money I was throwing away. A rare sight in Byzantium or anywhere else for that matter' *(Mimuses)*. 'Meteors streaked across the sky, mysterious lights were seen in the heavens, there were plagues of frogs, toads and lizards, it rained blood and the Stock Market fell one hundred and fifty points' *(World)*. 'Philosophy, not sodomy, is the Greek vice' *(Glory)*. 'I'm so old I have to be fumigated' *(News)*. 'I've always been full of pep — well, full anyway' *(Rosa)*.

As in the stage plays, Barnes pillages literature and popular culture. In *Mimuses*, the injunction not to overdo self-mortification, 'There's too much pride in too much humility', invokes Burton's *Anatomy of Melancholy* ('They are proud in humility: proud in that they are not proud'). Shakespeare is pilfered: for instance, Reverend Miller lifts from both *Hamlet* ('Outbreaks of lunacy trebled in Vermont, New Hampshire, Pennsylvania, Maine and New York—though there it was hardly noticed' recalls the gravedigger's explanation of why Hamlet's lunacy would not be noticed in England) and *Lear* ('nothing comes of nothing, they say'). Shaw too is scavenged. *Yesterday's News* suggests *Major Barbara*: the crone's statement that poverty is 'a disease more terrible than leprosy' and that she cured herself resembles Undershaft's contention that 'the worst of crimes' is poverty, which 'blights whole cities' and that he cured himself; and her question, 'Can conscience put hot food in your stomach and money in your pocket?' resembles his assertion, 'I wouldn't have your income, not for all your conscience, Mr Shirley' (Shirley is destitute). *Yesterday's News* also recalls Brecht. 'Murder's an ugly word—but bankruptcy is uglier' may be suggested by *The Good Woman of Setzuan*, wherein Shen Te says that pauper is an uglier word than prostitute.

Pillage from popular and other aspects of modern culture includes a traditional song ('Goodbye Dolly I must leave you though it breaks my heart to go' [*News*]), George Leigh Mallory's statement on why he climbed Mount Everest ('Why was I chosen? Why me?' asks Lilly, 'Because I was there?'), W. C. Fields' quip that he liked children only when fried or parboiled ('You never liked women', says Rosa, 'well, only with mustard'), and the aphorism 'There are no cold women, only clumsy men' ('There are no good girls, only frightened men' [*News*]). In *Glory*, the phrase 'Down, Julius', to delay a friend who is all too eager to ignite the pile of wood, is a familiar injunction to a faithful dog, as well as a sexual injunction.

Although not as frequently as in the stage plays, sounds rather than words sometimes, in Artaud-like fashion, convey meaning in these radio plays, as when Miller shrieks in pain that he is on earth rather than in heaven and when Rosa imagines the demolition of the wall of institutionalism. Brechtian social motifs fill these monologues—notably, as mentioned before, *Rosa*. The 113-year-old woman, who has known grinding poverty, contrasts with the indigent poor in *Rosa:* 'I've got a personal maid and nurse. I can pay so I'm not treated like old rope.' She exemplifies the capitalist ethos: 'Greed was the motive that kept me going. They're always insulting greed. All I can say is God help the ungreedy—the poor, the blacks, the starving millions. I'm a grabber. When I grabbed I prospered. When I stopped grabbing I struck trouble.' In *Confessions*, Lilly self-righteously mentions the riches he might have had if the supreme powers had not cautioned him that riches corrupt (another contrast with *News*, whose speaker, like Undershaft in *Major Barbara*, is unashamed of her actions), and the suicidal orator suspects that Christians might be con-men because they want him to surrender his worldly goods in expectation of a greater reward in the vague future *(Glory)*.

Within the medium of radio, more restricted than that of the stage, Barnes' people also turn on a sixpence. In *Confessions*, Lilly suddenly interrupts memories of his grey existence with instructions to imaginary satellites in magnetization orbit. In *World*, Miller prays fervently, describes the flight of his soul, counts the midnight bells, and sings a hymn. *News* rapidly shifts from sentimental recollections of a bygone era to contemporary gags to a philosophical rumination on ageing to a song. The most unexpected turn on a sixpence, however, occurs in the movement from the sixth to the final monologue, which Barnes writes realistically—suddenly 'playing it straight', so to speak—and does not portray a bizarre or grotesque character. Coming as it does after the earlier monologues, *Rosa* is shocking in its straightforwardness; and its realism is an unexpected splash of cold water on one's face, a shock into sobriety. Like the earlier monologues, *Rosa* concerns illusion and reality, but unlike them it explicitly rejects illusions (about moderate social reform), however passionately they may have been held at one time, and it embraces the reality of radical social change. Yet *Rosa* is true to its title character, who though passionate in her new conviction is too old and beaten down to do what she recognizes to be necessary.

While *Barnes' People* rings variations on familiar themes and recapitulates the author's techniques, it does so freshly and from new viewpoints. Furthermore, he employs radio, a different medium from the stage, in a distinctive and appropriate manner, so that hearing or overhearing the motivated monologues is an integral dramatic stratagem.

Notes

Chapter 1

1. Pp. vi, vii. Subsequent quotations from all of Barnes' published plays, and from introductions to them, will be cited parenthetically in the text. For publication details of these and other works cited in footnotes, see Bibliography. Quotations from Barnes' unpublished plays are from their typescripts (courtesy Peter Barnes) and will be cited, unless otherwise indicated, by acts and scenes.

2. Unless otherwise indicated, such information, as well as quotations and paraphrases of Barnes, derive from correspondence and conversations with him.

3. Quoted in 'Liberating Laughter,' p. 16.

4. Hobson, 'All Swing Together,' p. 53; Bryden, 'Tricks in Toryland,' p. 17.

5. Spurling, 'Arts: Bond Honoured,' p. 314; Shulman, 'Huntin', Seducin', etc.,' p. 17.

6. Wardle, 'Leonardo Clubbed,' p. 7.

7. Lewis, 'The Joke's on Us,' p. 14.

8. Esslin, 'The Bewitched,' pp. 36–37.

9. Harold Hobson, 'Royal Fantasia,' p. 38.

10. Robert Cushman, 'Bewitched, Bewildered,' p. 35.

11. B. A. Young, 'The Bewitched,' p. 8; Kenneth Hurren, 'Review of the Arts,' p. 616.

12. Wardle, 'Laughter!' p. 13.

13. Felix Barker, 'It's Not Funny,' p. 15.

14. Billington, 'Laughter,' p. 10.

15. Worth, *Revolutions in Modern English Drama*, p. 159; Hammond, 'Barnes, Peter,' p. 71.

16. Hinchliffe, *British Theatre 1950–70*, pp. 169–170.

Chapter 2

1. According to the Rehearsal Script, it was telecast on 21 August 1960. Hammond dates it as 1961 (op. cit., p. 69).

2. Interview with Martin Esslin, 2 July 1979.

3. Although 25 November 1969 (a date listed in the published text) was scheduled as opening night, it was postponed to 4 December. See notice in *The Times*, 25 November 1969, p. 17.

4. 'Ben Jonson and the Modern Stage,' p. 5.

5. Ibid.

6. 'My Ben Jonson,' typescript of programme broadcast on BBC Radio 3, 17 September 1972 (courtesy Peter Barnes).

7. Ibid.

8. 'Ben Jonson and the Modern Stage,' p. 20.

Chapter 3

1. Bryden, 'Tricks in Toryland,' p. 17.

2. Swift, *A Tale of a Tub*, p. 144.

3. 'Liberating Laughter,' p. 15. In America, Gogol's play is usually known as *The Inspector General*.

4. Shaw, *The Intelligent Woman's Guide*, p. 186.

Chapter 4

1. 'My Ben Jonson,' typescript of BBC Radio 3 Programme, broadcast 17 September 1972 (courtesy Peter Barnes).

2. Johannes Nohl, *The Black Death*, pp. 83–84. Barnes pointed to this passage as his source.

3. Rokeach, *The Three Christs of Ypsilanti*, p. 3. Dr Rokeach sued Barnes for plagiarism and lost. According to the court, factual material is not copyrightable; an idea is, but not that idea's expression; even if Dr Rokeach's material were copyrightable, Barnes' copying was well within the boundaries of fair use; and as the plaintiff admitted, *The Ruling Class* did not adversely affect the market or value of *The Three Christs*. *News and Comment*, No. 365, pp. A–7–9.

4. Ibid., pp. 314, 332.

5. Ibid., p. 126.

6. Ibid., p. 131.

7. Although England abolished the death sentence in 1964, its use in this scene is no more anachronistic than the thirteenth Earl's wearing a three-cornered hat. To him, ruling class tradition, exemplified by both, is important.

8. Although Barnes admits the reference is to *Romeo and Juliet*, the phrase also resonates a passage in Jonson's *The Alchemist*, wherein Sir Epicure Mammon, fantasizing his harem, hopes to become 'as tough/As Hercules, to encounter fifty a night.'

9. Barnes' one-act plays, including the two that comprise *Laughter!* contain few references to classical music and literature. Religious music in Latin figures in *Leonardo's Last Supper* ('Dies Irae') and *Noonday Demons* ('Gloria in Excelsis'), operatic music in *Tsar* (Gluck's *Orfeo and Eurydice*) and *Auschwitz* (Wagner's *Die Meistersinger von Nürnberg*). Their few anachronistic literary allusions include Samuel Johnson on death (spoken, appropriately, by the resurrected Leonardo) plus a reference to *Matthew*,

16:26 on gaining the world and losing one's soul, and two references to Shakespeare's *Julius Caesar*, both about bestriding the world like a colossus, spoken by and to the monk-tsar Ivan. The presence of such allusions is part of Barnes' distinctive artistic sigature. Although their paucity deprives these plays of some of the texture of the full-length works, their relative scarceness in the one-acters is an artistic merit, for this sort of texture might seem pretentious in such short pieces.

10. Shaw, *The Bodley Head Bernard Shaw*, Vol. II, p. 295.

11. Although Barnes' plays resemble E. E. Cummings' *Him* in this respect, the resemblance is coincidental, since Barnes was unfamiliar with Cummings' play until after he had written them.

12. 'Liberating Laughter,' p. 17.

13. *The Bewitched: Proof Copy*, p. 79 (courtesy Peter Barnes).

14. The scene recalls a passage in Shaw's *On the Rocks*. Having heard the Prime Minister rehearse a speech, a character comments, 'As I listen to you I seem to hear a ghost preparing a speech for his fellow ghosts, ghosts from a long dead past.' *The Bodley Head Bernard Shaw*, Vol. VI, p. 668. As with *Him*, resemblance does not mean influence. Barnes was unfamiliar with *On the Rocks*.

15. *Matthew*, 13:12, 25:29; *Mark*, 4:25; *Luke*, 8:18, 19:26.

16. Despite their affinity, in this respect, to America's Open Theatre, which flourished in the 1960s, Barnes was unfamiliar with this company's work. It is from the Open Theatre that I derive the word *transformationalism* to label Barnes' distinctive theatrical style. According to Peter Feldman, an actor and director with the Open Theatre, its 'transformations' are improvisations 'in which the established realities . . . of the scene change several times during the course of the action. . . . These changes occur swiftly and *almost without transition*, until the audience's dependence upon any fixed reality is called into question' (Feldman, 'Notes for an Open Theatre Production,' pp. 201–202). Jean-Claude Van Itallie, whose plays the Open Theatre performed, describes this technique: 'In *The Airplane* the actors . . . started as parts of the airplane itself as it took off, then they enacted a series of comedy improvisations which became increasingly realistic, then they were parts of the plane again as it crashed, and, finally, they faced the audience as the dead. In a later performance we added an in-flight movie and then, within that movie, a television show.' (Van Itallie, 'Playwright at Work,' p. 156).

17. Interview, 4 October 1978.

18. Wardle, 'Overloaded with Good Material,' p. 7.

Chapter 5

1. The script is divided into acts but not scenes.

2. In an interview prior to the film's release, Chaplin said as much. See Theodore Huff, *Charlie Chaplin*, pp. 293–294. In the film itself, Verdoux makes similar statements.

3. Although it is not a deliberate copy, Barnes' Hell Epilogue to *Clap Hands, Here Comes Charlie* resembles Bernard Shaw's centrepiece ('Don Juan in Hell') in *Man and Superman*. With each writer, Heaven reflects what he admires, Hell what he does not. In both works, the Devil does not want uncongenial spirits in Hell and urges them to go to the alternative establishment, the Devil left Heaven because he could not tolerate it, and the hero—who embodies the spirit of Heaven—elects to go there.

Chapter 6

1. In citing Jacobean plays Barnes has edited and adapted, I refer only to the acts. Scene divisions vary according to editors (some of whom use the convention of the French Scene, others not) and the five-act division of these plays makes quotations easy to locate with act citations alone. Barnes' Jacobean renderings are unpublished.
2. 'Hands Off the Classics,' p. 17.
3. Robert Gale Noyes, *Ben Jonson on the English Stage*, p. 222.
4. 'Hands Off the Classics,' p. 17.
5. Levin, 'The Ungentle Art of Doctoring Jonson,' p. 37.
6. 'Lambasting Levin,' p. 14.
7. 'Hands Off the Classics,' p. 17.
8. Act I consists of an abridged version of *Antonio and Mellida*, Act II of *Antonio's Revenge*. In citations, AM or AR precede act designations.
9. Interview with Martin Esslin, 27 September 1978. When Esslin suggested that the *Radio Times* print, with its listing of the play, a picture of the four collaborators, the man in charge was reluctant. 'You know how difficult it is,' he explained, 'to get four writers together at the same time to pose for a photograph.'
10. Unfortunately, and perhaps unintentionally, Barnes deletes the first line spoken to Hamlet the footman: ''Sfoot, Hamlet, are you mad?' (III).
11. *The Essays and Hymns of Synesius of Cyrene*, Vol. II, p. 258.
12. Brecht, *Gedichte*, Vol. V, p. 104.
13. Quotations from all of Wedekind's plays are from Wedekind, *Prosa Dramen Verse*. Citations to Barnes' plays are in the usual manner; to Wedekind's, ES or PB, followed by a page reference (to *The Singer*, solely the page reference). Translations are mine.
14. Grabbe, *Werke*, p. 474. Further citations will be by page, parenthetically in the text. Citations of Barnes' unpublished adaptation are by act and scene. Literal translations of Grabbe are mine.
15. Feydeau, *Théâtre complet*, Vol. III, p. 161. Hereafter, quotations will be cited parenthetically in the text. Translations are mine.
16. Barnes, 'My Ben Jonson,' loc. cit.
17. Ibid.
18. 'Ben Jonson and the Modern Stage,' p. 18.
19. Barnes, 'My Ben Jonson,' loc. cit.
20. 'Ben Jonson and the Modern Stage,' p. 19.

Chapter 7

1. 'The Playwright Who Can't Find a Stage,' p. 10.
2. 'Liberating Laughter,' p. 17.
3. Wardle, 'Overloaded with Good Material,' p. 7.
4. Hobson, 'All Swing Together,' p. 53.
5. Esslin, 'The Bewitched,' p. 37.
6. Claudia D. Johnson, 'Burlesques of Shakespeare: The Democratic American's "Light Artillery"', *Theatre Survey*, 21 (May 1980), pp. 55–56.

Bibliography of Published Works

(i) Plays and Adaptations by Peter Barnes

The Bewitched. London: Heinemann, 1974.
The Frontiers of Farce. London: Heinemann, 1977.
Laughter! London: Heinemann, 1978.
Leonardo's Last Supper and Noonday Demons. London: Heinemann, 1970.
Lulu. London: Heinemann, 1971.
The Ruling Class. London: Heinemann, 1969.

(ii) Barnes on Theatre

'Ben Jonson and the Modern Stage.' *Gambit,* 6 (1972), pp. 5–30.
'Hands off the Classics—Asses and Devilry.' *The Listener,* 5 January 1978, pp. 17–19.
'Introduction' to *The Frontiers of Farce.* See (i).
'Introduction' to *Leonardo's Last Supper and Noonday Demons.* See (i).
'Liberating Laughter.' *Plays and Players,* 25 (March 1978), pp. 14–17.
'The Playwright Who Can't Find a Stage.' *The Guardian,* 18 September 1979, p. 10.
'Staging Jonson.' *Shakespeare and Jonson: Papers from the Humanities Research Centre* (Canberra, Australia), ed. Ian Donaldson. London: Macmillan, 1981.

(iii) Secondary Sources

Barker, Felix. 'It's Not Funny.' *Evening News,* 25 January 1978, p. 15.
'Ben Jonson and the Modern Stage.' See (ii).

Billington, Michael. 'Laughter.' *The Guardian*, 25 January 1978, p. 10.

Brecht, Bertolt. *Gedichte*, Vol. 5. Frankfurt am Main: Suhrkamp Verlag, 1964.

Bryden, Ronald. 'Introduction' to *The Bewitched*. See (i).

'Tricks in Toryland.' *The Observer*, 2 March 1969, p. 17.

Cushman, Robert. 'Bewitched, Bewildered.' *The Observer*, 12 May 1974, p. 35.

Dukore, Bernard F. 'Peter Barnes,' in *Contemporary British Drama*, ed. Albert Wertheim and Hedwig Bock. Ismanning/München: Max Hueber Verlag, 1981.

Elsom, John. *Post-War British Theatre*. London: Routledge and Kegan Paul, 1976.

Esslin, Martin. 'The Bewitched.' *Plays and Players*, 21 (June 1974), pp. 36–37.

'Green Room.' *Plays and Players*, 21 (August 1974), pp. 12–13.

'Introduction' to *Lulu*. See (i).

'Peter Barnes Double Bill.' *Plays and Players*, 17 (January 1970), p. 51.

Feldman, Peter. 'Notes for an Open Theatre Production.' *Tulane Drama Review*, 10 (Summer 1966), pp. 200–208.

Feydeau, Georges. *Théâtre complet*, Vol. 3. Paris: Editions du Bélier, 1948.

Grabbe, Christian Dietrich. *Werke*. Emsdetten, Westf.: Verlag Lechte, 1960.

Hammond, Jonathan. 'Barnes, Peter,' in *Contemporary Dramatists*, ed. James Vinson. London: St Martin's Press, 1977, pp. 69–71.

'Hands off the Classics—Asses and Devilry.' See (ii).

Hinchliffe, Arnold P. *British Theatre 1950–70*. Oxford: Basil Blackwell, 1974.

Hobson, Harold. 'All Swing Together.' *The Sunday Times*, 2 March 1969, p. 53.

'The Importance of Being Married.' *The Sunday Times*, 7 December 1969, p. 53.

'Introduction' to *The Ruling Class*. See (i).

'Royal Fantasia.' *The Sunday Times*, 12 May 1974, p. 38.

Huff, Theodore. *Charlie Chaplin*. New York: Henry Schuman, 1951.

Hurren, Kenneth. 'Review of the Arts.' *The Spectator*, n.v. (18 May 1974), p. 616.

Lahr, John. 'Laughter.' *Plays and Players*, 25 (March 1978), pp. 26–27.

'Lambasting Levin.' *The Sunday Times*, 15 May 1977, p. 14.

Levin, Bernard. 'Possession is Nine Points of the Law.' *The Sunday Times*, 5 February 1978, p. 35.

'The Ungentle Art of Doctoring Jonson.' *The Sunday Times*, 8 May 1977, p. 37.

Lewis, Peter. 'The Joke's on Us.' *Daily Mail*, 5 December 1969, p. 14.

News and Comment, No. 365. Washington, D.C.: Bureau of National Affairs, 9 February 1978.

Nightingale, Benedict. 'Green Room.' *Plays and Players*, 21 (July 1974), pp. 12–13.

Nohl, Johannes. *The Black Death: A Chronicle of the Plague Compiled from Contemporary Sources*, trans. C. H. Clarke. London: Unwin Books, 1961.

Noyes, Robert Gale. *Ben Jonson on the English Stage 1660–1776*. New York: Benjamin Blom, 1966.

Rokeach, Milton. *The Three Christs of Ypsilanti*. London: Arthur Barker, 1964.

Shaw, Bernard. *The Bodley Head Bernard Shaw: Collected Plays with Their Prefaces*, Vols. 2 and 6. London: The Bodley Head, 1971 and 1973.

The Intelligent Woman's Guide to Socialism, Capitalism, Sovietism, and Fascism. London: Constable, 1949.

Shulman, Milton. 'Huntin', Seducin', etc.' *Evening Standard*, 27 February 1969, p. 17.

Spurling, Hilary. 'Arts: Bond Honoured.' *The Spectator*, 222 (7 March 1969), p. 314.

Swift, Jonathan. *A Tale of a Tub, The Battle of the Books, and Other Satires*. London: J. M. Dent, n.d.

Synesius of Cyrene. *The Essays and Hymns of Synesius of Cyrene*, Vol. 2, trans. Augustine Fitzgerald. London: Oxford University Press, 1930.

Taylor, John Russell. *The Second Wave*. New York: Hill and Wang, 1971.

Van Itallie, Jean-Claude. 'Playwright at Work: Off Off-Broadway.' *Tulane Drama Review*, 10 (Summer 1966), pp. 154–158.

Wardle, Irving. 'Laughter!' *The Times*, 25 January 1978, p. 13.

'Leonardo Clubbed.' *The Times*, 5 December 1969, p. 7.

'Overloaded with Good Material.' *The Times*, 27 February 1969, p. 7.

Wedekind, Frank. *Prosa Dramen Verse*. München: Albert Langen-Georg Müller, 1954.

Worth, Katharine J. *Revolutions in Modern English Drama*. London: Bell, 1972.

Young, B. A. 'The Bewitched.' *The Financial Times*, 9 May 1974, p. 3.